RESEARCH IMPACT AND THE EARLY CAREER RESEARCHER

Research Impact and the Early Career Researcher documents experiences and perspectives on the emerging concept of research impact from a range of disciplines and places them within an analytical and critical discursive framework. Combining personal reflections with research essays, it provides the reader with a multi-dimensional perspective on research impact and how it connects to the research lives and practice of early career researchers.

Research impact is playing an ever-increasing role in international research policy and government strategy. This book:

- Explores the arrival of impact into the national research consciousness
- Discusses how to build capacity and skills within research impact and how this might impact academic career progression in an international job market
- Offers advice on balancing national expectations with institutional expectations on research in terms of funding and career progression
- Offers suggested ways forward whilst actively challenging what constitutes research impact

Research Impact and the Early Career Researcher provides a much-needed research base for studies of research impact and the extent to which it has altered, changed, and influenced the research practice of early career academics. It is an essential guide for any new and early career researchers wishing to navigate the complex landscape in order to meaningfully contribute to the impact agenda.

Kieran Fenby-Hulse is an Assistant Professor in Research Capability and Development at Coventry University, UK.

Emma Heywood is a Lecturer and Researcher in Journalism, Politics and Communication at the University of Sheffield, UK.

Kate Walker is an Assistant Professor in the Centre for Advances in Behavioural Science at Coventry University, UK.

RESEARCH IMPACT AND THE EARLY CAREER RESEARCHER

Lived Experiences, New Perspectives

Edited by Kieran Fenby-Hulse, Emma Heywood and Kate Walker

Routledge
Taylor & Francis Group

LONDON AND NEW YORK

First published 2019
by Routledge
2 Park Square, Milton Park, Abingdon, Oxon OX14 4RN

and by Routledge
52 Vanderbilt Avenue, New York, NY 10017

Routledge is an imprint of the Taylor & Francis Group, an informa business

© 2019 selection and editorial matter, Kieran Fenby-Hulse, Emma Heywood and Kate Walker; individual chapters, the contributors

British Library Cataloguing in Publication Data
A catalogue record for this book is available from the British Library

Library of Congress Cataloging-in-Publication Data
Names: Fenby-Hulse, Kieran, editor. | Heywood, Emma, editor. |
Walker, Kate, 1969- editor.
Title: Research impact and the early-career researcher / edited by Kieran
Fenby-Hulse, Emma Heywood and Kate Walker.
Description: Abingdon, Oxon ; New York, NY : Routledge, 2019. |
Includes bibliographical references.
Identifiers: LCCN 2019003176| ISBN 9781138562042 (hardback) |
ISBN 9781138562073 (pbk.) | ISBN 9780203710104 (ebook)
Subjects: LCSH: Learning and scholarship--Philosophy. | Research--Evaluation.
| Inquiry (Theory of knowledge)
Classification: LCC AZ103 .R47 2019 | DDC 001.2--dc23
LC record available at https://lccn.loc.gov/2019003176

ISBN: 978-1-138-56204-2 (hbk)
ISBN: 978-1-138-56207-3 (pbk)
ISBN: 978-0-203-71010-4 (ebk)

Typeset in Bembo
by Taylor & Francis Books

Printed and bound in Great Britain by
TJ International Ltd, Padstow, Cornwall

This is dedicated to all the ECRs out there who are working hard to find their place in a challenging and changing research landscape.

CONTENTS

FOREWORD

Julie Bayley

Why do impact? Why play the impact game? Why expend effort – amidst so many other pressures – on something that sits so far beyond traditional expectations of an academic career?

First, it is essential to define what is meant by research impact. Amidst a range of definitions, perhaps the most simple is that from the UK's primary research funding body – UK Research and Innovation – who define impact as 'the demonstrable contribution that excellent research makes to society and the economy' (UKRI 2018). A more detailed definition by Research England for the Research Excellence Framework (REF) expresses impact as 'an effect on, change or benefit to the economy, society, culture, public policy or services, health, the environment or quality of life, beyond academia' (Research England 2018, p. 83). In short, research impact can be defined as the provable benefit of research in the 'real world'.

Research impact is, of course, in no way new. Applied research, technology transfer, knowledge exchange, and varied other ways of driving research into practice have existed in numerous guises for many years. Impact – by any name – is a longstanding feature of academia, with research routinely informing healthcare, education, policy making and wider practices within industry and commerce. University websites are replete with triumphant storytelling of collaborations with industry, public services and the charity sector, and government communiques awash with persuasive stories about the benefits research provides. However, whilst there are of course many examples of problem-focused research, traditionally the generation of societal benefits has been a more altruistic offshoot of research. Academic studies have far more routinely extended only as far as outputs and dissemination, stopping short of pursuing or monitoring any provable markers of change.

However, in recent years, the need to connect research to the economy and society has been intensified and accelerated by the introduction of more a formal impact agenda. Arguably, one of the most powerful examples of impact being catapulted into national research consciousness is the UK's Research Excellence Framework (REF). In the UK, a dual funding structure (Hughes et al. 2013) provides research investment through (i) competitive funding schemes run through a range of subject-specific research councils, and (ii) quality research (QR) income allocated on the basis of institutional achievements in research assessment exercises. Impact features as part of both funding mechanisms, with funding councils routinely requiring plans for how research can lead to non-academic effects ('pathways to impact') as part of the application process to ensure research is connected to need beyond the academy. For QR funding, UK research institutes are assessed cyclically on the quality of their research to determine funding and to produce national institutional rankings. Up to and including the 2008 'Research assessment exercise', this was achieved by reviewing outputs and factors such as doctoral activity, research funding, and the quality of the research environment only. Higher scores conveyed not only a financial but a reputational advantage. However, in 2011, the UK government added a new requirement – *impact*. Now called the REF, the academic sector was suddenly required to demonstrate the effects of research beyond the academic walls and within the 'real world'. Rules required institutions to submit case studies of impact occurring within the assessment window (2008–2013) of research conducted for the 20 years previously (1993–2013) at the institution. Suddenly, academics were no longer marked solely on the quality of their research publications, but also on the broader effects of their research. As a testament to the success of this element of REF, for the next REF cycle (submission 2021), impact weighting has been elevated from 20% to 25% of the total QR allocation, thus amplifying importance further. With impact now conferring an increased financial benefit for those most able to robustly demonstrate world-leading research impact, it is unsurprising that there has been a rapid growth in the desire to deliver impact.

In the immediate years since the 2014 REF cycle, there has been considerable exploration into how impact is achieved. Results from the analysis of REF 2014 (Kings College London & Digital Science 2015) show 3,709 unique impact paths from 6,647 case studies, demonstrating not only the breadth of impacts possible, but reaffirming that impact cannot be templated. Taken together or read in isolation, the case studies are extremely impressive, and doubtlessly showcase some of the most significant applications of research in recent years. However, for those seeking to generate impact from their own research, it is important to reflect epistemologically on the nature of this 'data'. By definition, this assessment-driven database is subjectively skewed to only include those examples selectively filtered, invested in and sufficiently honed for institutions to judge worthy of submission. By default, they offer no reflection of impact pathways which were not realised, nor the unsuccessful efforts of brokering research into challenging or un-receptive environments. As such, whilst providing a large and inspiring body of impact, we must recognise the REF case studies are neither gold standard models to be re-applied nor comprehensive maps of how to navigate research outwards.

The UK is, of course, not unique in its pursuit of impact, and is detailed here simply as a particular example of impact at scale. Australia's 'Excellence in Research Australia' (Australian Research Council 2015) is a similarly centralised assessment process, although unlike the UK purposefully focuses on impact *and engagement*. Likewise, New Zealand (Ministry of Business, Innovation and Employment 2018) has recently sought expert feedback on running a national science-specific impact assessment to assess the effect of research within this disciplinary sphere only. Canada has a particularly longstanding history of engaged research, although unlike the UK, Australia and Canada stop short of a centralised assessment system. Instead, impact is driven through the funding system, with most Canadian academic research funding agencies requiring strategies for knowledge mobilisation (in the social sciences and humanities), knowledge translation (in health) and commercialisation (in natural sciences and engineering) (see Government of Canada 2018 for information on these). The prevailing impetus in Canada is, thus, on the brokering of research outwards, rather than the pursuit of assessable and competitive effects.

Across the world, established and incoming impact agendas vary around the engagement vs. impact and broad vs. specific axes, but ultimately both reflect increasing national appetite to demonstrate the social value of research investment, and align with the need to strongly connect research with the broader non-academic community. Within all these economically and socially charged agenda, the sector is still resolving a range of challenges. For those in assessment driven arenas, the issues of attribution (of the effect to the research) and ownership (of the effect amidst other influences) are particularly marked. Processes such as REF favour persuasively causative narratives, requiring academics to show how their distinct research contributions have led to tangible and provable effects. More philosophically, there are ongoing debates around the default notion of 'benefit', and the resulting tendency to overlook negative impact. There are, of course, occasions where research has led to negative effects – classic examples would include the significant drop in immunisation rates caused by now debunked claims on the link between the measles, mumps and rubella (MMR) vaccination and autism in children (Flaherty 2011) – but aside from such infrequent neglectful practice, 'negative' is more routinely a mislabel. Rather than generating obviously positive impact (e.g. higher school achievement, improved health, financial profit), research instead may lead positively to ineffective or dangerous practices being *stopped*, with obvious benefit to those stakeholders involved.

With formal impact agendas a relatively recent introduction to the research environment, the sector has drawn on existing models and frameworks to inform how we drive social effects. Much of the traditional rhetoric about impact is underpinned by simple logic models expressing impact as a linear input-output-outcome-impact path (such as WK Kellogg Foundation 2004). More sophisticated models, such as the heavily influential Payback Framework (Buxton and Hanney 1996), similarly lineate impact as a clear function of (i) topic selection, (ii) research and resultant outputs, (iii) dissemination leading to secondary outputs (e.g. policy) and adoption, culminating in (iv) impact. Such stepwise models have considerable merit for identifying causative sequences which lead to impact – particularly with impact often taking many years to mature (Hughes et al. 2013) – but in practice rarely reflect the myriad of pathways which do or do not lead to impact. Through the experience of generating, not just recording, impact, those supporting impact within the sector are increasingly cognisant of the need to shift away from linear assumptions about research naturally maturing to impact and towards a tone of *effortful brokerage*. Dominant terminology is accordingly starting to shift from simplistic uni-directional 'transfer' models, and towards more bi-directional ('exchange') or multi-directional ('mobilisation') phraseology (Greenhalgh and Wieringa 2011). Models such as the Co-produced Pathway (Phipps et al. 2016) reflect the vital engagement of stakeholders throughout the research process to not only receive the results of studies (as would be the case in an in input-output model), but instead help frame, inform and drive forward the outcomes of research. Such advances are coupled with debates on responsible use of metrics (Wilsdon et al. 2015), a growing recognition that current scholarly metrics cannot demonstrate impact, and growing communities of practice such as the 750+ strong impact special interest group within the UK Association of Research Managers and Administrators (ARMA) membership base.

There are also challenges across disciplinary areas. For example, in arts and humanities subjects, impacts can be more amorphous and less tangible, such as bringing a lost story to life or invoking emotional connections to topical events. Some activities (e.g. art installations and performances) may even seek to instil unease within an audience to provoke thinking, reflection, and raise awareness. Unsurprisingly, such effects can be a challenge to capture, and whilst researchers can fall back on established social science evaluation methods such as interviews, questionnaires and other such means, the risk is that such reductionist means cannot capture or do justice to the effects being assessed. Conversely, whilst arts and humanities may struggle to capture immediate and engaged effects, fundamental scientists often struggle with the time lag and the translational chain (number of steps) from their research to effect. Discovery science is, quite necessarily, focused on exploration and knowledge extension, as separate from a clear social application. The world is awash with populist examples of where such research has led ultimately to significant real world benefits – DNA, Higgs Boson, pharmaceutical breakthroughs, medical imaging, to name a few – but when working at the exploratory stage, the ultimate benefit may be unclear. Moreover, the nature of the exploratory endeavour itself is something so implicitly valued within the science community that expectations of impact can be felt as anywhere from inappropriate, through distasteful, to insulting.

But what does this mean particularly for those early in their research careers? For those embarking on academic careers, thinking about research impact can generate a range of different feelings from fear to joy. Ultimately, this changing policy context is reshaping expectations of what it means to be a modern academic. Whilst the pace and formality of this may differ internationally, researchers must increasingly understand the relationship between their research and the wider environment, and build the skills and knowledge to be able to do this.

The risk, however, is that impact could be understood as undermining the traditional academic landscape, which was previously firmly rooted in grants and outputs for so many years. However, a crucially important tone that is often lost is the idea of *impact as an opportunity*. Never before have we had such a strong and formal basis to drive social and economic change through our research. Never before have we had – at a sector level – such opportunity to chase our research passion through to discernible effects for real people. Whilst this is not without effort or challenge, the policy focus on impact heralds a new era in academic practice with walls between academia and the public increasingly permeable. We have not only the chance, but also the momentum, to really *make a difference*.

For ECRs, there is now an incredible opportunity to embrace impact. By identifying and engaging with stakeholders, connecting research to a clear problem and expressing impact 'goals' which are made possible by the work, researchers can amplify the contribution of their work beyond outputs. More fundamentally, ECRs can *drive* understanding of how research can be most meaningfully connected to the non-academic world, and in so doing build critical reflections on the process of implementation and impact. Impact may resist templating, but as a community we can enhance our knowledge of how best to connect research to change. To best position themselves for impact, ECRs should look at both their national expectations around impact (such as funders' requirements and centralised assessment mechanism) and institutional expectations (e.g. how it features in progression routes), alongside reflecting on disciplinary challenges and opportunities. No discipline is ever automatically precluded from impact; the challenge is to work out how the research contributes and creates momentum towards real world change. This neither means blind acceptance nor uncritical compliance, but rather a need to understand and position ones work along the continuum from discovery to application. The need is to become *impact literate* (Bayley and Phipps 2017), developing sufficient critical judgement to understand *what* impact is possible, *how* it can be achieved through stakeholder engagement, and *who* – via appropriate skills and partnerships (see Bayley et al. 2017 on knowledge broker competencies) – can achieve it.

So why play the impact game? Well, imagine what the world could look like if you do.

References

Australian Research Council (2015). *Excellence in Research for Australia (ERA)*. Australian Government. [Viewed 3 October 2018]. Available from: www.arc.gov.au/excellence-re search-australia

Bayley, J. and Phipps, D. (2017) *Building the Concept of Impact Literacy*. Evidence and Policy. [Viewed 3 October 2018]. Available from: www.ingentaconnect.com/content/tpp/ep

Bayley, J.E., Phipps, D., Batac, M. and Stevens, E. (2017). *Development and Synthesis of a Knowledge Broker Competency Framework*. Evidence and Policy. [Viewed 3 October 2018]. Available from: https://doi.org/10.1332/174426417X14945838375124

Buxton, M. and Hanney, S. (1996). How can payback from health services research be assessed? *Journal of Health Services Research*. 1(1), 35–43.

Flaherty, D.K. (2011). The vaccine-autism connection: a public health crisis caused by unethical medical practices and fraudulent science. *Annals of Pharmacotherapy.* 45(10), 1302–1304.

Government of Canada (2018). *Natural Sciences and Engineering Research Council of Canada.* Government of Canada. [Viewed 3 October 2018]. Available from: www.nserc-crsng.gc. ca/index_eng.asp

Greenhalgh, T. and Wieringa, S. (2011). Is it time to drop the 'knowledge translation' metaphor? A critical literature review. *Journal of the Royal Society of Medicine.* 104(12), 501–509.

Hughes, A., Kitson, M., Bullock, A. and Milner, I. (2013). *The Dual Funding Structure for Research in the UK: Research Council and Funding Council Allocation Methods and the Pathways to Impact of UK Academics.* Cambridge: Department of Innovation and Skills, UK Innovation Research Centre.

Kings College London, & Digital Science (2015). *The Nature, Scale and Beneficiaries of Research Impact: An Initial Analysis of Research Excellence Framework (REF) 2014 Impact Case Studies.* [Viewed 3 October 2018]. Available from www.kcl.ac.uk/sspp/policy-in stitute/publications/Analysis-of-REF-impact.pdf

Ministry of Business, Innovation and Employment (2018). *The Impact of Science.* Ministry of Business, Innovation and Employment. [Viewed 3 October 2018]. Available from: www.mbie. govt.nz/info-services/science-innovation/funding-info-opportunities/nssi/impact-of-science

Phipps, D., Cummings, J., Pepler, D., Craig, W. and Cardinal, S. (2016). The co-produced pathway to impact describes knowledge mobilisation processes. *Journal of Community Engagement and Scholarship.* 9(1), 31–40.

Research England (2018). *Draft Guidance on Submissions.* [Viewed 3 October 2018]. Available from www.ref.ac.uk/media/1016/draft-guidance-on-submissions-ref-2018_1.pdf

UK Research and Innovation (UKRI) (2018). *Excellence with Impact.* [Viewed 3 October 2018]. Available from www.ukri.org/innovation/excellence-with-impact/

Wilsdon, J., *et al.* (2015). *The Metric Tide: Report of the Independent Review of the Role of Metrics in Research Assessment and Management.* [Viewed 3 October 2018]. Available from www. hefce.ac.uk/pubs/rereports/year/2015/metrictide/

WK Kellogg Foundation (2004). *Logic Model Development Guide.* [Viewed 3 October 2018]. Available from www.wkkf.org/resource-directory/resource/2006/02/wk-kellogg-founda tion-logic-model-development-guide

ABOUT THIS BOOK

Kieran Fenby-Hulse, Emma Heywood and Kate Walker

This book arose out of an Impact Summit held at Coventry University in 2016. The summit focused on challenges and priorities for research impact and consisted of a series of expert talks to help support those new to impact in understanding the opportunities and challenges research impact brings to the research endeavour. The conference highlighted that understandings and approaches to impact varied considerably and were particular to the nature of the research. There were no clearly defined processes or procedures for delivering research impact. As colleagues, researchers, and researcher developers, we wanted to explore impact further and were curious to understand research impact from the perspective of early career researchers (ECRs).

For the purpose of the book, we define ECR broadly. We include doctoral and postdoctoral researchers, lecturers, and emerging independent researchers. We also include those who are new to academia having moved from industry, business, or the third sector. This broad definition enabled us to capture the diversity of experiences of research impact as well as identify commonalities. As ECRs ourselves, we were keenly aware that impact can seem daunting, an almost insurmountable challenge for ECRs. In this book, we combine reflective narratives written by ECRs on their experiences of impact with a series of critical and empirical studies that explore the effect research impact has had on the working lives of ECRs.

To attempt to capture a diverse range of ECR experiences, we chose not to approach contributors, but rather to conduct a call for papers, which we shared via Twitter and relevant mailing lists. The array of submissions meant we had to dedicate a significant amount of time to understanding how the various contributions come together and the story we wanted to tell by placing them side by side. Writing and editing was, thus, a dynamic process. We were demanding of our authors, asking for rewrites and adjustments to ensure that the kaleidoscopic array of perspectives, interpretations, and critical studies spoke to one another. The aim was never to create a liner narrative, but an informal conversation.

Depending on your own interests and background, different chapters and sections of the book will prove more useful or relevant than others. It should be borne in mind that this is not a traditional text. It is neither a training manual, nor an academic monograph. Rather than offering a single perspective or voice on the subject, it brings together individual experiences, insight from professional practice, as well as empirical research to examine this complex issue. This innovative approach is reflected in the different voices encountered throughout the book. Some talk directly to the reader offering advice and guidance, others talk from their own experience, and some present the findings of research studies. You can read this book in a linear manner, or you may prefer to dip into different chapters as the time and opportunity arises. The reflections complement the preceding essay, but also function as standalone pieces of work. The book is organic in the sense that the first section focuses on the connection between impact and the individual researcher, before moving, in section two, to a discussion of how research impact work requires that we think through how we transfer, translate, and exchange our ideas. In the final section, we look more at research structures and how the notion of impact is encouraging networked, coproduced, and collaborative approaches to research, changing the shape of doctoral education, research training, and the spaces and places in which we work.

ACKNOWLEDGMENTS

This book couldn't have come into being without the advice and guidance of our colleagues and the support of Coventry University and the University of Sheffield. In particular, we would like to thank Maddalaine Ansell, Eleonora Belfiore, Laura Caulfield, Paul Manners, Wilfred Mijnhardt, Nick Turner, Phil Ward and Abigail Williams for their contributions to the 2016 conference and for inspiring us to take this book forward. We would also like to thank all those who took the time to submit abstracts for this collection – we wish we could have accepted them all. Special thanks goes to the collection's contributors for their engagement with what has been an unusual editing process. Finally, we would also like to give special thanks to Julie Bayley for her insight, support, and contribution throughout the book's development.

CONTRIBUTORS

Tony Bromley, University of Leeds (UK): Tony is a Senior Training and Development Officer at the University of Leeds. He was lead author of the UK researcher development sector evaluation impact framework and has published work on both the evaluation of impact of training and development activity and research.

Alex M. Clarke-Cornwell, University of Salford (UK): Alex is a Lecturer in Public Health, with a background in Mathematics and Statistics. Alex's research and teaching focuses around her experience of epidemiology and statistics, and the use of accelerometers to explore issues related to the measurement of physical activity and sedentary behaviour.

Jenna Condie, Western Sydney University (Australia): Jenna is a Lecturer in Digital Research and Online Social Analysis. She researches the psychology of cyber-urban living and what humans are becoming with technology in urban places. Jenna co-leads the Travel in the Digital Age (TinDA) project, which examines the intersections of travel, transport, technology and mobile lives.

Anna Mary Cooper-Ryan, University of Salford (UK): Anna is a Lecturer in Public Health, with a background in Psychology, working therapeutically with children and public health. Her teaching and research crisscross a range of topics focusing on global public health, systematic reviews, childhood, behaviour change, interventions, and oral health.

Rachel Cowen, University of Manchester (UK): Rachel is a Senior Lecturer and co-founder of the Centre for Academic and Researcher Development. She specialises in developing programmes to promote research and teaching and learning excellence and inspiring academic leadership nationally and internationally.

Ian Edelstein, Human Sciences Research Council (South Africa): Ian is a Research Specialist in the Human Sciences Research Council. He holds a PhD in Sociology from the University of Cape Town. Before joining the HSRC, he was head of communications and public affairs at the International Committee of the Red Cross – Pretoria Regional Delegation and a global adviser on urban violence and youth projects.

Kieran Fenby-Hulse, Coventry University (UK): Kieran is an Assistant Professor in Research Capability and Development and is responsible for designing developmental initiatives for researchers and research teams. His research focused on research leadership and creating innovative and inclusive research cultures. He is Managing Editor for the Journal of Research Management and Administration.

Vicky Gilroy, Northumbria University (UK): Vicky is a Senior Lecturer in Specialist Community Public Health Nursing and is currently on secondment to the Institute of Health Visiting as Projects and Evaluation Lead.

Judith Gracey, University of Manchester (UK): Judith is a Knowledge Transfer and Impact Coordinator, focusing particularly on the development of REF impact case studies.

Helen Graham, University of Leeds (UK): Helen is Associate Professor in the School of Fine Art, History of Art, and Cultural Studies. Helen's research lies at the intersection of political theory and participative and action-led forms of research. With museums, heritage and place as a focus, Helen investigates political dynamics of property, rights and claims; of democracy; of agency and affinity through experimenting with how small-scale participatory work can be combined with large scale 'whole system' action.

Ged Hall, University of Leeds (UK): Since 2011, Ged has worked at the University of Leeds supporting academics of all disciplines to generate the impact they want to see emerge from their research. He has led researcher development programmes, careers and academic writing development services. Before working in HE, he was a consultant in the oil, gas and utility sectors (essentially the knowledge broker that papers on impact processes / models often refer too). His research background is in physical chemistry.

Tracy Ann Hayes, University of Cumbria (UK): Tracy is a Lecturer in Health, Psychology & Social Studies, where she recently completed a PhD researching the relationship that young people have with the natural environment. She embraces transdisciplinary methodologies which utilise creative and narrative approaches.

Emma Heywood, The University of Sheffield (UK): Emma is a Lecturer and Researcher in Journalism, Politics and Communication. She is currently assessing the impact of radio on women's empowerment in Niger drawing on a previous

British Academy-funded project which investigated the role of local radio in NGO activities in the West Bank. She is also working with United States Institute for Peace's RESOLVE on a methodological guide to researching the prevention and countering of violent extremism.

Katie Hill, Share It CIC (UK): Katie is a Researcher specialising in social design and community participation. Katie worked on the Connecting Epistemologies project as a community partner through Leeds Love It Share It CIC, an independent research social enterprise of which Katie is a founding director. As well as working in the third and private sectors, Katie has held 12 temporary part-time and 9 freelance contracts with 8 universities.

Dee-Ann Johnson, University of Manchester (UK): Dee-Ann supports the professional development of early career researchers across a range of transferable skills. She leads on activities for researchers involved in public engagement and research impact and co-ordinates university-wide science communication initiatives, opportunities and strategy.

Peter Matthews, University of Stirling (UK): Peter is a Senior Lecturer in Social Policy at the Faculty of Social Sciences. His research focuses on understanding inequalities in the urban environment and efforts to tackle these. He has developed innovative coproduced approaches to carrying out research and is interested in social science evidence use in wider society.

Louise Maythorne, Bath Spa University (UK): Louise is a Knowledge Exchange Officer with responsibility for KE activity in each academic unit. She is responsible for brokering collaborative relationships between academic staff and research users in government, businesses and communities. Louise is responsible for third-stream funding, university consultancy and supporting colleagues with the intellectual property of their research.

Alex McDonagh, University of Salford (UK): Alex is a Lecturer in Critical and Contextual Studies. His research interests are broadly based in heritage and culture, with a particular focus on the ways that heritage and culture are formed in everyday and subaltern contexts and how digital media may affect the perception or agency of dominant cultural discourses.

Robert Meckin, University of Manchester (UK): Robert is a postdoctoral research associate in the Department of Sociology. He researches interdisciplinary knowledge-making communities, particularly in the biosciences, and he also uses creative and sensory methods to explore how non-experts reconstruct technoscientific knowledge in everyday life. He is interested in development opportunities for early career researchers and currently coordinates the Postgraduate Forum for Science, Technology and Innovation Studies (pfstis.co.uk).

Jessica Medhurst, Ocean University (China): Having completed a PhD in Victorian Children's Literature and Photography at the University of Reading, Jessica undertook a Knowledge Transfer Partnership at Seven Stories (The Antional Centre for Children's Books) with Newcastle University. She is currently a lecturer at Ocean University of China where she teaches 19th and 20th century British and American literature.

Helen Morley, University of Leeds (UK): Helen works at the intersection of contrasting expertise and experience and has used her backgrounds in engineering, philosophy and leadership to support researchers in developing effective, efficient and meaningful impact, primarily focusing on Arts and Humanities specialists. Having worked as a Teaching Fellow, Research Ethics Training Officer and Research Impact Officer, she is currently enjoying developing staff and PGRs as a Learning and Development Adviser at the University of Leeds.

Dave O'Brien, University of Edinburgh (UK): Dave is Chancellor's Fellow in Cultural and Creative Industries at the University of Edinburgh. His next book will be Culture is Bad for You? Inequality and the Creative Class, published by Manchester University Press.

Balungile Shandu, University of Johannesburg (South Africa): Balungile is a doctoral student in the Department of Education Leadership and Management. She holds a Masters degree in Social Sciences (Public Policy) from the University of KwaZulu-Natal. She completed a two-year internship programme at the Human Sciences Research Council as a Masters Research Intern. Her research interests include: Monitoring and Evaluation, Language Policies in Education and the Healthcare sector.

Rebekah Smith McGloin, Coventry University (UK): Rebekah is the Director of the Doctoral College and Centre for Research Capability and Development at Coventry University. She chairs the Postgraduate Research Training and Development Committee for the national Doctoral Training Alliance and is a serving UK Council for Graduate Education executive committee member. She is a member of the BBSRC Bioscience Skills and Careers Strategy Panel, a peer reviewer for the European HR Excellence in Research Award and was an expert panel review member for the UK Concordat for Researchers. Rebekah is also reviewer for the International Journal of Researcher Development.

Sandrine Soubes, University of Sheffield (UK). Sandrine is a Higher Education Researcher / Practitioner, specialised in postdoctoral researcher development and doctoral education. She works as a researcher development manager in the Faculty of Science, at the University of Sheffield. She has a particular interest in ethnographic research in HE contexts. Her research is concerned with mechanisms of academic reproduction through the use of Bourdieusian analysis and the field of research.

Isabella Streffen, University of Lincoln (UK): Isabella Streffen is Senior Lecturer in Fine Art. From 2013–14 she was Early Career Research Fellow at Oxford Brookes University, undertaking research into drones, and collaborative work with the And Or Project. She was awarded her doctorate in Fine Art by Newcastle University in 2012 for her work on strategies of military vision. Her current research focuses on artists' use of invisible spectrum technologies.

Mark Taylor, University of Sheffield (UK): Mark Taylor is Lecturer in Quantitative Methods (Sociology) at the Sheffield Methods Institute. His research interests are in the sociology of culture: in consumption, production and education, and its relationship to inequality. He is currently working on AHRC-funded projects on social mobility into cultural and creative work, and on data, diversity and inequality in the creative industries. Methodologically, he is interested in the analysis of survey data, and data visualisation.

Anh Tran, Coventry University (UK): Anh Tran is a Senior Lecturer in Humanitarian Engineering. Her research focuses on sustainable food, energy and water systems, and services in displacement and challenging remote context. Anh has a BEng and PhD from the University of Queensland, Australia.

Kate Walker, Coventry University (UK): Kate is an Assistant Professor in the Centre for Advances in Behavioural Science. Her research focus is on intimate partner violence and the development and evaluation of primary and tertiary interventions for the prevention of violence in adult and adolescent populations. Her work also focuses on sexual violence, including child sexual exploitation and image-based sexual abuse.

Diana Warira, African Institute for Development Policy (Kenya): Diana is a Communications Specialist with nearly 10 years of experience in development communications. Her research interests are in the link between the communication of research and effective public policymaking and programming. She's a communications officer and also an alumni scholar of the South Voices Network for Peacebuilding at the Woodrow Wilson International Center for Scholars.

Ke Yu, University of Johannesburg (South Africa): Ke is an Associate Professor in the Faculty of Education. She previously worked as Senior Research Specialist at the Human Sciences Research Council in South Africa. She holds a PhD in Educational Management and Policy Studies from the University of Pretoria in South Africa (2008). Her research interests primarily include research synthesis, research governance (research impact and ethics), and knowledge production with the advances of technology, as well as comparative studies on oriental, occidental and African culture and society.

PART I
Research impact and me

1

UNCERTAINTY AND CONFUSION

The starting point of all expertise

Ged Hall, Helen Morley and Tony Bromley

Our aim in this chapter is to examine the effect that the impact agenda, within the UK, has had on the process of developing an academic identity or becoming an expert in your chosen field. Our approach emerged from reflecting on a combination of our own experience in supporting impact within our institution (we work with researchers, at all career stages from PhD through to experienced professors, across the full disciplinary spectrum to support them in this career-long journey of increasing expertise) and published work, which covered three key areas:

1. Recognised research identities: imposter syndrome; aspirants; existentialists.
2. Key aspects of the researcher journey: intellectual; networking; institutional.
3. How researchers personally develop: behavioural; attitudinal; intellectual.

The outcomes of our reflection are the following proposals:

1. Uncertainty in your academic identity in response to impact is natural but can be overcome by engaging with the type of impact that most motivates and has a natural link to your research.
2. You can use the same skills you have already used in your research journey to respond to the challenges of developing impact.
3. As with your research development, you should draw on the networks and sources of expertise within your institution and the academy more widely.

In addition, we also offer specific advice on impact for fundamental researchers, both in response to our experience of concern from this group about the relevance of impact for their research, and as a means of reflecting on impact itself.

Research identity and experience

Researching is a human experience, researchers are people too and the processes, cultures, attitudes and challenges associated with research are all part of that human experience. One of the ways this manifests in a recurring theme that emerges from the literature is the personal uncertainty and confusion that is typified by statements such as 'Am I good enough?' This imposter syndrome (Clance and Imes 1978; Knights and Clarke 2014) can re-emerge at any stage of a career although it may be more publicly voiced in the earlier stages as an ECR. As we will see below, the challenge of responding to incorporating impact into your research practice can significantly contribute to researchers experiencing elements of imposter syndrome in ways that they may not currently be experiencing with their research.

A sense of being an 'imposter' is a common description of a research identity. Whilst Sukulku and Alexander argue for a narrow definition, with Imposter Phenomenon affecting a 'small subgroup of people who experience a clinical level of self-perceived intellectual fraudulence (2011, p. 74), Knights and Clarke (2014) take a broader view and identify two other types of insecure identities: 'aspirants' and 'existentialists'. They found that aspirants were continually working towards an idealised perfect academic that they recognised was unachievable with rejection (of grants and papers) constantly throwing them off track. Existentialists were continually looking for validation, nearly always external, of their work and its value. All three types of identity may face challenges in engaging with those outside the academy as they pursue impact, as there is a wide range of possible reactions from non-academic partners that could lend evidence that the researcher might be not good enough, provide imperfect impact pathways or evidence, or fail to provide sought-after evaluation.

All three insecure identities emerged from a continuous exposure to the judgement of others. This sense of constant examination, within an academic career, has been suggested to be without comparison in other professions (Gabriel 2010). This judgement, within the UK, has been systematised through the Research Excellence Framework (REF), which introduced non-academic impact assessment into the UK's regular research assessment, and in the Teaching Excellence Framework (TEF) that has emerged more recently. In 2017, Jo Johnson MP, the then Minister of State for Universities, Science and Research and Innovation in the UK Government, announced the possibility of a Knowledge Excellence Framework (KEF) (Johnson 2017) to evaluate engagement, collaboration and commercialisation. This systemic series of judgements builds on and increases the potential stresses that emerge from the cumulative critique in a career that may have started with a small seminar presentation as a PhD student through to the rejected multi-million pound grant application as a senior professor. Although all three frameworks express an institutional assessment publicly, the institutional assessment is inevitably a composite of individuals' inputs. Inputs that will be known, and assessed, locally within the institution.

Prior to the inclusion of impact within REF 2014, it was possible to avoid the agenda (within the UK and the EU) by not applying for particular funding streams (UK Research Council and the EU's framework funding). Impact may have provided a safer and appealing environment, especially for existentialists (Knights and Clarke 2014), for those who chose to engage. However, this formalised assessment may have reduced the desire of those who already engaged in impact to do so (Chubb and Reed 2018) and added yet more insecurity for those who had not chosen this path previously. Regardless of any of this history, 'impact' has certainly added to the uncertainty and confusion across the academic sector with debates about the definition of impact (the introduction to this book discusses definitions of impact), referred to by David Phipps as 'definitional dystopia' (Phipps 2016), and academics critiquing its effect on the nature of universities (Collini 2012).

Our argument, in this chapter, is that those who have always chosen to engage with impact beyond the academy must now demonstrate, prove and measure their impact. Whilst those who did not previously consider this to be part of their academic role must now learn new skills and behaviours and enter new networks. This therefore puts both types of researcher, no matter what career stage they are at, back at the beginning of an intellectual journey to either begin to develop impact in their research or provide better evidence of the existing impact of their work and grow the impact that emerges from it. This place is again one characterised by the uncertainty and confusion they felt when they first began to read the existing literature to carve out a niche for their fledgling career.

This is often further exacerbated for researchers who locate their academic identities at the very fundamental end of their particular discipline. For these researchers, no matter whether they are scientists, social scientists or in the arts and humanities, there can be an even deeper confusion and uncertainty about whether impact can ever be for them. We will come back to this question in the final part of our chapter.

To analyse the effects that impact has on a researcher, i.e. it takes them back to a place of relative non-expertise, compared to the expertise they demonstrate in their research fields, we looked at previous research that discussed the journey from PhD research to first non-contract academic post (or a tenure position in North American universities). The work of McAlpine et al. (2010) provides a framework to consider this journey. Their work is based on empirical research from the Canadian university sector and the three strands they proposed that exist on this trajectory, Intellectual, Networking and Institutional, give us an excellent framework for thinking about the effects impact has on any researcher. Towards the end of the chapter we provide some specific advice for fundamental researchers.

The Intellectual strand is essentially the contribution the researcher has made and is making to their chosen field via the publication, presentations and curriculum artefacts they produce. The authors acknowledge the effect of external forces such as funders' expectations, strategic grant calls, developing collaborations and the pressures to co-author internationally in this area. Now, if we add in the expectation to have impact, beyond the academy, the researcher must first identify what this impact could be, learn how to enable this impact (whilst managing the time and resource burden it may generate), develop skills in the evaluation of this impact (which may not be directly measurable) and navigate new contexts outside the academy. Even the most experienced of researchers who has never considered this before can see this is a daunting intellectual task. This may even also lead them to question whether engaging with impact may take them too far from their evolving academic identity.

The Networking strand is the various local, national and international networks the person is connected to. Any network and a person's visibility in that network are built on relationships and interactions. These relationships and interactions can take a significant time to develop and have fluctuations in the net input to or output from the network. Again, the consideration of impact may lead to the researcher needing to develop entirely new networks, ones into which their current networks do not provide any meaningful bridge. This will add a sense of isolation and take yet more effort to establish a sense of respect from those who already inhabit that network, which is not unusual amongst researchers in the early stages of their PhDs when the big names in the field were just that – names on a paper and not real people with different characters.

The Institutional strand provides the income and resources to sustain and move forward along this academic trajectory. This includes part-time teaching positions and scholarships at PhD level, through post-doctoral funding and salary and set-up costs for first-time academic positions. The availability of these resources and income at a particular university or for the particular career phase of the individual may enhance or hinder the person's development in the other two strands. For instance, if travel funds are not available at a university, or if the funds do exist but the individual is not currently in a role that is eligible for them, then they could struggle to attend 'that conference' that will turbo-charge their intellectual and / or networking strand. When we consider impact, we again have to ask what monetary and / or person resources are available at a particular university (for instance, at our own institution, which is not unusual within the UK, there are professional staff whose roles can assist with impact and internal funding at school, faculty and institutional level to help with starting and maintaining the crucial external networks) and whether this resource is only available to people at a particular stage of their career. Researchers at any stage may ask how this additional work fits into their current workload or what funding exists. Again, we have gone back to a state of uncertainty and confusion.

This whole cycle of returning to uncertainty and confusion was highlighted in a commentary, published in the same book, by Driver (2010) on McAlpine et al.'s (2010) chapter. Driver made the point that every new position or research direction he had taken in his career had produced 'learning curves'. It is therefore likely that impact will be another learning curve.

This leaves us to deal with three questions:

1. How to overcome the intellectual challenges associated with impact?
2. How to overcome the networking challenges associated with impact?
3. How to overcome the institutional challenges associated with impact?

If we ask anyone to consider the transitions in their research career, by reflecting upon these three strands, we can find ways in which they overcame similar challenges as they moved from early stage researcher into their first open-ended academic post. It is also likely that the most important strand to consider first is intellectual.

Impact and the intellectual strand

Many books written to assist with the PhD process suggest that motivation and maintaining that motivation is the crucial component in succeeding (Cryer 2006; Hall and Longman 2008; Petre and Rugg 2010; Phillips and Pugh 2015). Motivation, or the reason why you became a researcher, is again the under-pinning of a recent book for advice on becoming a productive researcher (Reed 2017). We therefore suggest that motivation should again be a guiding force for your intellectual journey in learning how to generate impact from your research. As you begin your process of clearing the uncertainty and confusion associated with impact, ensure you are seeking to generate impact that motivates and excites you. This motivation will help to protect you from being overawed by the challenges of impact in the same way as it does when you face challenges in your research.

We are often asked by researchers (of any career stage) who are new to impact, which forms of impact the UK Research Councils and the REF value more than others. We believe the honest answer is actually none because of two particular points:

1. The definitions of impact used by the Research Councils and in the REF (HEFCE 2011) are so broad that they do not exclude any form of impact, other than the proviso that it needs to be beyond the academy.
2. In REF2014 there were highly graded case studies for a huge range of very different forms of impact.

We acknowledge that there are pressures that the Research Councils face in demonstrating the worth of research to government. Also in any complex funding landscape there are specific funding streams that may be much more impact focused. For instance, within the UK the Global Challenge Research Fund (UKRI, n.d. a) is specifically targeted at impact that occurs within official development assistance (ODA) compliant countries, whilst the new Industrial Strategy Challenge Fund (UKRI, n.d. b) is specifically focused on the UK Government's long-term plan to raise productivity and earning power in the UK. Whilst we acknowledge that there is no clear correlation between the extent of the impact demonstrated by REF2014 and these new and substantial forms of research funding within the UK, there is discussion within the UK HE sector that the inclusion of impact within REF may have had a positive influence on the UK Government's view of the sector's value.

However, we believe the Research Councils and the panels that determine the REF results are adroit at not skewing their judgements due to these external biases, precisely because these judgements are made by people drawn from the academic community. (For readers unfamiliar with the research funding system in the UK, it is important to know that decisions about research funding are taken by the research community itself, commonly known as the Haldane Principle. This applies to both strands of the UK's dual support system: 1. funding for specific applications and 2. funding received directly by an institution based on the outcomes of the regular research assessments, such as REF2014.) These individually assess whether a researcher has thoroughly considered what impact may emerge from the proposed research their application is describing and then assess the evidence of the actual impact at the end of the process, but they do not bias one form of impact over another. This assertion is based on the fact that both systems use peer review, which is the best tool we have available to remove individual subjective bias (as noted by Smith et al. 2011). The scope for peer processes to remove bias towards one form of impact was also noted by Derrick (2018). Furthermore, as we have already noted, the definition of impact (used in assessing UK grant applications and REF impact case studies) is massively broad. Therefore, you do have the same freedom in choosing which type of impact to pursue just as you do in choosing which research questions are most stimulating for you.

Once you have decided the type(s) of impact that could emerge from your research, that truly motivates you or speaks to your core values, you can then use your highly developed research skills to research answers to the question 'What skills / intellectual capabilities do I need to pursue this form of impact?'. The particular choice of impact and a pathway to it, including this skill development, is highly specialised and context dependent (Bayley and Phipps 2017) and will therefore likely require you to seek support, advice and guidance.

This acknowledgement of 'a gap' in your capabilities may not be very comfortable for you but you need to remember the vulnerability you felt in the past when this happened to you, and remember how you asked for help then. Thinking about the help and support you received from teachers, mentors and peers (Allen et al. 2004) will help you to break this intellectual development question down further to become 'Who may know what skills I may need and how I may develop them?'. Therefore, in essence, you need to be able to ask those around you, who you are comfortable with, this question and, with universities being what they are, there is likely to be an expert not far away within your existing network.

If this local search doesn't prove fruitful then you can resort to the same literature search skills you always use to find the authors of papers who have researched impact (and all the various terms used in this arena, such as knowledge mobilisation) in a range of contexts. This is exactly the process that one of us used when moving into the field of providing training for impact:

1.   Find local experts (TB was an already a friend and colleague and an evalua-
     tion expert).
2.   Access institutional support (e.g. research support professionals and funding).
3.   Read papers (not all written by those local experts).
4.   Build relationships with those local and external experts.
5.   Enter the debate to keep re-thinking, reflecting and learning about impact
     and how it occurs.

This is a process you can follow as well because that is exactly the process you
used to develop the intellectual strand of your career journey.

Impact and the networking strand

The networking strand is, perhaps, the most obvious area of uncertainty and confusion
with regard to impact. This is because, before you start on your journey to your
potential impact, you are unlikely to have specific contacts in the impact context, and
your academic network may not have this expertise either. It is also likely to be the most
important area to focus on, if Reed's assertion that impact is best achieved through a
relational approach (Reed 2016) (based on empirical research he was involved in (Reed
et al. 2014)), is true; through our own experience, we believe that it is. For many
researchers, at any stage of their careers, the level of confusion and uncertainty is such
that they may be unable to describe any groups, people or organisations who may
benefit from their research (over any time scale), whilst others may only be able to
tentatively suggest one or two people or groups who may benefit, but they are likely to
have no prior connection to those networks. In addition to this networking uncertainty
there is also the potential for challenges within the intellectual strand, which may reinforce 'imposter syndrome' feelings, when connecting with those new networks.

In order to be successful in delivering impact, it is crucially important to know
what your impact could be, or what the 'destination' is. Without some idea of this
'destination', or impact goal, it becomes impossible to decide what actions you
could take to help realise that impact. It is also impossible to fully evaluate your
impact without some benchmark – usually both a baseline and a hoped-for outcome are necessary. You may well have multiple impact goals (destinations) in
mind. However, you will need to prioritise them to ensure you aren't stretched
too thin and end up achieving nothing. Of those multiple destinations, which are
most likely? Are some more difficult to achieve? Which are the most significant?
And which do you care most strongly about?

When individuals reflect on previous times in their lives when they have had to
establish new networks and get to know new people, they often refer to the fear of
'being different' and 'not fitting in'. This fear often translates into avoidance tactics
(either finding other activities to make you too busy to begin the process of
interacting with new contacts or 'hiding' from those new contacts in new situations, for instance checking email during a conference coffee break rather than
entering into conversations with new people) or clinging onto identities that they

have developed in their other networks. Therefore, when you reflect on your past examples like this, what have you done to prevent these avoidance tactics or overcome your specific internal barriers that initially stopped you engaging? In our experience, these actions are likely to include:

1. Using introductions into the network, usually from someone you already have some connection (or trust) with.
2. Establishing a relationship with one or two people in the network, usually via smaller events / gatherings of that network.
3. Spending time gathering information about the network. Who is powerful and influential? What are the 'rules' (implicit or explicit) of the network? What is their shared language and identity and how does it differ to my own identities (for example, teacher, researcher, research leader, etc.)? This tactic may be part of an early stage of tactics 1 and 2.
4. Undertaking small tasks (e.g. administrative tasks) for the network to become known within the network.

It is this latter activity which often allows you to undertake something you do know how to do in order to move from 'known by a few' to 'known by many'. This final tactic resonates with much of the advice on how to grow impact, which suggests that it is easier to move from significant impact with a few beneficiaries to many beneficiaries than it is to move from minimal impact with many beneficiaries to significant impact with all of that population (Reed 2017). In order to develop your impact goal, run through these simple actions:

1. Take a look at the Gateway to Research (UKRI, n.d. c), maintained by UK Research and Innovation, which lists all the funded research in the UK and their likely impact. Narrow down with keywords relating to your research and only look at examples from the last 2–3 years. The EU also maintains a similar database (European Commission, n.d.).
2. Review the published impact case studies from REF2014 (HEFCE 2014). Use the search tools to narrow down your reading to focus on case studies that include keywords linked to your current or future research project. Which groups were described in those case studies? What benefits did they accrue? What actions did the researcher(s) undertake to help make this impact achievable and how did they evaluate it? Make notes about the types of groups and benefits that appeal to you.
3. Discuss these appealing ideas of impact with people within the networks you already have. This should include academic colleagues, staff in research, public engagement and impact support roles to test out your ideas and get feedback. If you don't know staff in these roles then the process of getting to know them could uncover brokers into the networks you may need to enter.
4. Identify one or two people in those new networks to approach to test out your ideas further and begin the process of entering those networks.

In step one, we asked you to note the examples of impact that 'appealed' to you. This is very important for a number of reasons. Firstly, you are an academic and therefore one of the key components of your identity is academic freedom. We believe that you should exert the same freedom in choosing the nature of the impact you want your research to enable and what actions you want to pursue to enable that impact. For instance, you may be happier to achieve some form of social impact rather than commercial impact. However, as with any freedom, we encourage you to make fully informed choices after you have investigated the potential impacts your research could have and the various routes to that impact. Also any freedom comes with balancing responsibilities and in the case of impact this is the responsibility of contributing something back to those who ultimately fund most university research (in the UK this being taxpayers).

Secondly, building new networks and relationships requires investment (time, energy and sometimes cost) on your part. In order to justify that investment to yourself, you must be convinced of the importance of the impact goal from your perspective.

Finally, in order to build and maintain trusting relationships with those who could benefit from your research, they must believe that you have a shared goal and a shared motivation to reach that goal. If, at any point, they believe that your motivation is lacking or your interests lie elsewhere, then their trust in you will immediately start to wane.

Impact and the institutional strand

This final strand focuses on the resources that are available to you at your institution for your academic development. Remind yourself of how you found out about those resources and how you overcame the confusions associated with learning new acronyms, understanding organisational structures, discovering appropriate internal funding schemes and understanding all the formal and informal mentoring that exists. This may be especially true if you are new to the institution.

However, it is possible that your institution may not have fully designed and implemented systems, funding and structures to help you with impact. This level of embeddedness of support for impact has recently been shown to be variable across the UK (we are not aware of any international comparisons) and much less well embedded than support for developing academic excellence (Galan-Diaz 2017). Therefore, this strand may also generate confusion and uncertainty regarding how your institution can help you because your institution is still in the process of making those decisions. As Galan-Diaz notes, 'preparedness regarding impact support in HEIs is on an improving trajectory towards being embedded' (2017). This reference to 'trajectory' is similar to your own trajectory in developing your approach to impact but with a focus on purpose, process, and people.

The following questions may help you to locate what resources your institution can provide (no matter how large or small that support may be):

1. In your institution's top team, whose remit do you think impact falls in? For us, at the University of Leeds, this would be the Deputy Vice-Chancellor for Research and Innovation.
2. What support structures report into that person?
3. What governance structures report into that person?
4. In your area of your institution, whose remit within the leadership group (in this area) do you think impact falls in?
5. Does your institution have support structures that assist with engaging with the press, the public, businesses, etc.? What do these various areas offer as support?

These questions are induction-style questions, and even if you have been at your institution for a number of years, thinking of yourself as a new inquisitive member of staff will help put you in the right mindset to explore them. However, as the level of embeddedness of impact at your own institution increases it will be useful to re-visit these questions regularly.

Personal and professional development 'lens'

Within this chapter so far, we have alluded at times to aspects of the individual as a researcher and how they may change and evolve through the development of their career. We explore this further now by considering impact through the lens of the individuals' personal and professional development as a researcher. A few key questions to explore:

1. What skills and attributes do researchers need to work in research today?
2. What is your conception of what it is to be a researcher today?
3. How has your conception of what it is to be a researcher today developed?
4. How does your conception compare to the reality of being a researcher today?

Question 1 we will explore further in the following paragraphs. Questions 2–4 are for you to explore personally.

In respect of the skills and attributes of researchers we consider two models, one descriptive and one conceptual. The 'descriptive' Researcher Development Framework was developed by the UK Vitae organisation (Vitae 2011) based upon research taking the views of researchers across all stages of a research career. The framework describes 'the knowledge, behaviour and attributes of successful researchers', and is organised into four domains (each with multiple subdomains that each contain multiple descriptors):

Domain A: Knowledge and intellectual abilities: The knowledge, intellectual abilities and techniques to do research

Domain B: Personal effectiveness: The personal qualities and approach to be an effective researcher

Domain C: Research governance and organisation: Knowledge of the professional standards and requirements to do research

Domain D: Engagement, influence and impact: The knowledge and skills to work with others to ensure the wider impact of research. Vitae (2011)

If we consider the RDF as a reasonable description of what is needed to be a successful researcher today, then we can see how diverse and wide-ranging the skills and attributes needed actually are. The individual considering this wide range and diversity may feel considerable uncertainty and ultimately imposter syndrome, especially when we consider that the impact context we discuss in this chapter is only one part of one of the four RDF domains.

However, is it that all the aspects listed in the RDF are those that you personally need to excel in to be a successful researcher and successful in impact, or is it that you can seek out the support of others to fulfil all of these skills? The networking that we have discussed is an extension of formalisation of the 'third space' within universities (Smyth 2014). The 'third space' has significantly developed in universities and is occupied by professionals in, for example, impact of research, obtaining research funding, commercialisation of research, public engagement, and professional development. Build them into your research team!

Moving on from the RDF descriptive model, let us now consider, in respect of impact, a conceptual model relating to researcher development. Evans (2011) considered the question 'What is researcher development?', in the first instance looking to the published literature to see the approaches used in characterising researcher development. Evans found that 'the literature encompasses a wide range of (usually implicit) interpretations of and foci on researcher development' (2011, p. 19). She categorised these 'interpretations and foci' as:

1. 'broad brush consideration of career paths, advancement and development of practising and aspiring researchers'.
2. 'development of employability-related and societal growth-relevant skills'.
3. 'acculturation and socialisation within research cultures and environments'.
4. 'capacity building issues, policy and practice'.
5. 'the development of individuals into "better researchers" by the acquisition of specific skills and knowledges and the adoption of different outlooks, concerns, values and foci' (Evans 2011, p. 19).

Through this examination, we add even more potential skills for consideration in addition to those highlighted by the RDF. We might now have an overwhelming conception of what it is to be a researcher of which impact is just one of the challenges in a developing identity. Are you sure of what your conception of a fully accomplished researcher is?

What can be lost in a consideration, such as that described above, about what it is to be a researcher, is a notion of developmental achievement and progress for the researcher; the very things that build confidence that can mitigate thoughts of uncertainty and imposter syndrome.

However, Evans (2011) offers a different approach in her conceptual model characterising researcher development as having three main components, each characterised by sub-components:

- Behavioural development (with sub components processual change; procedural change; productive change; competential change).
- Attitudinal development (with sub components perceptual change; evaluative change; motivational change).
- Intellectual development (with sub components epistemological change; rationalistic change; comprehensive change; analytical change).

For the researcher in this conceptualisation of development, development is simplified to: 'is there development in my behaviour, attitude, and intellect?'. Further, relating to previous discussion in this chapter and specifically impact, the developmental emphasis from Evans' model (Evans 2011) should be about attitudinal development. For the researcher, are you experiencing attitudinal change (as described in Evans 2011) in respect of impact as your research identity develops? Also, as the higher education system evolves, is your conception of your research identity, and impact's place in it, evolving in a complementary way or a divergent way?

Specific advice for fundamental researchers

In this final section of our chapter we try to draw out specific advice for those who identify their research at the fundamental end of the particular discipline they associate with. However, we note that this advice applies to all researchers. As we noted earlier in this chapter, fundamental researchers can be particularly uncertain and / or confused by impact. In our experience, this can arise from four different reasons:

1. The researcher cannot even begin to think of any potential impact from their research.
2. The researcher can envisage impact from this research but it is so far in the future that they struggle to feel any ownership or responsibility for its emergence.
3. The researcher can see so much potential impact from their research that they struggle to decide how to prioritise their efforts and may become overwhelmed with learning new skills for all these different contexts.
4. The researcher can see potential impact from their work once it has meshed with many other bodies of work.

For fundamental researchers, the intellectual uncertainty and confusion that is felt in the four scenarios we described above is subtly different. The first scenario is the most demoralising because, as a researcher, we take pride in our abilities to see into problems and questions and find routes to an answer. That is, after all, a definition of research and being a researcher. Therefore, to be bereft of ideas or even a methodology to generate them strikes at that identity. In this scenario, it is therefore easier to ignore impact and argue that it is not for them, as individuals, or not even appropriate for that area of study.

Our suggestion to address this is to consciously seek to explain your research to as broad an audience (by audience we mean any size from a 1:1 to 1:many situations in both the live and online spaces) as your uncertainty and confusion allow you to deal with. You will need to think about how to structure this explanation and prevent yourself from making assumptions about the audiences such that it is as engaging and accessible as possible. The first occasion you see interest, deep interest, in the audience (this may be just from one person), you may have found someone who can help you to work out what your impact could be. Think of this as a chance for some research with the following questions: 1) What element(s) of the research has this person found so interesting? 2) Why are those area(s) interesting to them? 3) What may emerge from this interest for them? If these audiences have all come from academia, then you will have to add a fourth question: 4) Could this interest lead to impact beyond the academy and, if so, what is the nature of that impact? However, if you have had the nerve to reach out beyond the academy then you are likely to be closer to an answer, or perhaps many answers, for what your impact may be.

Even after these conversations with different audiences you have then only taken the first step on your intellectual journey (and perhaps attitudinal) relating to this potential impact. However, you do at least now have a goal, an objective. Again, if you think about this in a research context, once a researcher has decided on the questions to ask and therefore the research objectives are clarified they can then choose an appropriate methodology. This is what you now need to do with impact. Therefore, you should start with a literature search to determine if similar impact from similar research has been generated previously and, if so, how? You could also use Vicky Ward's (2017) analysis of the knowledge exchange framework to narrow down a suitable impact methodology for your area of work..

The second scenario has implications for the networking strand of your identity development. If impact feels too far in the future, it is hard to imagine what networks you will need to help you to generate it. However, in this scenario you can imagine what the nature of that impact may be. In order to think through what networks you will need to achieve this impact, we ask you to consider ideas from the 'knowledge mobilisation' literature. Put simply, knowledge mobilisation is 'the process of moving knowledge to where it can be most useful' (Ward 2017, p.477). Therefore, you are the first initiator of some fundamental knowledge that must be moved, added to, or evolved to become useful. Therefore, you should think clearly about the person(s) who will take on the next stage of that long process and look to build networks and relationships with those individuals in what may be different disciplines. We have used the word 'discipline' because those individuals and networks are likely to still be within the boundaries of academia. Ward's framework (2017) will assist you in thinking through what knowledge you need to mobilise, to whom, by what mechanism and for what purpose.

In the third scenario (i.e. which of the many types of impact should I prioritise?), we want to remind you of our earlier point on academic freedom. Which impact do you want to prioritise? This decision is likely to be influenced by your values and motivations. It may also be influenced by pragmatic reasons. For instance, if you have strong connections into another discipline, which is that first port of call on the knowledge mobilisation journey, and have very little connection with the first ports of call towards your other potential impact, you are perfectly free to choose, what may be, this easier route. Finally, you may also want to consider external influences on your choice such as your department's policies or the wider policy context.

The confusion in the final scenario can arise from an internal debate relating to attribution, i.e. whose impact is this? Our initial advice to you here is that impact is owned by those who make the change, experience the effect or gain the benefit. The reason we say this is because they are people with every right to apply or not apply the tools, thoughts and results that your research has contributed to. Therefore, in your academic identity you do have 'ownership' of your publications but within the realm of impact you are solely an influencer. Now think back to all the mentors and those who have influenced you in your development as a researcher, but ignore those you have done specific research with: how many of these influencers are authors or even acknowledged on any of your publications? For fundamental researchers, the ultimate owner of the impact can be a huge number of steps away. However, to reduce this level of uncertainty we would suggest that you attempt to keep yourself informed of how the first and second steps in the chain towards that ultimate impact have utilised and evolved the knowledge you provided them with.

Conclusion

In developing this chapter we primarily set out to examine the effect of the impact agenda on the process of development of an academic identity. Much of that examination centres on consideration of what it means to be a researcher today. 'Being a researcher' is a constantly evolving concept, but the process of identity development itself can be characterised, as we have done in this chapter. And the process can have aspects that 'chime' well with the research process. Understanding impact in your area can start with a literature review; a fundamental 'pillar' of research.

What it means to be a contemporary researcher certainly includes development of impact within researcher identity. As the times change, there may be new facets of being a researcher that come to the fore. But core characteristics of how the multitude of aspects of any researcher identity develop are like to remain consistent.

Learning points

- Reflect on your values to find the impact that motivates you.
- Expect to feel confused and don't let that trouble you.
- You don't have impact by yourself – so build your networks, and use those that already exist (within and outside your institution).
- Celebrate when the mist rises and then help others to get there too.

References

Allen, T.D., Eby, L.T., Lentz, E. and Lima, L. (2004). Career benefits associated with mentoring for proteges: A meta-analysis. *Journal of Applied Psychology*. 89(1), 127–136.

Bayley, J.E.Phipps, D. (2017). Building the concept of research impact literacy. *Evidence and Policy*. 13(4). [Viewed 22 August 2018]. Available from: doi:10.1332/174426417X15034894876108

Chubb, J. and ReedM.S. (2018). The politics of research impact: academic perceptions of the implications for research funding, motivation and quality. *British Politics*. [Viewed 22 August 2018]. Available from: doi:10.1057/s41293-018-0077-9

Clance, P.R. and Imes, S.A. (1978). The imposter phenomenon in high achieving women: dynamics and therapeutic interventions. *Psychotherapy: Theory, Research and Practice*. 15(3), 241–247.

Collini, S. (2012). *What are universities for?*London: Penguin Group.

Cryer, P. (2006). *The research students' guide to success*. Maidenhead: Open University Press.

Derrick, G. (2018). *The evaluators' eye: impact assessment and academic peer review*. London: Palgrave Macmillan.

Driver, J. (2010). Commentary. In: L. McAlpine, and G. Akerlind, eds. *Becoming an academic*. New York: Palgrave Macmillan. pp. 193–195.

Evans, L. (2011). What research administrators need to know about researcher development: towards a new conceptual model. *Journal of Research Administration*. 42(1), 15–37.

European Commission (n.d.). *Project databases.*. [Viewed 23 August 2018] Available from: https://ec.europa.eu/info/research-and-innovation/projects/project-databases_en

Gabriel, Y. (2010). A space for ideas, identities and agonies. *Organization Studies*. 31(6), 757–775.

Galan-Diaz, C. (2017). Institutional support for impact remains at the relatively early stages of embeddedness. *LSE Impact of the Social Sciences Blog*. 14 November. [Viewed 22 August 2018]. Available from: http://blogs.lse.ac.uk/impactofsocialsciences/2017/11/14/institutional-support-for-impact-remains-at-the-relatively-early-stages-of-embeddedness/

Hall, G. and Longman, J., eds. (2008). *The postgraduate's companion*. London: Sage.

HEFCE (2011). *Assessment framework and guidance on submissions*. REF2014. [Viewed 22 August 2018]. Available from: www.ref.ac.uk/2014/pubs/2011-02/

HEFCE (2014). *Impact case studies database*. REF2014. [Viewed 22 August 2018]. Available from: http://impact.ref.ac.uk/CaseStudies/

Johnson, J. (2017). *How universities can drive prosperity through deeper engagement*. Gov.UK. [Viewed 22 August 2018]. Available from: www.gov.uk/government/speeches/how-universities-can-drive-prosperity-through-deeper-engagement

Knights, D. and Clarke, C.A. (2014). It's a bittersweet symphony, this life: fragile academic selves and insecure identities at work. *Organization Studies*. 35(3), 335–357.

McAlpine, L., Amundsen, C. and Jazvac-Martek, M. (2010). Living and imagining academic identities. In: L. McAlpine, and G. Akerlind, eds. *Becoming an academic: international perspectives*. New York: Palgrave Macmillan. pp. 125–154.

Petre, M. and Rugg, G. (2010). *The unwritten rules of PhD research*. Maidenhead: Open University Press.

Phillips, E. and Pugh, D.S. (2015). *How to get a PhD: a handbook for students and their supervisors*. Maidenhead: Open University Press.

Phipps, D. (2016). Knowledge mobilisation. 2016 Research Impact Summit [online talk].

Reed, M.S. (2016). *The research impact handbook*. Huntly: Fast Track Impact.

Reed, M.S. (2017). *The productive researcher*. Huntly: Fast Track Impact.

Reed, M.S., Stringer, L.C., Fazey, I., Evely, C. and Kruijsene, J.H.J. (2014). Five principles for the practice of knowledge exchange in environmental management. *Journal of Environmental Management*. 146(15), 337–345.

Smith, S., Ward, V. and House, A. (2011). Impact in the proposals for the UK's Research Excellence Framework: shifting the boundaries of academic autonomy. *Research Policy*. 40 (10), 1369–1379.

Smyth, K. (2014). *The university as a third space?*3E Education. 28 July. [Viewed 22 August 2018]. Available from: https://3eeducation.org/2014/07/28/the-university-as-a-third-space/

Sukulku, J. and Alexander, J. (2011). The imposter phenomenon. *International Journal of Behavioural Science*. 6(1), 73–92.

UKRI (n.d. a). *Global challenges research fund*. [Viewed 23 August 2018]. Available from: www.ukri.org/research/global-challenges-research-fund/

UKRI (n.d. b). *Industrial strategy challenge fund*. [Viewed 23 August 2018]. Available from: www.ukri.org/innovation/industrial-strategy-challenge-fund/

UKRI (n.d. c). *Gateway to research*. [Viewed 23 August 2018]. Available from https://gtr.ukri.org/

Vitae (2011). *Developing the Vitae researcher development framework*. Vitae. [Viewed 17 November 2017]. Available from: www.vitae.ac.uk/researchers-professional-development/about-the-vitae-researcher-development-framework/developing-the-vitae-researcher-development-framework

Ward, V.L. (2017). Why, whose, what and how? A framework for knowledge mobilisers. *Evidence and Policy*. 13(3), 477–497.

REFLECTION

Start small, think big: The hard path to success for the early career researcher

Kate Walker

One often hears, as an early career researcher (ECR), about the importance of 'disseminating' researchers' work effectively and demonstrating its 'real-world impact' beyond the academic context; that is, not just 'sharing' knowledge with interested parties but ensuring it is consumed in some form or another by those it was designed to benefit. The increased emphasis on demonstrable benefit by key players like the funders, regulators (e.g., Research Excellence Framework (REF)) and the public is a welcome one; however, there is a lack of consensus with regard to what these stakeholders and researchers themselves define as impact, and how they measure or count it (Watermeyer and Hedgecoe 2016). Therefore, as a researcher navigating these waters, I have some work to do to develop a clear, comprehensive and realistic impact plan that meets the expectations of these various groups.

Impact is prominent in the UK higher education context. This is particularly the case in relation to research where expectations have risen in part due to the REF, a prescriptive framework in relation to what we have to achieve with our research. As such, there are three distinct elements that I must demonstrate in my work and ultimately be assessed on: the quality of my outputs (e.g. publications, performances, and exhibitions), their impact beyond academia, and the environment that supports my research (Research Excellence Framework [2021] 2017). Based on this, I need to produce 3★ or 4★ publications that are world-leading research in terms of originality, significance and rigour (Higher Education Funding Council For England 2017). I need to formulate case studies demonstrating impact that is outstanding in terms of reach and significance – with impact for the purpose of the REF defined as 'an effect on, change or benefit to the economy, society, culture, public policy or services, health, the environment or quality of life, beyond academia' (Higher Education Funding Council England 2017).

The REF, in many ways, is a positive framework and aspiration for me to work towards; as a researcher, it makes me accountable to governing bodies, my organisation and, most importantly, to the public. Requirements of the REF focus my thinking on the rationale for my research and what can be achieved, and it discourages me from doing research just for research's sake. However, these expectations can feel overwhelming and unattainable for an ECR, when you are attempting to forge a research path which inevitably has to start small. It can be difficult to hold on to your own research vision if you think there are alternative, quicker routes to satisfying REF requirements. ECRs are, as a result, quite susceptible to experiencing cognitive dissonance (Festinger 1962), i.e., a discomfort caused by holding conflicting elements of knowledge. However, to right the conflict that this may cause, I discuss the following concepts that I hope may prevent the feeling of dissonance that an ECR could experience. I would promote: small is a good start; learn your trade developing your networks and collaboration portfolio; work with leaders in your field (and other disciplines) and learn from them; and (most importantly) learn from your failures – however frustrating they may be. Oh, and please celebrate your successes no matter how minor they may seem.

Small is a good start

The highlights of my portfolio include developing an intervention for men who have used violence in relationships (which is delivered locally), scoping out the characteristics of perpetrators of child sexual exploitation (CSE), and examining non-consensual sharing of sexually explicit media in university students. These are important pieces of research, but to some extent are small-scale and difficult to quantify and qualify in terms of impact that is outstanding in significance and reach. For example, my colleagues and I have developed an intervention using a solution-focused approach for partner violent men in the community (see Bowen, Walker and Holdsworth, in press) and as through-care provision for those in prison (i.e., working with them in prison and following them back out in the community and continuing the work there). We know that engagement vis-à-vis these interventions has been promising based on service providers' reports and the low attrition rates recorded, and we have informal reports from families, service users and service providers of successful integration of those who have offended back into their families. We have moderate quality evidence that individuals have stopped using violence. At a local or grass-roots level, we have evidence of small successes and making a difference, but at this stage it is too small scale to align with the type of difference required for the REF. However, there is clear value in this work, with early evidence of curbing violent behaviour, albeit at a local level. What is important is that I (a) conduct the research at the highest level of quality regardless of scale and (b) that I effectively capture this information of outcome and impact. This is how the work can be used to generate new and bigger research opportunities. We know we need to upscale and robustly evaluate, both of which at times feel unachievable, but this needs to be reframed as something that is attainable by being realistic about the steps to success. To enhance our future funding applications, we have partaken in accreditation discussions with the Ministry of Justice, where I hope to build upon my small start.

Learn your trade developing your networks and collaboration portfolio

Starting with your small projects, learn what works well, what doesn't work well, what are the challenges and most importantly engage with collaborators, partners and advisors on the way. From a small internal pump prime funding to examine non-consensual sharing of sexually explicit media (revenge pornography), a colleague and I are now developing our plan for world-leading research. I started small-scale, published (Walker and Sleath 2017; Walker et al., under review), presented at national and international conferences, ran interactive workshops and I am currently devising a seminar series. This takes time, commitment and tenacity and becomes particularly difficult when trying to include world leaders in your workshops / seminars with little or no funding to cover their costs. I have, however, made some excellent contacts and collaborators along the way, including other academics, practitioners (e.g., revenge-porn helpline providers, NSPCC) and I am currently extending the reach to include educational psychologists, teachers, parents and policy makers. It has been suggested that collaboration arises from and is most effective utilising different levels within the research system: micro-level (individuals, research groups), meso-level (departments, institutions), and macro-level (institutional sectors, in particular, colla-borative agreements between university and industry, or regions) (Franceschet and Costantini 2010) and this is a formulation that I have followed. This now gives me the groundwork to develop a bidding strategy, which will enable me to undertake the large-scale research, developing prevention and intervention strategies around con-sensual and non-consensual sharing of youth-produced sexually explicit media in adolescents. I believe as such this can meet the demands of the REF. It's obviously not plain sailing: the bidding is a highly competitive process, success rates are low and falling (Matthews 2015), the process is slow, writing bids is time-consuming, devel-oping bids takes us away from actually doing research and writing those 3★ and 4★ papers, and in itself bid writing is not a 'REFable' activity. However, I hope by 'learning my trade' and 'developing networks / collaborators' it, at least, places me in a stronger position to achieve this research vision.

Work with leaders in your field (and other disciplines) and learn from them

Learning from experts can be as simple as read, read, read and read (a mantra I believe that is commonly preached to our students). By reading 4★ papers in your field, you can understand what is required from you, and specifically what comprises world-leading research in terms of originality, significance and rigour. You can identify people you want to collaborate with; indeed, doing this has facilitated an international collaboration for me with a Professor in New Zealand. The same principle goes for bidding. If possible, get sight of successful bids and read, read and read. Learn from other people's successes: through working with a colleague, who recently landed an exceptionally large grant that screams 'big data' and world-leading research and impact, I understand what is required if I am to generate my own successful big win. Join in on other people's bid (early on in your career and early on in the bid) and do the legwork so you can learn skills and techniques. This is about being strategic – get your names on papers, bids and projects. This might mean moving away from your own vision, but it is an invaluable training ground. I have worked with a colleague who is world-leading in relation to research into child sexual abuse; this has led to a small-scale scoping study around child sexual exploitation, which is a departure from my research on intimate partner violence. I have now developed my skills in relation to responding to tenders (i.e., invited bids for project work), and importantly this has evolved to us working together currently on a larger scale tender which could lead to a research project with the potential for significant impact. What starts as a departure and a learning platform could result in an exciting opportunity to make a difference.

Learn from your failures

As an academic and particularly as a researcher, I learned early on that I need to be resilient. It was clear that I was joining a profession where I was continually being assessed or reviewed by numerous people, e.g., by students, about my teaching/ marking; by peers, informally, on research bids, reports, papers; by academics, for- mally, through journal reviews, ethics submissions; and by funders, through evaluation of my proposals. At times, this can be soul-destroying, particularly if you have a run of rejections. However, you need to learn from these failures. Firstly, don't see them as failures, but opportunities, i.e., opportunities to learn, re-craft, improve and try again. I have a grand vision of a longitudinal study, investigating the behaviours of partner violent men, in order to develop a framework of desistance and ultimately inform interventions. This proposal has got to the final stages for a couple of funders, but unfortunately recently was rejected again at the second stage. Such failure again is disheartening, and I didn't confront it for a month (I would advise taking a break before processing the feedback). Without doubt, though, it has improved with each iteration, my skills have developed and my belief in the value of this research has not wavered. The feedback from reviewers is positive and offers some sound advice about how this can be adapted, therefore potentially increasing the change of it being funded elsewhere. This encourages me to learn from such failure / rejection, dust myself down and try again. In doing so I follow the philosophy noted by Brian Tracy (CEO of Brian Tracy International), 'Failure is a prerequisite for great success. If you want to succeed faster, double your rate of failure' (Tracy 2014).

Celebrate your successes no matter how small they may be

This final point is very simplistic. As noted above, as a researcher, you need to be resilient and accept a fair bit of rejection / failure and learn from these. However, in doing this, don't lose sight of the successes you have, no matter how small. Remember and celebrate the good you have achieved, especially where you know that as a result of your work, you have made something better for someone out there.

References

Bowen, E., Walker, K. and Holdsworth, E. (in press). Brighter Futures: An integrated brief solution-focused and cognitive behavioural program for intimate partner violence perpetrators in the community. *International Journal of Offender Therapy and Comparative Criminology*.

Festinger, L. (1962). *A Theory of Cognitive Dissonance*. London: Tavistock Publications.

Franceschet, M. and Costantini, A. (2010). The effect of scholar collaboration on impact and quality of academic papers. *Journal of Informetrics*. 4(4), 540–553

Higher Education Funding Council England (2017). *The Second Research Excellence Framework*. HEFCE. [Viewed 20 July 2018]. Available from: www.hefce.ac.uk/rsrch/ref2021/

Matthews, D. (2015). Success rates: Surge in applications to 'struggling' research councils. *Times Higher Education: The World University Rankings*. October 29. [Viewed 14 February 2018]. Available from: www.timeshighereducation.com/news/success-rates-surge-applica tions-struggling-research-councils

Research Excellence Framework [2021] (2017). *What is the REF?*. REF2021. [Viewed 20 February 2018]. Available from: www.ref.ac.uk/about/whatref/

Tracy, B. (2014) 17 March. [Viewed 7 March 2019]. Available at: https://twitter.com/bria ntracy/status/445633322509938689

Walker, K. and Sleath, E. (2017). A systematic review of the current knowledge regarding revenge pornography and non-consensual sharing of sexually explicit media. *Aggression and Violent Behavior*. 36, 9–24.

Walker, K., Sleath, E., Hatcher, R.M., Hine, B. and Crookes, R. (under review). Non-consensual sharing of private sexually explicit media among university students. *Journal of Interpersonal Violence*.

Watermeyer, R. and Hedgecoe, A. (2016). Selling 'impact': peer reviewer projections of what is needed and what counts in REF impact case studies. A retrospective analysis. *Journal of Education Policy*. 31(5), 651–665.

2

DEVELOPING AN ACADEMIC IDENTITY

What's the time Mrs Wolf?

Tracy Hayes

My chapter offers a creative interpretation of my experiences and interests to explore how doctoral research has impacted on me and how my past has shaped my understanding of research and research impact. I invite the reader to join in a playful exploration, through my allegorical relationship with wolves, of what it means to become an academic. If we want to understand the impact of our research, we first need to understand ourselves. I draw on an amorphous body of literature, from diverse sources such as children's author Enid Blyton; Jungian psychologist Pinkola Estes; and *Children's Geographies*, long recognised as a place that utilises creative methodologies, resulting in interdisciplinary work that is challenging, creative and exciting (Kraftl, Horton and Tucker 2014). I pay homage to and further develop that tradition, whilst embracing concepts of playfulness (Bateson and Martin 2013) and transformational learning (Eyler and Giles 1999). As Eyler and Giles (1999, p.133) argue, 'Transformational learning occurs as we struggle to solve a problem…we are called to question the validity of what we think we know or to critically examine the very premises of our perception of the problem'. What happens when the problem we perceive is ourselves? My objective for sharing my story here is to encourage you to pause, consider what impact your research and experiences have had on you, and to explore what you can learn about yourself. One potential outcome from undertaking this reflexive process is that it can enable us to move forward in our careers with more self-awareness and confidence, whereby we stride out, rather than tiptoe. And we can then more effectively support others to do the same, as we transform from early to mid-career researcher, and beyond.

For me, the wolf has come to symbolise the development of my academic identity, counter-balanced by my wider identity as embodied within my relational roles of wife, parent and child (Burke and Stets 2009). The most recurrent question within this process has been *who am I?* I have often found it easier to say who /

what I am not than to say what I am – something that will probably resonate with many early career researchers. I interpret my inner dialogue (the conversations I have in my head) by linking the emotional (my feelings) and cognitive (my thinking) processes (Mezirow 1990; Theodosius 2012) that have occurred as part of the transformational process whereby I have come to be the person I am. The process of undertaking and completing a PhD has fundamentally changed me as a person. I am not who I was. As highlighted by Jarvis and Parker (2005, p.1), 'It is in relationship – in the interaction of the inner person with the outer world – that experience occurs and it is in and through experience that people learn'. At times, my learning has been troubling and unsettling (Meyer and Land 2003) and I share this with you as a way of encouraging you to consider how / why you have come to be the person you are – what impacts have your research experiences had on you? And then to consider in what ways this may impact on your relationships with the world around you, your relationship with yourself and how this may have impacted on your research. To structure my reflexive narrative, I am utilising a conceptual model, a map of reflective writing (Moon 2004) as it effectively captures the ongoing, exploratory nature of my reflections. To paraphrase Owens' discussions (2010, pp.25–26) about the work of C.G. Jung, a reflective map is a conceptual tool, useful for signalling the prominent spatial and temporal landmarks, translating what I have learnt from my travels into tools of discovery that may be useful for deciphering human experience. Within the map are key stages: setting the context through description of events; feeding in additional ideas; reflexive thinking relating reflection to actions; acknowledging learning; moving on to more reflection and review of purpose (Moon 2004). In folklore and mythology, the wolf is symbolic, taken to represent keen intelligence; deep connection with and expression of instincts; appetite for freedom; and a feeling of being threatened, lack of trust in oneself or others. I have often felt silenced by others, unable to express myself through my 'outer voice' and as a result I have developed the ability to listen and attend to my inner voice. Through reflexivity I have learned how to weave these together. Writing this has been an emotional experience, resulting in learning, knowledge and understanding: perhaps most important of all, it has proved empowering. We do not start our doctoral studies as a blank page. We are drawn to areas of research and develop questions based on our specific interests for a reason. Therefore, I argue, it is neglectful to ignore the influence of our past and present interests in this process. Our past impacts our present and our future – our research impacts on our identity as much as our identity impacts on our research.

I have described myself elsewhere as an accidental youth worker (Hayes 2013a), however I am a very deliberate researcher, exploring the relationship that humans have with nature (see more on this later). How did I reach this point? After graduating with a BSc in Natural Sciences I wanted to educate and inspire others about the natural environment, to share my enthusiasm and sense of wonderment. I began working with young children, families and adults, then realised that young people were being inadvertently excluded by not offering opportunities that were accessible, relevant or attractive to them. Resolving to help change this, I qualified as a youth worker, before

moving on to social science research for my doctorate. Pausing to reflect on my transformation from natural to social scientist raises the question: does there have to be a
distinction, or is this a false dichotomy based on traditional methodologies? Over the last
three years I have found a home within the Royal Geographical Society (RGS, n.d.),
particularly the Geographies of Children, Young People and Families (GCYFRG, n.d.)
research sub-group. Does this mean that I am a geographer? Or is this yet another facet
of my increasingly complex identity, something that has always been implicit in my
approach to learning and is now becoming explicit as I shine a reflexive light upon it?
To understand this, I need to go back to my beginnings.

My early life

As a young child, I loved reading, especially about nature, and from a very early
age I buried my nose in a book. However, the kinds of books I read, and the
knowledge embodied within them, has changed over the years. I reflect on my
books as I question how I came to be the person I am. What tales do my books
have to tell about me? What impact has my reading had upon me? Where did my
fascination for wolves come from, and how does Enid Blyton (Enid Blyton Society
2018) fit in all of this? The last two, apparently disconnected, questions have in my
reflections become imperceptibly intertwined. I will address the wolf question
later, however the Blyton question is one I have been pondering since a conversation with a colleague, getting to know each other through swapping stories of
experiences from childhood, growing up into adulthood, failed past relationships
and happy current ones. I admitted: 'Enid Blyton made my childhood' in an attempt
to explain my approach to outdoor learning – an approach that embraces thinking
like a child, emphasising the concepts of playfulness, imagination and stories (Hayes
2013b). She responded, 'Me too!' We laughed, acknowledging that it was not 'cool'
to admit this! For her, it was the boarding school stories, midnight feasts and
mysteries that appealed. For me, it was the magical folk, enchanted woods and
faraway trees, and the overwhelming sense that life was an adventure. I spent many
happy hours playing with my twin sister in our back garden, looking for pixies,
pretending to be a fairy, concocting magic potions from petals and rainwater. The
world described by Blyton came alive in our garden and in our imaginations.
However, it was quickly outgrown and then forgotten as I moved on to more
'grown-up' books, with an ever-decreasing focus on nature and an increasing focus
on relationships with people (especially boys).

As I grew up, it became apparent that my parents did not believe in higher education for girls. 'A waste of time and money, you'll only get married and have children. No need
for university, best get a job until you find a husband.' I married young, only 19 years of age,
and over the next few years produced four wonderful children. We grew up together.
Barely out of adolescence, I embraced the opportunity to continue playing, to read
children's books and have adventures outside. We made use of outdoor spaces such as
gardens, woods, fields and parks to have adventures. Reacting to my own gendered
upbringing, I resolved to be different as a parent and eschewed Blyton's books in

favour of less 'girlie' books; along with my dolls they were donated to charity and I began investing in more grown-up reading on bird watching, gardening and cookery.

My children grew older, providing time and space for me to begin to study. I registered with The Open University (2018) and after six years successfully achieved BSc (Hons) in Natural Science – First Class. I started volunteering for a local conservation charity, helping with groups designed to encourage families to explore nature; then I was employed to organise the groups. My research and teaching impacted on my book collection: art, crafts, poetry, identification guides and scientific surveys all made their way on to my shelves. A postgraduate Certificate in Education for Sustainability added yet more weighty tomes. I moved on to environmental youth work, and continued to study: first a certificate, then a Masters in Youth Work and Community Development – more books! And journals and study guides. The children's books were packed away: the favourites carefully boxed and stored; the others passed on to charity shops and gifted to friends with younger children. Then I started learning to teach and followed an introductory course, Philosophy for Children (2018). I restarted buying children's books. I began to understand that these books have an ability to convey important messages in a concise, succinct, understandable way – through both words and pictures. On holidays to Cumbria I discovered a new love for Beatrix Potter (Beatrix Potter Society 2018) and treated myself to a collection of her books, plus toys to match. However, it was not just the stories that appealed to me, it was the author herself. I drew many parallels between her life and mine, her experiences resonated with mine – as, indeed, I hope my experiences are resonating with you. Like Beatrix and her Cumbrian husband, my new husband and I shared a love of being outdoors. We holidayed in Scotland and I encountered wolves – real, live, howling wolves – trapped in a wildlife park. I wanted to set them free.

Becoming an ECR

My youngest child left home and we moved to Cumbria as I commenced my doctoral research: my love for the place determined my choice of university. Books were shed along the way as we attempted to downsize to a smaller house. However, within a short space of time even more studious books were added to my collection. Alongside these more children's books crept in: Aesop's fables, Icelandic fairy tales and various nursery rhymes, bought with the intention of helping to bring to life my oral and written presentations (see for example: Hayes 2014a). One day I awoke with a story in my head, soon followed by several more. My subconscious was making sense of my research findings and my experiences, weaving them together through a creative, interpretive process. I attempted to explain this to my doctoral supervisors, it was not something I had planned to do, it just seemed to happen. I openly acknowledged that I drew inspiration for my writing from Rachel Carson (Lear 2018) who had written a fable to demonstrate what would happen to the natural world if people continued to use pesticides (Carson 1962). Her approach was markedly different from those who use scare tactics to attempt to change behaviour. She has been described as a 'gentle subversive' (Hamilton-Lytle 2007) yet her words had a significant impact on me, and on the way that I was researching. However, her work still differed from mine in that it seemed to be planned, a result of a conscious effort to write, whilst my creative writing felt subconscious: it mostly happened when I was not expecting it. Whilst most of my stories were about people, other characters crept in: Boggarts, bunny rabbits and bears (Hayes 2015) – lots of bears!

I began sharing my stories at conferences, cautiously at first, expecting to be rebuked as non-academic (Hayes 2014b; Hayes 2018). That did not happen; instead I was praised for being different, for making my work accessible and understandable; they became part of my methodology (Hayes 2014b; Hayes 2018) which made use of a blended methodology of hermeneutics, autoethnography and action research. But what to do with them next, what was their purpose? And perhaps more importantly (to me anyway) why was my brain working in this way? The first question was relatively easy: I developed a concept called 'Adventure Bears', a small handmade fabric teddy bear designed to be played with outside which I gifted to recipients with a short story making the links to playing outside. By the completion of my doctorate there were more than 200 having adventures across the world (see Hayes 2018 for more on the Adventure Bears). I determined to address the question as to why my brain was working this way (creating simple stories, often involving toys) by using the metaphor of reflection as looking into a mirror whereby I look into myself (Uzat 1998). I can see me surrounded by my experiences, people, places, objects, toys; my mind is alive with images (Parker 2013) and metaphors – which help to capture '...the essential nature of an experience' (Lawley and Tompkins 2000, p.6). My book collection becomes a metaphor for the different phases of my life, as I have grown and developed into the person I am now. One book catches my eye: Enid Blyton's *Nature lover's book* (1944); a book purchased with the aim of helping me to develop inspiring and engaging activities for families and young children, based on embracing storytelling, both as a pedagogical approach and as a means for communication. I have not looked at it for years. I open it and begin to read: the words feel familiar; memories stir deep within me and I begin to appreciate the impact they have had on me over the years. The lilting, sing-song text speaks to me, calling to the little girl within the body of this much older early career researcher.

'*Enid Blyton, really? But I thought you were a youth worker? Wasn't she a sexist and a racist? She had some very bigoted views...and I hate to mention it, so very middle-class!*' Back to today: a colleague's reaction at the mere mention of Enid Blyton. I acknowledge that Blyton has proved to be a controversial figure (Tucker and Reynolds 1997), and that arguably she was all of those things, but she is of a certain time and place, a socio-cultural construction (Jones and McEwen 2000). This is reflected in her stories that may appear quaint and old-fashioned amongst more modern children's literature. However, her work helped to shape and guide my childhood: rereading the stories and poems I realise that I have absorbed them into my subconscious, they have affected the way I think and write, impacting on the way I put words together to share my experiences. I determine to find out more about the impact this has had on me growing up, and to consider how this may continue to impact on me now, within my research practice. This process will include considering other key authors from my childhood who may also have impacted on my research. Most of my childhood books are long gone, only my memories of them remain. Undoubtedly some have imperceptibly impacted on me in a way that I cannot discern, the authors and characters lost from my conscious memories. However, some stand out in distinct form, allowing greater consideration.

Discovering my inner wolf

By now you may be wondering where the wolves fit into all this. They crept into my life unnoticed. I remember reading *White Fang* (London 1906) as a child, relishing reading this story which explores complex themes including morality, redemption and how animals may view humans. It is predominantly told from the viewpoint of the titular canine character and offers an alternative perspective – something I really liked as a child (and still do), and a technique that was also characteristic of many of Blyton's stories. But the book was lost as I grew up. My 40th birthday was marked with a gift of a toy wolf (a present from the wildlife park) along with homemade cards decorated with wolves. These were enjoyed, and then quietly packed away in my treasure box; the wolves retreated to the background. In 2013, I was invited to join a leadership training programme, aligned to my doctoral research. This proved to be a pivotal moment in my life: surrounded by confident, outwardly more successful professionals, I crumpled into a mass of insecurity; engulfed by the dreaded imposter syndrome, I felt a fraud and a fake, out of my depth. Each night of the four-day course I returned home, howling at my husband, '*Who am I? What am I doing here? What's my purpose?*' I was deep in the pain of self-doubt, mired in a liminal space, '...a place of ill-defined purpose ... of transition ... a state of mind that is blurred such as that between the state of dreaming and being awake' (Wilson 2012, p.32). However, this process of self-discovery proved to be a threshold moment, a rite of passage (Norris 2011). One afternoon, we played a game. Unseen by the others, we had to choose a picture of an animal to enact in the woods. Without conscious thought, I sprang across the room first and silently pocketed the picture of a wolf. I felt myself come alive in the game: one minute I was stalking prey; the next I was leading the others in a hunt; then silently observing the group from a distance. Afterwards, the others expressed their surprise and delight at my performance. The week finished with a group exploration of the impact we thought we had had on each other. This was torture for me. Wracked by self-doubt I had been unable to relax and participate fully within the group, something they openly acknowledged. They wanted more of the Tracy they had experienced in the game. I came away with a determination to find her.

I bought a book. 'Healthy wolves and healthy women share certain psychic characteristics: keen sensing, playful spirit, and a heightened capacity for devotion' (Pinkola Estes 1992, p.2). The words resonated deep within me, but as someone unfamiliar with psychology, this was not an easy read. I lingered over each chapter, using it to reflect on my life and experiences. I gained a growing awareness of my own identity, of how it has been shaped and influenced by others (real and fictional) over the years; this was accompanied by a flourishing of confidence in my academic abilities. I learned that identity is a socially constructed, continually evolving state (Jones and McEwen 2000); it has multiple dimensions and is an embodied reflection of lived experiences. Jones and McEwen (2000, p.412) exhort us to 'listen for how a person sees herself' if we want to understand them. I openly acknowledge my inner wolf, a metaphor that represents the instinctive, intuitive, primitive emotions I contain within. I am now able to release these to help me survive the wilderness of the (academic) world (Brown 2017). I understand my need to play (Pinkola Estes 1992, p.365) and how this impacts on my use of stories and toys within my research to highlight key points and to appeal to a transdisciplinary audience. The magical folk, enchanted woods and faraway trees of Blyton's world have informed my way of interpreting the world, and I still hang on to the overwhelming sense that life is an adventure – or at least it can be, if we choose to perceive it that way. The toys and stories I use are everyday objects which are fun, comforting, a reminder to be childlike – childish even (see Macfarlane 2016). 'They serve as a link to our past, our memories and reflections – allowing us to make connections through time and space. And yet as we recall those moments of childhood, we are looking back through time, through the eyes and awareness of an adult' (Hayes 2018). This prevents us from truly reliving those moments as they were or feeling the impact that they had on us at the time; however, through critical reflexivity we can consider the impact they may continue to have. Through the process of critical reflection, I have found my voice and learned how and when to howl. This was much needed as I navigated my way through the final stages of my doctoral study and the thorough examination process that brought it to an end.

The impact on me and my research

My recently completed doctoral research was a qualitative study titled *Making sense of nature: a creative exploration of young people's relationship with the natural environment* (Hayes 2017), which I conducted using an alternative, storied approach. But, I am not an Arts or Humanities student. I am a transdisciplinarian, demonstrated by how I conduct my work (research process) and how I interpret my findings (research outputs). Like Ingold (2000, pp. 1–2), I have sought out ways to cross the divide that '…separates the "two worlds" of humanity and nature'. Transdisciplinarity enables us to focus on approaches that capture people's imagination and their attention – for example through stories, fables, poetry, song. I view my research as emergent, open-ended, innovative and creative, and I embrace methods that invite introspection, reflexivity and dialogue (as exemplified here; also see Hayes 2016). I have found this an effective way to explore and understand situations whilst remaining mindful of the potential impact of my values, beliefs and emotions. My aim is for my research to influence, affect, or move readers / audiences through aesthetic, evocative representation and naturalistic generalisations. Using a storied, transdisciplinary approach has also enabled me to present my research findings in accessible formats and to reach both academic and non-academic audiences. I want my stories to be aesthetically pleasing, to be well-crafted and have artistic merit; however, more than that, I want them to be useful – to serve the purpose of provoking dialogue about a topic. They are more than simply a pleasing story. They have purpose and impact, which extends beyond research, beyond the academy, into practice and pedagogy.

As a transdisciplinarian storytelling lecturer, I do not feel the need to conform to outdated expectations or to follow 'somebody else's rule' (Frank 2012, p. 1). I want my work to reflect a wide range of interests and my writing to feel fresh and modern. However, as my reflexive narrative demonstrates, I have not always found it easy to be a creative researcher. As highlighted by many others (see for example, the work of Patricia Leavy 2016; Carolyn Ellis & Art Bochner 2000; Brené Brown 2017 or Helen Kara 2017), I have felt the need for permission to work creatively – or more accurately, to be enabled to give myself permission (Brown 2017). I have needed people to support me to convince others that it is legitimate to take a creative approach to research. And I have been fortunate in having that support from my supervisors, examiners and colleagues. I thank them all – with their care, support and guidance I have been awarded my doctorate. However, that is not the end of the story: as Helen Kara highlights, there is still '…a long hard fight ahead to convince people in certain quarters that useful knowledge exists beyond the bounds of academic convention…' (2017). I will continue to fight this fight as I move onwards with my post-doctoral plans, which include exploring the actual, as opposed to allegorical, relationship between humans and wolves (and wolf-dogs like White Fang).

Conclusion

How does the allegorical wolf relate to me being an academic and to evidencing impact? Parodying the quote that started this chapter, wolves can symbolise a group of academics who gather in packs at conferences, in constant need of nourishment and mental stimulation to maintain their academic identity. With recent changes to academic funding, increasing pressure to quickly evidence the impact of our work (see for example: Reed 2016; 2017) and a heightened sense of accountability, many fear the academic world as we know it may be teetering on the brink of extinction. I have a role to play in ensuring this doesn't happen; as a researcher and as a lecturer I have meaning and purpose. I have learned how to hunt down opportunities, to carefully observe and contemplate the world around me before pouncing into action. I have developed a sense of trust in myself, my abilities, of when and how to allow myself to be vulnerable. Arguably, most significant of all, I have realised the importance of being true to myself, of being authentic (after Brown 2017) and of the impact this approach can have on me, and on others around me. I relish the chance to relax by a fire and recuperate after a long day of work and I understand the need to frolic, play and socialise with others. I am also now adapting to an additional role, as the supervisor, mentor and supporter of other, newer, earlier career academics. We cannot escape the need to evidence the importance and impact of our work and to show what we have achieved. But we do have a choice about how we do this, about how we perceive and conceptualise our impact. My approach demonstrates how stories can be used not only as a way of engaging wider audiences, but as way of ensuring a research methodology that is both communicative and engaging. It is a participatory way that enables us to consider the potential audience, the 'users' of our work, from the outset of our research, rather than waiting until we are finished.

As I conclude this chapter, I imagine Enid playfully asking me the timeless question, evocative of playgrounds across the world (Opie and Opie 1969): '*What's the time Mrs Wolf?*' To which I firmly reply, '*It's MY time – and our time. We work best as a pack.*'

Learning points

- Research has the power to transform us – our studies impact on us, as well as on others.
- Reflexivity is vital: if we want to understand our impact, we first need to understand ourselves.
- By becoming more self-aware and confident we can more effectively support others, as we progress from early career to more mature researchers.

References

Bateson, P. and Martin, P. (2013). *Play, playfulness, creativity and innovation.* Cambridge: Cambridge University Press.
Beatrix Potter Society (2018). *About Beatrix Potter.* Beatrix Potter Society. [Viewed 14 February 2018]. Available from: http://beatrixpottersociety.org.uk/
Blyton, E. (1944). *Nature lover's book.* London: Evans Brothers Limited, reprint 2008.
Brown, B. (2017). *Braving the wilderness: The quest for true belonging and the courage to stand alone.* London: Vermilion.
Burke, P. and Stets, J. (2009). *Identity theory.* Oxford: Oxford University Press.
Carson, R. (1962). *Silent spring.* London: Penguin Group, reprint 2000.
Ellis, C. and Bochner, A.P. (2000). Autoethnography, personal narrative, and personal reflexivity. In: N. Denzin, and Y. Lincoln, eds., *Handbook of qualitative research.* Thousand Oaks, CA: Sage. pp. 733–768.
Enid Blyton Society. (2018). *Author of adventure.* Enid Blyton Society. [Viewed 14 February 2018]. Available from: www.enidblytonsociety.co.uk/index.php
Eyler, J. and Giles, D. (1999). *Where's the learning in service-learning?* San Francisco, CA: Jossey-Bass.
Frank, A.W. (2012). *Letting stories breathe.* London: The University of Chicago Press Ltd.
GCYFRG. (n.d.). *About the group.* GCYFRG. [Viewed 14 February 2018]. Available from https://gcyfrg.wordpress.com/welcome/

Hamilton-Lytle, M. (2007). *The gentle subversive: Rachel Carson, silent spring, and the rise of the environmental movement.* Oxford: Oxford University Press.

Hayes, T.A. (2013a). The accidental youth worker. In: B. Humberstone, ed., *Outdoor learning as a means of promoting healthy and sustainable lifestyles and social inclusion for young people.*. European Outdoor Learning Seminar. [Viewed 14 February 2018]. Available from www. eoe-network.eu/fileadmin/PDFs/EOE_12th_European_Conference_Papers.pdf

Hayes, T.A. (2013b). Seeing the world through their eyes: Learning from a 5 ½ year old, a rabbit and a boat ride with aunty. *Horizons.* 63, 36–39.

Hayes, T. (2014a). The challenges of social inclusion in outdoor education: Can tortoise and hare learn together? In: P. Varley, and S. Taylor, ed., *Being there: Slow, fast, traditional, wild, urban, natural. 2013 Adventure conference proceedings.* Fort William: University of the Highlands and Islands. pp. 43–54.

Hayes, T.A. (2014b). Methodological mud wrestling! Openness and criticality: Evaluating and publishing our research. Fourth international conference on value and virtue in practice-based research. July 2014. York St John University.

Hayes, T. (2015). A playful approach to outdoor learning: Boggarts, bears and bunny rabbits! In: B. Evans, J. Horton and T. Skelton, eds., *Play, recreation, health and well being, vol. 9 of Geographies of children and young people.* Singapore: Springer. pp. 155–172.

Hayes, T.A. (2016). Sharing stories: An interactive, interdisciplinary approach to pedagogy and research. Storytelling: Global reflections on narrative, 9th global meeting. July 2016. Mansfield College, Oxford.

Hayes, T.A. (2017). *Making sense of nature: A creative exploration of young people's relationship with the natural environment.* PhD thesis. University of Cumbria.

Hayes, T.A. (2018). Dr Bear and the adventure bears. *Children's Geographies.* 26(4), 461–464.

Ingold, T. (2000). *The perception of the environment: Essays in livelihood, dwelling and skill.* London: Routledge.

Jarvis, P. and Parker, S., eds. (2005). *Human learning: An holistic approach.* Oxon: Routledge.

Jones, S.R. and McEwen, M.K. (2000). A conceptual model of multiple dimensions of identity. *Journal of College Student Development.* 41(4), 405–414.

Kara, H. (2017). *The importance of creative research methods.* [Viewed 14 February 2018]. Available from: https://helenkara.com/2017/07/11/the-importance-of-creative-research-methods/

Kraftl, P., Horton, J. and Tucker, F. (2014). *Children's geographies.* [Viewed 9 November 2015]. Available from: www.oxfordbibliographies.com/obo/page/childhood-studies

Lawley, J. and Tompkins, P. (2000). *Metaphors in mind.* London: The Developing Company.

Lear, L. (2018). *The life and legacy of Rachel Carson* [Viewed 14 February 2018]. Available from www.rachelcarson.org/

Leavy, P. (2016). *Essentials of transdisciplinary research: Using problem-centered methodologies.* Oxon: Routledge.

London, J. (1906). *White Fang.* New York: Macmillan.

Macfarlane, R. (2016). *Landmarks.* Milton Keynes: Penguin Books.

Meyer, J. and Land, R. (2003). *Threshold concepts and troublesome knowledge: Linkages to ways of thinking and practising within the disciplines.* Edinburgh: ETL Project.

Mezirow, J. (1990). How critical reflection triggers transformative learning. In J. Mezirow, ed., *Fostering critical reflection in adulthood.* San Francisco, CA: Jossey Bass. pp.1–20.

Moon, J. (2004). *A handbook of reflective and experiential learning: Theory and practice.* Oxon: Routledge Falmer.

Norris, J. (2011). Crossing the threshold mindfully: Exploring rites of passage models in adventure therapy. *Journal of Adventure Education and Outdoor Learning.* 11(2), 109–126.

Opie, I. and Opie, P. (1969). *Children's games in street and playground: Chasing, catching, seeking, hunting, racing, duelling, exerting, daring, guessing, acting, pretending.* Oxford: Clarendon Press.

Owens, L.S. (2010). The hermeneutics of vision: C.G. Jung and Liber Novus. [Viewed 14 February 2018]. Available from http://gnosis.org/Hermeneutics-of-Vision.pdf. Originally published in *The Gnostic: A Journal of Gnosticism, Western Esotericism and Spirituality*. 3, 23–46.

Parker, J. (2013). Imaging, imagining knowledge in higher education curricula: New visions and troubled thresholds. *Teaching in Higher Education*. 18(8), 958–970.

Philosophy for Children (2018). *Philosophy4Children*. [Viewed 14 February 2018]. Available fromwww.philosophy4children.co.uk/

Pinkola Estes, C. (1992). *Women who run with wolves: Contacting the power of the wild woman*. London: Rider.

Reed, M.S. (2016). *The research impact handbook*. Huntly, Aberdeenshire: Fast Track Impact.

Reed, M.S. (2017). *The productive researcher*. Huntly, Aberdeenshire: Fast Track Impact.

RGS (n.d.). *About us*. [Viewed 14 February 2018]. Available from: www.rgs.org/about/the-society/

The Open University (2018). *About the Open University*. [Viewed 14 February 2018]. Available from: www.open.ac.uk/about/main/

Theodosius, C. (2012). Feeling a feeling in emotion management. In D. Spencer, K. Walby, and A. Hunt, eds., *Emotions matter: A relational approach to emotions*. Toronto: University of Toronto Press. pp. 63–85.

Tucker, N. and Reynolds, K., eds. (1997). *Enid Blyton: A celebration and reappraisal. NCRCL papers 2*. London: National Centre for Research in Children's Literature.

Uzat, S.L. (1998). *Cognitive coaching and self-reflection: Looking in the mirror while looking through the window*. [Viewed 23 August 2018]. Available from http://files.eric.ed.gov/fulltext/ED427064.pdf

Wilson, P. (2012). Beyond the gaudy fence. *International Journal of Play*. 1(1), 30–36.

REFLECTION

Reflexivity, doubt and social tensions in collaborative research as positive research impact

Alex McDonagh

In this reflection, I aim to tell you about how my PhD research has impacted on both me and the participants involved. I first highlight some of the early anxieties related to my role as a researcher and my anticipation of what was to come in my research project. I then go on to address some of the impact the research project has had on myself through the development of relationships and my growth in confidence as a researcher. The impact on the participants is then discussed in terms of their reaction to the project. As well as acknowledging my own doubt as a researcher, I share some of the ways I was able to overcome these doubts and maintain self-confidence throughout the research process. I conclude with some of the ways that the project has demonstrated the potential for wider impact and the significance of my anxieties and reflective approach as integral to that impact.

My PhD project looked at the impact of developing a digital heritage inter-pretation and explored the impact on heritage meanings as communicated in a digital object, but also the impact of the digital development process on users of heritage sites. Often there are traditional heritage meanings that receive primary attention; for example, historical narratives associated with heritage sites. Smith (2006) identifies these meanings as part of an authorised heritage discourse (AHD). My research project aimed to engage with non-authorised heritage discourses in addition to AHD. The heritage focus here is Towneley Park in Burnley, Lancashire, which contains a number of traditional heritage aspects as well as everyday leisure aspects. Along with the AHD meanings in the park, I have aimed to illuminate some of the different ways that we engage with park heritage spaces. I have used a phe-nomenological methodological approach (Tilley 1994; Bender et al. 2007) which embraces the role of our bodies and emotions in understanding landscape meanings. This has consequently involved interviews and field visits to the park with park users. Taking a grounded theory approach, the interviews were open-ended and I left the field visits open for the participants to choose a route through the park. The key to the research approach has been to provide the participants with the freedom to communicate the park to me from their own point of view.

Based on the narratives gathered, a digital representation of the park, called *Digital Towneley*, was developed in collaboration with the participants. Feedback interviews with the participants helped to highlight the impact of both the research process and *Digital Towneley* itself.

My early anxieties

In the early stages of the research, I had several anxieties linked to my role as researcher. My initial contact with participants through telephone and face-to-face conversations caused me some anxiety, similarly identified by Trussell (2010), related to the potential unknowns involved in ethnographic work. I was apprehensive about how I would come across to the participants and ultimately how well I would handle the unscripted interviews. My own emotional investment in the project was therefore clear from an early stage. Trussell's approach had highlighted to me the importance of acknowledging the researcher's positionality as a way of understanding ethnographic research more fully. In the context of park heritage, I also adopted ideas which embraced both emotional and corporeal factors (de Certeau 1984; Smith 2006; Bender et al. 2007). My role as a researcher would be to perform heritage narratives in the park space alongside the participants.

The 'data' I sought were the meanings most significant for the participants in relation to Towneley Park and the ways in which the participants interacted with the park. To this end, I tried to avoid imposing my own epistemologies on the participants in order to minimise my influence on how they communicated the park to me. This meant that the purpose and form of *Digital Towneley* remained unknown for much of the research project as it relied on what the participants would tell me and show me. This caused me some anxiety as I found it difficult to explain this concept to the participants and as a result I was concerned at times that I was not projecting a convincing research identity. In response to this, I drew strength and confidence from the literature that had inspired me, leaning on ideas that supported the potential of my approach to illuminate under-represented heritage voices (Waterton 2005; Smith 2006).

As a researcher, I felt that I had a responsibility to accurately represent these heritage voices. I knew well from my research that heritage issues can be emotional and important for the people involved, and so I began the project with an awareness of how heritage issues may be emotional and important for the participants. I was nonetheless surprised by how passionate the participants were about the park and their use of it. From the beginnings of the interviews, it was clear that the park space extended into many aspects of the participants' lives. Although this felt overwhelming at times, I kept a reflective diary to track my own feelings and agency in the research process. This followed the approach of Bender et al. (2007) and helped me to understand not only my own feelings but also some of my interactions with the participants.

Impact of the project on me

I turn my attention now to two participants, Helen and Gareth, both of whom I interviewed and visited the park with (pseudonyms have been used for all participants here to protect anonymity). Helen is a member of a voluntary group that cares for the park space. I became a member of the group because it is a significant part of the running of the park. I also felt obliged to attend the group meetings because: (i) I did not want to offend Helen; and (ii) I wanted to foster a good relationship with Helen and other park users to recruit participants for the project.

During the start of my field trip around the park with Helen and Gareth, we had open-ended conversations about various aspects of the park, but also about our lives more generally. My research journal captured some of the concerns I had about my perceived role as researcher:

> We made some small talk about what I might do after my research – I felt it necessary to mention the possibility of continuing the research at Towneley; I have become aware recently about the potential offence that may be taken if I suggest that I will just move on afterwards. [Field Visit with Helen and Gareth: June 2014]

From my contact with the participants, I had become aware of how important the park is to each of them. My research journal identifies that, from my perspective at least, I had developed an affective engagement with Helen and Gareth. Put simply, I cared about their feelings; how they viewed my intentions was important to me and, in this sense, my research participants had already impacted on my life and social connections.

I was mindful and wary of the potential for my academic interest to make me distant and insensitive to the participants' perspectives (Waterton 2005) and I felt manipulative because I was aware that there was an unequal power balance. The participants had something that I wanted: their knowledge, experience and perspective. These thoughts highlighted for me my own motivations as a researcher and I was concerned that my own research narrative would override the heritage narratives of the participants.

On this subject, I was put somewhat at ease through discussions with my supervisor. Just by vocalising and articulating the situation with another person, I was able to break out of the mental loop that I had formed from my close attachment to my research. My supervisor provided me with a helpful perspective and I was able to see the value of my involvement in the voluntary group as a fair trade-off for participant involvement in my own research. This reduced my feelings of guilt and helped me to draw confidence that I was taking reasonable steps to gather research data.

Impact of the project on the participants

An aim of my methodological approach was to work towards representing the participants' varying uses and opinions about the park. However, while I aimed both to engage participants on their own terms and to avoid imposing my own epistemologies, my approach also appeared to have an impact on the relationships I developed with the participants. During the field visit with Helen and Gareth, we reached a pathway junction where some of the negative impacts were revealed. To avoid imposing my own perspectives, I had let the participants decide where we would go. For Gareth, this didn't work well:

> It is frustrating, he says, to have to think what the important parts of the park are. My impression is that I have irritated him. [Field Visit with Helen and Gareth: June 2014]

It was evident that my approach here fell short of allowing the participants to use the park in their own way. Although I had left the decisions up to the participants, my role as researcher clearly affected the dynamic of our walk. Gareth felt a pressure to identify 'important' parts of the park and this was frustrating because I had not provided guidance on how to categorise such 'importance'. Despite aiming to be transparent and collaborative, my approach may at times have appeared to conceal a secret research agenda.

In contrast, two other participants, Ruth and Derek, expressed satisfaction with the project and appeared to show genuine appreciation of my approach:

> It was nice to have somebody take an interest.
> It's like somebody taking an interest after years of being, you know, out there in the wilderness, cos we know it's here, but nobody else knows it's here. [Ruth and Derek, Feedback Interview: April 2015]

Here, Ruth and Derek were identifying the interest I had shown in their own narratives of the park in contrast to the traditional narratives put forward by the local authority custodians. These responses are representative of several of the participants' reactions to the project and they highlight some of the success that the project had in engaging the local park users.

Communicating views as starkly different as these compared to Gareth's reactions was a challenge and this made me anxious that my research would be a failure; that my outcome would be offensive to the participants. Although there were positive reactions from participants like Ruth and Derek, by unwittingly irritating Gareth my anxiety had been magnified.

Here, my literature review provided me with guidance and I drew confidence specifically from the study by Bender et al. (2007). In putting together an exhibition of their findings, they explained how some local residents had become angered by the exhibition's interpretation of the local environment. It reminded me that the impact of my research on the participants may be positive or negative. It was a tangible example for me that things could go wrong even for the academics who we seek to emulate, and that this need not mean disaster.

Impact achieved by the project

The success of developing relationships was integral to the narratives that I was able to create and share with the participants. The *Digital Towneley* project was a product of those relationships, and Ruth and Derek perceived *Digital Towneley* to have the potential to challenge the authority of the local council and to champion the voices of the local community. They felt that the project may have the potential to influence local government funding decisions. In one exaggerated example, a participant stated that *Digital Towneley* was 'important for the whole country' since he felt that it communicated the benefits of park spaces to the nation.

Other participants saw the project as an honest reflection of their own feelings and experiences about the park. These everyday elements of Towneley heritage were impactful for the participants insofar as they communicated important stories of memory and experience within the park. For some participants, *Digital Towneley* was seen as a concrete object that represented a legacy of park experiences made accessible to friends and family. These participants felt they had left their mark.

Conclusion

The open-ended nature of the interviews and field visits did cause me to doubt my effectiveness as a researcher and presented frustration for some participants like Gareth. However, as the participant reactions of Ruth and Derek demonstrate, my approach also fostered trust and appreciation by engaging with participants on their own terms. As such, the project had positive impacts on the participants.

My concern for the participants' feelings was evident from my reflexive diary and this acted as a reminder of my responsibility as a researcher and my role as custodian of the participants' stories. This helped to prevent distancing myself from the human significance of the park spaces, and so develop some accurate interpretations of the participants' park. This helped to develop the impact of *Digital Towneley* on participant's ideas of legacy and future as well as the potential for political (local government) impact. It is therefore through my research project's impact on me that I was able to influence the impact of the project on others.

In relation to the above, I hope that the following points may be useful to you in your own early career researcher journey: 1) identify some reflective studies in your field that discuss openly the emotions involved in carrying out research (e.g. Trussell 2010) or that openly highlight mistakes and pitfalls (e.g. Bender et al. 2007); 2) avoid the echo chamber of your own thoughts by ensuring that you discuss your research practice with your supervisor or other counsel; and 3) in light of the above, be prepared to be imperfect and to make mistakes.

References

Bender, B., Hamilton, S. and Tilley, C. (2007). *Stone worlds: narrative and reflexivity in landscape archaeology*. Walnut Creek: Left Coast Press.

De Certeau, M. (1984). *The practice of everyday life*. London: University of California Press.

Smith, L. (2006). *The uses of heritage*. London: Routledge.

Tilley, C. (1994). *A phenomenology of landscape: places, paths and monuments*. Oxford: Berg.

Trussell, D.E. (2010). Gazing from the inside out during ethically heightened moments. *Leisure Studies*. 29(4), 377–395.

Waterton, E. (2005). Whose sense of place? Reconciling archaeological perspectives with community values: cultural landscapes in England. *International Journal of Heritage Studies*. 11(4), 309–325.

3

BEYOND THE IVORY TOWER

Impact and the arts practitioner

Isabella Streffen

Is the new impact agenda a particularly valuable opportunity for practice-led early career researchers (ECRs) whose research is frequently situated and experienced outside academia? What might be the potential complications? How might it influence research design for new projects? With these questions in mind, I will reflect on my experience as an ECR in visual arts, focusing on three case studies relating to my own research. I will discuss notions of longitudinal impact and how this intersects with the specificities and requirements of the Research Excellence Framework (REF), the UK's national audit on research in terms of both the research outputs submitted and the impact of those outputs. I will explore the notion of *the package* – a term used for a single REF output that consists of numerous elements often in different formats (for example, a submission that consists of several exhibitions, a book chapter and original artworks) – and how this has structured my career trajectory and decisions since my PhD completion in 2013 through four short-term postdoctoral posts at four different institutions.

This text foregrounds the experiences of practice-led researchers in the arts as that is my area of expertise, and because comparatively few publications examine the unique sets of possibilities and problems that many such researchers face. I use the term 'practice-led' throughout, though I might just as easily use 'practice-based' (Candy, 2006), this is not the moment to focus on these specific philosophical refinements. And although I specifically discuss visual art projects, similar issues arise for performers, dramaturges, musicians, composers, dancers, choreographers, creative writers, designers, curators and conservators alike.

Practice-led research is still contentious within the academy. It occurs, of course, in many different disciplines where it is not named as such, where the term 'pracademic' (Posner, 2009) might be used instead to encompass researchers in allied health, engineering, management and business arenas who would not usually be included by the traditional definitions in use in the arts. A 'pracademic' has been identified as one who 'spans both the ethereal world of academia as a scholar and the pragmatic world of practice': people who need an expert level of understanding of a practical field in order to identify areas that need rigorous examination (Walker, 2010, p.1). I will discuss this further in the next section.

Postdoctoral research for practice-led researchers and the 'pracademic'

Arts and humanities ECRs whose work already spans the public sphere may appear to have the advantage in terms of the 'impact agenda', but is this really so? It could certainly be argued that the impact agenda's focus beyond academia does offer some useful opportunities to practice-led ECRs. This, however, is comparative, as practice-led ECRs are often excluded from taking up postdoctoral research roles and fellowships, with most opportunities conservative in the type of research that they are prepared to support, at least in practice, if not directly in intent. This is evident from a cursory glimpse at the various postdoctoral schemes awardee lists, which are dominated by research projects carried out using traditional methods (i.e. research that will culminate in journal articles or monographs), though this does not imply that those projects are less innovative, challenging or important. For example, The Leverhulme Trust's awards for Early Career Fellowships made 62 awards in the humanities in 2017, two of which are practice as research enquiries (Leverhulme Trust, 2017). It's a similar story in previous years. There are, of course, exceptions to this rule of thumb, and a small number of practice-led researchers have convinced funders that their research priorities are best served by investigating through practice: this strategy seems to be particularly efficacious in medical humanities, eco-critical geographies, creative technologies and cognate areas. I speculate that these interdisciplinary clusters are more open to diverse methodologies because of the nature of interdisciplinary research itself.

It is interesting to ask whether 'pracademic' researchers, whose work is also likely to take place in the public domain, face the same level of difficulty in accessing postdoctoral opportunities. It certainly appears that impact can be comparatively straightforward to demonstrate in 'pracademic' disciplines, where impact is defined as an effect on, change or benefit to the economy, society, culture, public policy or services, health, the environment or quality of life. (REF2021, 2018). Projects producing quantitative data seem to be at an advantage here, as it is, perhaps, easier to clarify whether someone's health is affected in specific ways than whether culture has benefited from a specific project or social capital has been built as a result of art's 'multilayered interpretation emphasizing connections and ambivalence' (AHRC, 2007, p. 16). Impact in relation to the arts is hard to measure; in trying to do so, we rely on interpretation and affect, which is much further away from quantitative data analysis. It is comparatively easy to demonstrate engagement through collecting data on audience figures, sales, visitor numbers and so on. It is possible to measure benefits to a community in terms of a boost to the local economy, or perceptions of well-being. The problem, though, is that there is no clear scientific correlative: the impact could be accidental, rather than a result of the research project.

A recent impact event that I attended offered some exemplars of key methods of identifying impact: the commissioning of creative works; positive reviews of creative publications and performances; citation in a public discussion or consultation; visitor or audience numbers, or numbers of participants; independent testimony; evidence of use of process or technology; critiques or citations in user's documents; change in behaviours, outlook etc.; community awareness of research; contracts and industry funding; increased cultural awareness and non-academic publications and performances. This, however, is not replicated by institutional interpretation of REF guidance documentation, which generates a much narrower definition.

To summarise, impact is clearly a valuable opportunity for practice-led researchers and pracademics alike, but not disproportionately so. Substantial work still needs to be done in developing indices and metrics that are sensitive enough to capture the impact of practice-led research in the terms demanded by REF2021.

The exhibitionary turn as impact strategy: Possibilities and complications

Anecdotal evidence suggests that a variety of disciplines are looking to the form of the exhibition to develop and demonstrate public engagement and impact at the planning stage of projects. This is not limited to arts and humanities disciplines, but includes social and hard sciences. It's possible that this is a result of the 'curatorial turn' (O'Neil, 2007) that emerged in the art world from the 1980s onwards, where the exhibition is identified as a form of 'institutional utterance' perhaps mirroring the ambitions of institutions for the research that their employees place in the public sphere. In discussing this question, I am acutely aware of my (still) early career status: I can't afford to make professional enemies, so I prefer not to be precise about roles and projects. I have not found any scholarly studies specifically on this as yet, but have personally collected data from jobs advertised on www.jobs.ac.uk over approximately five years (2013–2018), which indicates an upward trend in the number of postdoctoral roles that have exhibition development or delivery as their main focus. Typically, this involves a funded position for a fixed-term, usually short-term, Post-Doctoral Research Assistant (PDRA) without specialist exhibition skills (usually with a PhD in the subject matter of the research project rather than a specialist in researching through exhibitions). I have described this shift as 'the exhibitionary turn' as it appears to indicate an identification of the exhibition as a useful tool for a wide range of research projects, and a rise in interest in translating academic research into something accessible by a far wider public. It would be useful to conduct this as a formal research project, to evaluate how much impact the 'impact agenda' is having on the history of exhibitions.

The opportunities of this type of impact-data-driven work can be significant, and they are clearly understood to be so by the Research Councils funding such projects. An investment of £100,000 or so in developing a significant exhibition with all the associated digital support, evaluation, and benefits to building capacity for exhibition-making across academia (rather than in the professional curating sector), can potentially be highly rewarded in assessment terms and consequently prestige. It would be interesting to know if such projects are considered less 'risky' than projects that are conceived as curatorial in the first instance, or into curating as a methodology.

Complications of this 'exhibitionary turn' include increased difficulties for practice-led specialists in exhibition-making accessing the posts that help grow precarious early careers into robust established and permanent appointments. These PDRA roles and their concentration on theme expertise rather than methodological expertise usually exclude curatorial specialists, and perhaps commensurately affect the experience of the exhibition itself for audiences. Another potential problem is that exhibitions developed by non-specialist project teams are more likely to illustrate rather than demonstrate research, and so not achieve the required levels of research excellence increasingly demanded by departments hungry for three and four star assessments. Finally, a note of caution should be rung in the context of the 'impact agenda' coming to dominate the practice of exhibition-making to the extent that practice-led exhibition projects (in which the research is conducted through the exhibition itself) are deprioritised as departments focus their support and limited resources on 'add-on' projects.

Broadly speaking, the opportunities of the exhibition as a tool for impact would appear to outweigh the potential problems, and the exhibition as a translation tool for academic research should be viewed as a potential route for sharing and embodying complex research findings. I will discuss my experience of this type of project in further detail in the second case study below, where I reflect on being part of the Picturing Finance project team.

Case studies

This section discusses three separate case studies that relate to the progress of my research career since completion of my PhD in early 2013. I undertook four postdoctoral roles (at the universities of Sunderland, Manchester, Oxford Brookes and Bath Spa) before gaining a permanent lectureship at Lincoln in 2016, where I am now a Senior Lecturer in Fine Art (no longer with ECR status as it is now defined due to the shifted REF date of 2021). My research is planned to be submitted to Panel D Unit 32 Art and Design: History, Practice and Theory, and has been internally and externally audited for submission to both Unit 32 and Unit 33.

The case studies cover the consideration of a work submitted for REF2014 as a longitudinal submission for 2021; the concept of the 'package' where outputs like exhibitions, books and artworks are framed by traditional peer-reviewed written articles, books or chapters; and how the details of the forthcoming REF2021 and the impact agenda have influenced my decisions around the structure and area of my research.

My research is predominantly conducted through the production of original artworks and exhibitions, and through written arguments in the form of book chapters and articles. I focus on how we are enabled to see and experience things quite differently as a co-product of new technologies, how this functions at the intersections of art and literature, and how this affects exhibitionary experience.

Illuminating Hadrian's Wall *(2010): Proposed longitudinal study*

My work *Illuminating Hadrian's Wall* (Streffen and Hadrian's Wall Heritage, 2010) took place across the length of the UNESCO World Heritage Site at Hadrian's Wall in March of 2010, and was submitted to REF2014 during my research fellowship at Oxford Brookes University (June 2013–June 2014, 0.5fte), alongside my 2012 work *Hawk & Dove* (digital video). In 2003, the works were framed for submission as research into site-specificity that considered the political implications of heritage sites using a unique pseudo-ethnographic methodology to form part of Oxford Brookes's research environment statement (Whitty, 2013). Both of these projects were large-scale public artworks with large teams working to deliver them. *Illuminating Hadrian's Wall* had a high profile (international press and broadcast coverage) and a high level of grant capture (£350,000), though my Director of Research took the decision to focus more on *Hawk & Dove* as my role in that project was considered less difficult to quantify.

Here, one of the complications of working as a professional artist in a research context becomes clear: who owns what? It was difficult to separate my role as a researcher from my role as producer, project manager, etc. The work emerged from a competitive residency developed by Inspire Northumberland, for which I wrote a research and development proposal in 2009. The proposal focused on landscapes of military power and their use as heritage objects. Early meetings with staff at Hadrian's Wall Heritage Ltd revivified a plan to make a large-scale work for The Wall, and in late 2009 it was announced that the team would deliver 'a line of light from coast-to-coast' 'a major site specific project connecting the North East to the North West' (Thrush, 2009), and that I was appointed as Lead Artist to 'conceptualise the creative theme'. On reflection, I was not fully prepared for this project, and this was a key factor in obfuscating my role (for example, I did not take part in press calls, and the most visible person throughout was the Production Team Lead). It is important to state what a hugely complex project this was. It involved hundreds of partners, thousands of participants and audiences, complex health and safety issues, and three individual events, as well as the wall-lighting and the production of my artist's film *Scintilla* (2010) subsequently shown at nine sites across the Hadrian's Wall Corridor.

The *artistic* idea behind the project was quite simple: people would come out into the dark together to make a symbolic gesture that saluted the past, echoing a Roman gesture of 'defensive integrity' that had not been seen on that site for more than 1600 years. The *impact* idea behind the project encompassed the following aims: to attract 18,000 visitors (approx. 12,000 from outside the region); to generate direct expenditure of £750,000 from day and overnight visitors (above and beyond the historic annual average for that month); to contribute to business productivity through 2 new full-time posts and 30 temporary paid positions, to engage with 200 businesses across the wall corridor; to build capacity within the regions to create, manage and make world-class festivals with 25 individuals from partner organisations to benefit from upgraded skills; to develop the skills of 70 volunteers for the Volunteer Network; and to build international partnerships with members of UNESCO's trans-national 'Frontiers of the Roman Empire' group.

The *research* idea behind the project was to look at what kind of site-specific artwork deliver these artistic and impact objectives. This involved exploring assumptions that art provides a conceptual insight into history, and that it provides a symbolic rather than a literal narration. The processes or methodologies that were employed were conceptualization, field-work and the event itself. A subsequent three-stage qualitative and quantitative evaluation was commissioned by Hadrian's Wall Heritage as part of its strict project management process, but also as part of its commitment to Arts Council England and the terms of its grant.

The project achieved more than was expected, as it caught the public imagination through a national competition to be an 'Illuminator' (individuals who comprised the volunteer lighting team), for which over 4,000 people applied and 520 were selected. It also attracted 50,000 visitors (Henderson, 2010); generated direct expenditure of £3million; reached a world-wide audience of 855 million people thanks to 544 media articles including a two-minute section by Chinese state broadcaster CCTV, with the website achieving 110,810 visitors.

And it's this data, along with the focus on impact for REF2021, which made the project one of interest to my current university, though it has no place in my current research plan. The emerging rules on portability and the possibility of submitting impact case studies to REF2021 that trace the impact of a project over a longer period of time were discussed with my current Director of Research. This was partly instigated by me, as I was anxious about having the required number of submissions, given the specific pressures of REF and the time required for the development of similar large-scale projects (*Hawk & Dove*, for example, took nearly 4 years from start to completion). Multi-disciplinary workshops relating to REF submission have been useful in this context, as it has been possible to see how other researchers 'worked' projects to use every potential output and line of enquiry. I discussed this in my studio diary in slightly more cynical terms 'wanting to squeeze out any last drop of anything interesting from a project, long after you've ceased to be interested in it'. The art world moves faster than academia on the whole, and this is an area of friction between having an identity as a practitioner, and research culture more generally.

I dedicated some time to compiling all of the data that I could find, from newspaper reports to sales figures, to information on where *Illuminating Hadrian's Wall* had been cited as an exemplar. But as Hadrian's Wall Heritage Ltd (the main source of data) closed in 2014 after English Heritage suffered in excess of 40% budget cuts (Pearson, 2014), it was felt that further investigation would not be the best use of my research time. I was not sorry to abandon this approach, as I preferred to concentrate on my current research projects. This project was at a very early stage of my research career, and had I been structuring such a project now, I would have developed a method for capturing the impact data at the time, even though I could not have anticipated a research career back in 2010.

Show Me the Money *(2014–2016) and the notion of 'the package'*

By the time that I started work on the *Picturing Finance* project in 2014, I was an independent researcher who had experience of preparing for REF submission. *Picturing Finance* (subsequently *Show Me the Money: The image of finance 1700 to the present*; Streffen, 2014–2016) was an AHRC-funded follow-on project led by Principal Investigator Dr Peter Knight at the University of Manchester, and co-investigators Dr Paul Crosthwaite (University of Edinburgh) and Professor Nicky Marsh (University of Southampton), in collaboration with Mr Alistair Robinson, director of the Northern Gallery of Contemporary Art. I was recruited to the project as Postdoctoral Research Associate on a part-time (0.5fte) 15 month contract (April 2013–July 2014) with the remit of curating an exhibition, or most specifically to 'translate academic research into public events' (Knight et al., 2012).

The aims of Knight's research were to stimulate public debate on the historical construction of 'the myth of the rational market' and to engage the wider public in the research insights of the Culture of the Market Network through a public exhibition on the visual imagination of finance, and to help rethink the idea of 'financial literacy' (Knight et al., 2012). Knight et al. wanted to use images of finance and 'the market' over 300 years to show how a particular myth came to be naturalised, as they often appear as immutable economic laws rather than cultural and historic constructions.

Additionally, Knight et al. considered impact at an early stage of the project (reflecting their experience and seniority, perhaps) and developed an impact statement defining the beneficiaries of the research: 'the general public; school children via an educational outreach programme to be organised by the gallery; the financial services industry, and creative practitioners seeking to represent and engage with them; and policy makers seeking to understand and regulate the practices of the financial sector.' (Knight et al., 2012).

The main outputs of the research were identified in the project bid document as a catalogue, a website, an exhibition or installation, and 'other' (in that order, where 'other' leaves space for hoped-for influence on policy). My work included writing a chapter for the catalogue published by Manchester University Press in June 2014 (Knight et al., 2012); proposing, securing and the nitty-gritty of curating works for a first iteration of the exhibition; and developing a method of capturing impact data through the website.

During 2013, three further venues were secured for a tour (Chawton House Library, the John Hansard Gallery and the People's History Museum) and further funds were raised (from internal applications and Arts Council England). The investigatory team had wanted a multi-venue tour if it could be achieved, and I was able to bring in my personal research to raise the further research question of how a curator can articulate a position that interrogates local history and contexts in terms of their potentially productive relationships with the 'horizon of internationalism' (Smith, 2012, p. 91) through developing methodologies to create site-specific curatorial compositions that interweave narratives from different discourses. In other words, I developed an addition to the project that looked at explicitly curatorial questions (which were not included in the project bid and therefore are independent research), of how site-specific exhibitions can be created that speak to both the local and particular, and the broader picture of places and ideas. The project team was supportive of this, and I planned which works would show (and how they would show) at each venue in relation to the site. Sadly, the nature of fixed-term contract research frequently leaves ECRs in the position of having to leave posts before the work is completed, particularly in cases where the original project is expanded.

I left the project in July 2014, prior to the second impact-focused event and iteration of the show at Chawton House. This was a significant personal disappointment, as I was unable to take part in the events due to starting a new role on another project at Bath Spa University. Working with this project team with their focus on measuring impact left me very much more aware of requirements for public accessibility and the developing impact agenda, which is why it appears here as a case study, and this will be expanded on in the final case study.

Securing a permanent post at Lincoln brought new responsibilities in terms of REFable outputs. One of the key issues around the *Picturing Finance* project was how, in relation to new REF regulations about researcher independence, it could be argued that I was an 'independent researcher' at that time, as the new REF guidelines do not permit that an output in its own right is enough to establish independence. My *The Money Shot* chapter was internally and externally 'audited' and a discussion arose about 'packaging' my research in order to lever the best possible REF evaluation. This is common in practice-led projects, where outputs of different kinds are often presented together as one 'output', and seems to be generated by lack of confidence in departments housing practice-led researchers. In the last few years, REF information meetings and conversations with external consultants have communicated a strong message that practice-led outputs are considered not to need 'qualifying' equivalent texts, yet this is encouraged at unit level within institutions. This culminates in a disproportionate demand on practice-led researchers to deliver both the practice-led research element and an additional traditional article or book chapter as a single output, effectively requiring twice the amount of work. The impact agenda plays a part in this, as discussed in the earlier section on 'the exhibitionary turn', with audience figures, new commissions and shifts in thinking as a result of artworks being key methods of recording and measuring impact. This will be discussed in more detail in the next case study.

For the purposes of *Show Me The Money*, it was proposed that I 'package' my book chapter, the exhibition tour and a yet-to-be-written article as a praxiological investigation into exhibitionary meaning that did not replicate the findings of the investigative team of *Picturing Finance*, but produced a constellation of meanings that could not be made known by other methods and which thus articulate the site-specific exhibitionary. The package would, therefore, comprise a practice-led investigation and two peer-reviewed traditional publications (each of which could, under REF submission rules, be submitted as a separate output). At the time of writing, this 'output' remains unresolved, though my current institution is keen for me to prioritise the journal article that 'binds' the outputs together, and places it in this institution and not in the one where the initial research took place.

My experience on *Picturing Finance* was a key factor in enabling my transition into a permanent role and through it I learned a new way of thinking about 'impact' and what it might mean in my future research projects.

The **And Or** *project and interdisciplinary work between art and literature (2014 onwards)*

My 2017 research plan articulated my plans for REF2021 submission. I have discussed a portion of this in the previous case study *Show Me the Money*, and in this section I will describe what is called 'Package B: Reading and writing art after the internet', and explain its history.

'Package B' has its roots in research undertaken during my fellowship at Oxford Brookes University, where I predominantly worked on two things: research relating to drones in art [not discussed in this essay], and a collaborative, interdisciplinary research project called *&/* (And Or) which involved both Dr Sarah Archino (currently Assistant Professor of Art History at Furman University) and Dr Síofra McSherry (currently Postdoctoral Fellow in American Literature at the Freie Universität in Berlin). '*And Or* is a research project and a digital space reimagining the relationship between art, interpretation, exhibition and theory… In establishing new ground within the dematerialised realm of digital, we seek to create a third space where writing and art can be brought together in new configurations' (Archino et al., 2018, p. 176). *And Or* itself contains two strands of research: the formulation and continuing renegotiation of this third space; and a line of questioning that includes the institutional structures of exhibitions, publications and peer review. The project emerged from overlapping concerns we each had within our separate disciplines. Since 2014 we have developed three exhibitions together with a number of conference papers and publications, and a fourth exhibition to be launched in the winter of 2018. The project was largely developed when we were all still precarious ECRs in contract research or hourly paid teaching posts, where we had little or no institutional support or leverage. As a result, this project has developed much more slowly than we would have liked. Nevertheless, it has been an important project because of its comparative lightness and hybridity: we were selected to speak about our first exhibition *Command Plus* (with poet Nia Davies and artist Molly Morin) at the College Arts Annual Conference in Chicago in 2014 on a panel with the director of the Carnegie Art Museum, the senior public programs specialist at the J. Paul Getty Museum and the Deputy Director of the Art Institute for Museum Education. This led to discussion about our project at an unexpectedly senior level and culminated in our inclusion in Routledge's Research in Museum Studies 2018 publication *Academics, Artists and Museums: 21st Century Partnerships* (Archino et al., 2018).

At the same time that I was developing this work in collaboration with my peers, I was also developing individual and other collaborative works that also addressed the idea of art and writing colliding in internet-specific ways. I was invited to be part of the artwork *Ways of Something*, curated by Lorna Mills and shown extensively throughout Europe and North America, including Istanbul Moving Image Festival, 2015; The Photographer's Gallery, London, 2015; Transmediale, Berlin, 2015; Art Athina Film, Athens, 2016; Western Front, Vancouver, 2015; Gene Siskel Film Center, Chicago, 2015; Carnegie Museum, Pittsburgh, 2016; Centro Cultural São Paolo, Brazil, 2017; Flatpack Film Festival, Birmingham, 2017; Dreamlands, Whitney Museum of American Art, 2017; Museum of the Moving Image, New York, 2018. It was reviewed in numerous journals and press articles, and was voted best digital artwork of 2014 by *hyperallergic* (110,000 subscribers). It was subsequently sold to the Whitney Museum of American Art. There's plenty of scope for investigating its impact, but similarly, it's important to remember that this is an enormous collaboration between 58 artists, so my contribution is a fragment, and proportional.

In discussions with my Director of Research, it became clear that my work with *And Or* and my individual research was part of a wider investigation of reading and writing art after the internet, and that my numerous projects, exhibitions and artworks in this field should be 'packaged' together for REF submission. This body of work comprises numerous separate outputs of different kinds, and investigates by practice the conditions of making and interpreting art and its convergences with literature after Web 2.0. Individual outputs, in addition to *Ways of Something*, the *And Or* exhibitions and publications, include: my media archaeology of the GIF *#unicornthings* exhibited first as part of *The New Black* exhibition at Resonate 2015, and subsequently reconfigured for live performance at *Finishing School* at Bethnal Green Working Men's Club later the same year; my text piece *The Catalogue of Unsatisfied Desires* and the Unsatisfied Desires twitter-bot (@UnsatisfiedD) which examine desire and social media; my work *A Silver Nutmeg and A Golden Pear* for curatorial intervention #exstrange; and my 2014 sound work *Something About The Girl* which addresses the figure of the disappearing female in fiction. It is possible that other individual outputs which research the same theme or use similar methodologies will be added to this package between the time of writing and 2020.

It's here that an advantage of practice-led research in the arts can be clearly seen, as all of this work takes place, beyond academia, in the cultural sector, and subsequently can be associated with audience numbers, evaluation data relating to visitors, sales figures and social media analytics. My strategy for this 'package' has developed from my experience with Knight, Crosthwaite and Marsh on *Picturing Finance* (2012), and I have deliberately ensured that I have relevant data on all of these individual projects towards the impact element of their REF assessment.

Conclusion

Not unexpectedly, impact can be a valuable tool for the practice-led researcher if they can avoid the pitfalls of time-intensive data collection, omitting impact from the research design stage, and illustrating the work of other researchers. In theory, impact also opens up new avenues for interdisciplinary partnerships, but this seems somewhat mitigated by the development of the exhibition as an impact tool, and the marginalization of practice-led researchers in that process.

My experiences as I have navigated my way to independent researcher status have demonstrated the importance of research design to allow an appropriate amount of focus on impact. There's a definite danger in over-focusing on the comparatively small 25% weighting of impact in the whole assessment, however, and it is important that the drivers of research remain: what needs to be known and what problems need solutions. It is important to maintain a critical approach to the types of evaluation and review that researchers are encouraged (both positively and punitively) to undertake, as well as the power structures at play and their impact on the society of which we as researchers are a part.

Finally, it is too early to offer any view on the impact of impact on my career. Impact's importance is likely to be reiterated in subsequent REF cycles, so it is a pragmatic decision to think about it now. One of the key factors in the research avenues that I have decided to tread in the last two years, and how I have decided to frame my research, is how it might be shown to have impact. Making this conscious and explicit decision has changed the way that I structure and conceive projects: they have become less organic, and consequently slightly less interesting as there seems to be less opportunity within them for experimentation and play, the hallmarks of practice-led research.

Learning points

- Use professional evaluation tools to help you to identify what data can be collected, and ensure that evaluation is part of your project planning (Arts Council England's models helped me to think through impact for REF).
- Encourage research groups to discuss and think collaboratively about impact.
- It's easy to overlook possible impact data – swap skills with a critical friend in another discipline to extend your thinking.

References

AHRC (2007). *Social Impact of Artist Exhibitions: Two Studies.* AHRC. [Viewed 30 August 2018]. Available from: https://ahrc.ukri.org/documents/case-studies/social-impact-of-a rtist-exhibitions-two-case-studies/

Archino, S., McSherry, S. and Streffen, I. (2018). A third place: the &/ Project. In: I. Costache and C. Kunny, eds., *Academics, Artists and Museums, 21st Century Partnerships.* New York: Routledge. pp. 176–190.

Candy, L. (2006). *Practice Based Research, A Guide.* [Viewed 1 September 2018]. Sydney: Creativity & Cognition Studios, University of Technology. Available from www.ma

ngold-international.com/_Resources/Persistent/764d26fd86a709d05e8d0a
0d2695bd65fd85de4f/Practice_Based_Research_A_Guide.pdf

Henderson, T. (2010). Illuminating Hadrian's Wall brought £3m into local economy. *The Journal*. 18 August. [Viewed 12 March 2019]. Available from: www.thejournal.co.uk/news/local-news/illuminating-hadrians-wall-brought-3m-4452567

Knight, P., Crosthwaite, P. and Marsh, N. (2012). *AHRC Follow-on Funding Proposal: Picturing Finance, an Exhibition on the Visual Imagination of Financial Capitalism*. [Unpublished Grant Proposal].

Leverhulme Trust (2017). *Awards Made*. [Accessed 1 September 2018]. Available from www.leverhulme.ac.uk/awards-made/recent-awards

O'Neil, P. (2007). The Curatorial Turn: From Practice to Discourse. In: J. Rugg, and M. Sedgwick, eds., *Issues in Curating Contemporary Art*. Bristol: Intellect. pp.13–28

Pearson, A. (2014). Hadrian's Wall Trust to close down after English Heritage pulls plug on support. *The Journal*. 25 March. [Viewed 12 March 2019]. Available from: www.thejournal.co.uk/news/north-east-news/english-heritage-withdraws-hadrians-wall-6873928

Posner, P. (2009). The Pracademic: An Agenda for Re-engaging Practitioners and Academics. *Public Budgeting and Finance*. 29, 12–26.

REF2021. (2018). *Draft Guidance on Submissions REF 2021*. REF2021. [Viewed 30 August 2018]. Available from: www.ref.ac.uk/media/ref,2021/downloads/Draft%20Guidance%20on%20submissions%20REF%202018_1.pdf

Smith, T. (2012). *Thinking Contemporary Curating*. New York: Independent Curators International.

Streffen, I. (2014–2016). *Show Me the Money: The Image of Finance 1700 to the Present*. [Exhibition]. At: Northern Gallery of Contemporary Art, Sunderland; John Hansard Gallery, Southampton; Chawton House Library, Hampshire; People's History Museum, Manchester.

Streffen, I. and Hadrian's Wall Heritage Ltd (2010). *Illuminating Hadrian's Wall*. [Art installation]. At: Hadrian's Wall.

Thrush, K. (2009). *Arts Council Project Proposal for Illuminating Hadrian's Wall*. [Unpublished Arts Council England Application].

Walker, D. (2010). Being A Pracademic: Combining Reflexive Practice with Scholarship. Keynote address, Australian Institute of Project Management Annual Conference, Darwin, 10–13 October. [Accessed 1 September 2018]. Available from www.researchgate.net/publication/267995102_Being_a_Pracademic_-_Combining_Reflective_Practice_with_Scholarship

Whitty, P. (2013). *Environment Template UOA 34, Oxford Brookes University*. [National Research Audit submission]. [Accessed 12 March 2019]. Available from: https://results.ref.ac.uk/(S(01e1x4s1xl4vsi34b5xnpf1v))/Submissions/Environment/130.

REFLECTION

Thinking laterally: A public health practitioner's view of impact

Victoria Gilroy

Introduction

The aim of this reflection is to explore the challenges and opportunities that arise from integrating my roles as both a practitioner and academic and examine how this can influence, guide and drive real-world impact. By reflecting on my personal experience to date, I consider the importance of recognising the differences between practice and academic contexts and how these can sometimes present unexpected barriers and opportunities for the early career researcher (ECR). To support my debate, I will use an example of a small research project where I was the principal investigator and was able to draw on my experience as both a practitioner and researcher. By reflecting on my personal experience, I look to articulate the lessons learnt, which may benefit and reassure others who are embarking on a similar journey.

Background

As a qualified specialist community public health nurse with over 30 years of experience working in the National Health Service, I was practised in a range of clinical and managerial roles; however, working and taking a role within higher education presented a significant and different challenge to me. This, I feel, was due to discovering that there are different underlying philosophical premises that inform academic institutions compared with those that inform practice. Academia, from my perspective, focuses on the process of generating new knowledge and evidence, whereas fundamentally, the primary role of practice is the actual 'delivery' of something in the here and now. This, as a concept in itself, can lead to an inner tension, as on the one hand for *practice* there is an implicit need to 'get the job done', while conversely in *academia* a key feature is taking time out to explore, consider, contemplate and reflect. The systems and processes that govern these two different worlds are constructed to support their overall goals, but the navigation of two such separate yet interlinked systems was in itself challenging. Arguably, I am simultaneously highly experienced as practitioner, whilst far less experienced within the academic world, and thereby find myself experiencing old, new and different challenges at the same time. I felt I had limited time to learn how to navigate new systems due to the fact that I, like many of my colleagues, had been bound up with a high teaching workload, with little scope or time to reach my full potential as an ECR. However, throughout all of this, what remained a constant for me was that as a practitioner it is vital that research relates closely to and advances practice, and that it must have real-world demonstrable impact. In philosophical terms, I see my role as a practitioner within academia as a vehicle to support the development of evidence-informed best practice through educating others.

The project

A particular opportunity arose which enabled me to capitalise on my dual areas of practice. Within public health, childhood nutritional health and the reduction of obesity are key national priorities (Gov.UK 2017). Given their direct contact with children, school nurses, therefore, have a significant role in delivering this agenda; yet at this time, there was little research that offered guidance and support regarding the education needs and requirements of school nurses delivering interventions to children and young people. In response to a national funding call by The Burdett Nursing Trust, we submitted a proposal to explore how nursing-focused research can support the reduction of maternal and childhood obesity. The call was particularly attractive given that it provided me with the opportunity to stay true to my values to ensure that any research I embarked on would inform and shape practice.

The University, in partnership with The School and Public Health Nursing Association, (a National Charity which aims to support the professional role of the school nurses through research, practice development and education), was awarded funding for the development of training and resources to support school nurses to enable them to provide evidence-based advice to young people on nutritional health. On reflection, I feel that the strength and success of our application was due to the direct connection between practice and research; we were able to articulate how research in the early stages of the project would impact and inform the co-creation of the practical and 'fit for purpose' resources required to improve and develop the practice of school nurses.

My role as the Principal Investigator (PI) of the project comprised leading the scoping of the research, including integrating the views of both school nurses and young people. This information would then be utilised to develop an evidenced-based training resource including a film and mobile app to be used by the school nurses in their work with young people. As this was a practice-driven project and based on my knowledge / experience as a practitioner, for me the pathways to impact were clear; if we used the research evidence to develop the resources, which in turn promoted best practice and facilitated opportunity and capacity for school nurses to work with young people, ultimately more young people would be more supported to healthier choices thereby achieving impact in relation to tackling obesity. However, due to the limited time and capacity of myself as the PI and the practitioners and young people who were part of the project, it required lateral thinking in order to create a model that could be replicated and was sustainable in real-world practice.

Opportunities

The project was initiated from a practice perspective and so it was vital that the research remained grounded in the reality of practice. This meant that stakeholder input, advice and steering was an integral part of the research and development process and would aid in moving the work forward. My background as a practitioner was immensely valuable here as I was able to identify potential collaborators through my existing connections. I approached a practising school nurse, with whom I had worked closely in the past, and we worked jointly with a professional association (the School and Public Health Nursing Association – SAPHNA). This co-creation approach allowed us to produce an ultimately successful resource, i.e., one that was evidence-based but fit and appropriate for use in practice.

However, we also recognised the need to connect with our research colleagues more substantially to draw on university support. We, therefore, sought and engaged in a collaboration with my university colleagues who, given our difficulties with capacity, supported me as the PI to carry out the initial research to inform the project deliverables and a final evaluation of the project. An experienced Reader was recruited as part of the project steering group. Their support to me as the PI allowed me to navigate the new and unfamiliar academic systems.

Budget management was a skill that I had developed in previous roles. However, for many colleagues it can be a daunting part of being the PI in a research study. Fortunately, my mentor had significant experience in the academic systems and was able to guide me and support me to overcome any barriers, both in the university and in practice. On reflection, having a role model like this was a crucial factor in the success of the research delivery model.

Challenges

The process of putting together the proposal and gaining ethical internal approval was the first challenge on my journey. I had to learn who to contact, which forms to complete and how to negotiate the workload. Whilst this is likely felt by all ECRs, as an experienced practitioner transitioning into academia, it was a particular challenge to me as I was out of my comfort zone having been used to navigating practice systems with success on a daily basis, yet now being faced with unfamiliar processes, procedures, rules and regulations.

One of the most significant challenges for me was creating the capacity to deliver the project within the agreed time scales. The need for creativity in our approach was essential. As a master's student some 10 years previously, I had found the process of studying to be isolating. The result of my study, whilst of value, disconnected me from my day job as a health visitor. This view has recently been validated by Shaw and le Roux (2017), who debate the notion that the higher education system can been seen as a 'functionally differentiated social system' with a different set of rules and boundaries from practice. This is a useful way to frame the disconnection between the practitioners' lived working environment and the process of studying at master's level. Ultimately, my master's sat on the shelf, and I continued with the demands of practice. This left me feeling there had to be a better, more applied and engaging way to use the capacity of our master's students.

Whilst elements of the process were smooth, especially the co-production with practice (this notably is one of my core professional skills), other elements of the research journey were not as easy to navigate, particularly those not a core part of my practitioner role. There were significant ethical challenges including a lack of understanding at the university of the working reality in a practitioner's world, and on my part, naivety in expecting this to be understood. There are lessons for us all in this, specifically that we need to develop a shared understanding and acknowledgement of the pressures and constraints of our differing contexts; by developing mutual respect and understanding we can support each other to navigate the systems which can at times present as obstacles to progress, from both perspectives.

Thinking beyond project impact

As an experienced practitioner, I was very aware of the difficulties for health-care professionals in pursuing academic qualifications due to time and resources. I was particularly aware that very few school nursing students complete a master's degree after exiting the course with a professional qualification. So, as part of this project bid, I negotiated an opportunity to create funding for two master's students, who were to be integrated into the project plan. This built capacity not only in the project, but addressed a key real-world need about skill development and engagement of the clinical workforce into research. Through this more lateral thinking, I was able to concomitantly: contribute to the learning experience of students; deliver research at a very competitive cost; and engage in research that was going to inform practice in a very direct way. Both students successfully completed their master's degree and reflected that they felt their contribution had direct impact on practice.

A key component of the success of this project has been the co-production of research questions and processes at every stage of the project, by building on and developing my practice links. As a practitioner, I recognised that this was key as it directly connected the practice context to the project. A steering group was established including academics, practitioners and representatives of the local youth partnership group. Young people were involved and able to steer the direction of the research, leading to the identification of a need for focus groups in the research. These then produced data which could be used to inform the development of the products built though a deeper understanding of these individuals' perspectives across the practice setting. Co-production was crucial in the scoping of the school nurses' views, ensuring that the messages, ideas and concepts that they were communicating through the focus groups and survey were translated fully into an evidence-based training tool that is now being cascaded nationally to the school nursing teams by SAPHNA trainers.

It is clear that research which engages practitioners and service users as active participants in its design and delivery has value on multiple levels. The key benefit for me has been realised through working with the wider community of practice and service users to increase the impact of research going forward and to maximise beneficial change. Through creative thinking and co-production, we were able to develop a robust study that maximised the capacity of all involved, and minimised significant barriers to the wider engagement of practice in the development and delivery of research to directly inform practice.

Reflections on the practitioner-academic

There is extensive literature that highlights the gap between theory and practice, and points to the need to support practitioner engagement in research and applying research to practice (see, for example, Allan et al. 2011; Chan 2013). For me, the primary driver in getting involved in this research project was the potential for reducing this gap. The language used and the processes involved can act as barriers to engagement in the research process by practitioners (Edward 2015). Experience suggests that research is often described in practice as something that is done by 'others' with little bearing on the real world of practice. For me, getting involved in this research project had the potential to dispel this myth through the integration of my role as a practitioner and an academic. I needed a project that could break down these somewhat artificial barriers; that aimed to embed the value of research in openly and explicitly informing practice.

From my perspective, there is a need to break down the barriers of academic research to support more collaboration and partnership with practice. Through co-production, knowledge-sharing and experience we can enable practitioners to work alongside academics to support shared understanding and move away from some of the traditional research and the 'them and us' attitude that still exists. Through my journey, I have acknowledged the value of my practitioner-researcher voice within the academic environment; it has supported my confidence in the world of academia and given me the ability to champion a greater focus on practice-led projects.

Conclusion

If I were asked to use this model again, I would say 'yes!' without hesitation. My advice to colleagues who are in my shoes – i.e., who are overwhelmed with the day job and concerned about the impact of research on practice – would be to think laterally, consider how they can involve a wider group in the co-production of their proposal and ultimately the delivery of their research project. The key for me was to draw on the skills of my mentor to guide me through technical aspects of the project, so I recommend identifying your mentor early and use them as a valuable resource to learn from and gain experience. The project is now almost finished; next steps include publishing the research findings and presenting them to the wider workforce.

References

Allan, H., Smith, P. and O'Driscoll, M. (2011). Experiences of supernumerary status and the hidden curriculum in nursing: A new twist in the theory-practice gap? *Journal of Clinical Nursing.* 20(5–6), 847–855.

Chan, Z.C. (2013). A systematic review of creative thinking/creativity in nursing education. *Nurse Education Today.* 33(11), 1382–1387.

Edward, K. (2015). A model for increasing appreciation, accessibility and application of research in nursing. *Journal of Professional Nursing.* 31(2), 119–123.

Gov.UK (2017). *National child measurement programme, England 2015 to 2016 school year.* Gov. UK. [Viewed 8 June 2018]. Available from: www.gov.uk/government/statistics/nationa l-child-measurement-programme-england-2015-to-2016-school-year

Shaw, C. and le Roux, K. (2017). From practitioner to researcher: Designing the dissertation process for part time coursework masters students. *Systemic Practice and Action Research.* 30(4), 433–446.

PART II

Research impact and collaboration

4

KNOWLEDGE EXCHANGE AS IMPACT

Louise Maythorne

In its broadest sense, knowledge exchange (KE) is the exchange of expertise between academics and non-academics in pursuit of social and / or economic advancement. It is this mechanism of exchange that allows a researcher to put their academic research to work in another context, hopefully resulting in a positive impact that can be identified and measured. In the context of UK Higher Education, however, the emphasis is often placed on specific commercial methods of delivering this exchange – for example, technology transfer, spin-out companies and the licensing of intellectual property (IP). This interpretation of KE misses the diversity of exchange, and in so doing makes it more difficult for researchers to understand the opportunities that KE offers to advance the impact of their research.

The impact agenda is one that touches ECRs in particular and consequently the opportunities that KE presents as a mechanism for impact are especially compelling for this audience. In this chapter, I discuss the rise of the KE agenda in the UK Higher Education landscape, pointing to the importance of KE fluency in order to navigate competing priorities. In the first section, I unpack the distinctive properties of knowledge exchange, arguing for an understanding of KE as a non-linear and iterative process of exchange that necessarily lends itself to impactful work outside academia. I explore five pathways to impactful knowledge exchange, identifying the activities and approaches that facilitate it. In the second part of the chapter, I discuss three of the properties of knowledge exchange that overlap with the professional priorities of ECRs, highlighting the value of knowledge exchange for this career stage in particular. In the final section, I revisit the idea of knowledge exchange as an agent of impact, focussing this time on the impact it can have on the institutions and policies of the higher education sector.

The context of knowledge exchange in UK higher education

Knowledge exchange has been an area of growing investment in higher education in the UK over the past twenty years. Since the UK's Higher Education Funding Council for England (HEFCE) introduced dedicated funding for knowledge exchange activities in universities in 1999 with the Higher Education Reaches-Out to Business & the Community Fund, this locus of activity has grown exponentially. With HEFCE funding in 2017 worth £160m (HEFCE 2017) and additional scrutiny for university KE activity proposed by the Knowledge Exchange Framework (Johnson 2017), the centrality of knowledge exchange to the Higher Education landscape seems certain.

In addition, to support the institutional pursuit of knowledge exchange through the Higher Education Innovation Fund (HEIF), individual researchers are encouraged by funders to embed KE within their research. For example, the Arts and Humanities Research Council (AHRC) writes:

> Putting Knowledge Exchange at the very heart of its strategy the AHRC works to ensure that arts and humanities academic interests are diversified and enhanced through opportunities to engage in knowledge exchange and partnership work across our entire funding portfolio; to encourage co-creation and co-production of research agendas; to have a significant and transformative effect on the creative and cultural life and health and well-being of the nation; and to enlarge the contribution to the arts, public engagement and policy formation. (AHRC 2015)

Here we see that knowledge exchange is 'at the heart' of the AHRC's strategy and is understood in explicitly impactful terms. In a similar vein, the Natural and Environmental Research Council (NERC) provides Knowledge Exchange Fellowships that 'focus on accelerating and amplifying economic impact and improvements in the quality of our lives' (NERC 2017). By embedding knowledge exchange as a mechanism for impact at the heart of their strategies and grants, funders are reinforcing knowledge exchange as a mechanism for impact and ensuring that researchers are literate in these values.

One of the consequences of the growing importance of knowledge exchange to Higher Education is the plurality of definitions for KE. This tension is significant for ECRs contemplating their role in the university system because understanding and navigating these definitions is a helpful way of crystallising an understanding of research impact. At its core, the tensions around defining knowledge exchange revolve around the extent to which the exchange should have commercial value. HEFCE explain the process of awarding Higher Education Innovation Funding (HEIF) to universities:

> All funding is allocated on the basis of performance, using a combination of measures of income as a proxy for impact on the economy and society. This aims to achieve the greatest impact from public funding of knowledge exchange. (HEFCE 2017)

In this context we can see the emphasis on income from KE activities as a means of quantifying its impact. By contrast, the Research Councils UK policy position is distinctively different in appraising the commercial value of KE. In *Impact through knowledge exchange: RCUK position and expectations* (RCUK 2014, p.1), it is stated:

> [We] recognise that knowledge exchange between academia and public services and third sector is central to delivering key societal and cultural benefits and does not always lead to immediate or direct commercial benefits. [We] support knowledge exchange not necessarily to generate a financial return to an individual, research group, institution or the Councils, but to deliver the widest range of benefits to the UK economy and society from the excellent research, people and facilities in which they invest.

Although sometimes assumed to be exogenous, these diverse definitions of knowledge exchange have now become subject to scholarly attention and researchers have sought to unpick and clarify definitions of KE and innovation (Cruickshank et al. 2012; Davenport 2013; Hagen 2008 amongst others). For ECRs seeking to gain a deeper grasp of research impact and the contribution that KE approaches can afford to their research, it is important to understand the nuances and cultural dimensions of how knowledge exchange is defined and practiced. In the next section we consider what 'doing' knowledge exchange may look like, and how these activities lend themselves to creating and measuring impact.

Knowledge exchange as an agent of impact: Definitions and activities

Knowledge exchange has been defined as 'the iterative cycle of sharing ideas, research results, expertise or skills between interested parties that enables the creation, transfer, adoption and exploitation of new knowledge in order to develop new products, processes or services and influence public policy' (Lockett et al. 2008). Although a helpful starting point, this definition conflates various types of engagement, each with distinctive properties, under a single umbrella term. Further, it assumes that 'interested parties' reciprocate an equally high level of interest in the knowledge at hand. Although this may lead to the highest quality of exchange, it is of course not always the case. An academic may be reluctant to receive the knowledge being shared by their partner organisations, or the non-academic partners may not feel enthused by the academic materials being presented. Some communities of interest or policymakers in particular may participate in knowledge exchange activities with less commitment or enthusiasm than their academic colleagues or vice versa – so while KE may be said to be taking place, the quality and sustainability of that exchange is not optimal. I suggest in this section some of the pathways to KE that can help ensure successful partnerships and balance the interests of both parties.

In his 2013 work, Davenport proposes a taxonomy of innovation that unpacks four types of innovation: technology transfer, knowledge transfer, knowledge exchange and knowledge creation. Each of these types of activity makes fundamentally different assumptions about the nature of the knowledge being created, the originators of the knowledge, and the structure of the collaborations. These approaches may be summarised as follows (Davenport 2013):

Technology transfer: Relies on applied research with an emphasis on science and technology. Partnerships are commercial and IP is patented. Mechanisms include: spin out, IP / legal advice, licensing, contract research, collaborative research, investment funds, incubators.

Knowledge transfer: Draws on a wider range of disciplines. Partners are commercial or non-commercial and IP may be patented. Mechanisms include: contract research, consultancy, collaborative research, knowledge transfer partnerships (KTP), secondments.

Knowledge exchange: Is inclusive of all disciplines and recognises the contribution of the arts and humanities. Partnerships are commercial or non-commercial and IP is generated but generally not patented. Mechanisms include: research, rapid prototyping, KTP, consultancy, secondment, sandpits, co-design workshops, social networking.

Knowledge creation: Is inclusive of all disciplines and recognises the potential for creative practice and design to play a leading role. Partnerships are commercial or non-commercial and there is an emphasis on foreground IP. Mechanisms include: fabrication labs, hack labs, co-design, sandpits, workshops, social networking, crowdsourcing, KTP, secondments.

This taxonomy provides helpful context for knowledge exchange and disentangles it from different but related processes. The focus on an iterative process of exchange, as opposed to a linear assignment of knowledge, is, I argue, what sits at the heart of effective and *impactful* knowledge exchange. This process of iteration necessarily involves collaboration. By collaborating closely on the design, execution, uses and the legacy of the work, the potential impact of that piece of work can be maximised.

Against these considerations Oancea et al. (2015) have identified five pathways and roles that make KE an effective agent of impact: (1) participation; (2) visibility; (3) use; (4) benefits; (5) diffusion. I consider these in turn.

Participation, and *the importance of collaborators from non-academic settings*, is central to the process of exchange. There are multiple ways in which this participation can be embedded in the research: from co-creation of the project from the initial design phase, to employing an 'expert' advisory board, to engaging with the research participants in designing the final outputs of the research. The focus here is on both designing opportunities for participation in the research and flattening the hierarchy of the participants:

The paradigm of collaboration is an innovative way of working in which everyone's knowledge is given equal status and knowledge exchange becomes a two-way channel, rather than a one-way flow of information from academics (Rasool 2017, p.320).

The importance of participation to the knowledge exchange process is that it maximises the project's ability to meet the needs of the collaborators, creating impact in more meaningful ways and, in turn, increasing the opportunities for both planned and serendipitous impact by increasing the opportunities for others to input into the work. While it is true that successful knowledge exchange should be planned in the sense that it should be part of a project's design, the planned process of collaboration often generates serendipitous impact by introducing the work to new actors, suggesting new routes of inquiry, seeding further collaboration or identifying opportunities to impact in ways that could not have been anticipated at the beginning of the project. It is worth noting, therefore, that far from limiting serendipity, KE often fosters it.

A second pathway to impact, central to effective knowledge exchange, is the *visibility of the project to the audience(s) for that work.* Activities in this area may be simple acts of dissemination: the publication of a report, a project website or twitter feed, an exhibition or similar, but may also be an exercise in public engagement. Here we see the value of participatory approaches, where the intended audience for the work has the opportunity to be exposed to it and to influence it. The evaluation of the knowledge exchange activity by these users is also key to ensuring successful impact. If knowledge exchange is understood as an iterative process, then regular evaluations and adjustments ensure that the knowledge that is being exchanged is valued by both parties.

The third pathway, identifying early on *the potential users or collaborators,* is a well-established mechanism for impact. Indeed the Economic and Social Research Council of the UK (ESRC) recommends to grant-holders that any activities designed to promote KE are designed with specific objectives in mind and suggests, in turn, that Theory of Change and Stakeholder Mapping approaches can help to identify the purpose of these activities (ESRC 2017). This systematic, yet holistic, approach means that although you should 'allow space for serendipitous connections and events to take place at any stage during or after your research' (ESRC 2017), the framework for planning and executing KE activities is one in which impact upon specific communities can be identified and calculated more easily than if it were not embedded in knowledge exchange.

The fourth element of impactful knowledge exchange is a strong sense of how the work will bring *benefit.* The UK Research Excellence Framework, as well as similar initiatives in international contexts and research funders, incentivises researchers to identify and articulate the benefit their work will bring to non-academic contexts. It should be noted that while there may be a difference between the benefits that are envisioned in the development of the project and those that are auditable at a particular point in the project's lifecycle (as KE is an iterative process and auditing should therefore not only occur at the end) the point to note is that both processes require a clear sense of benefit and an ability to articulate that benefit. Knowledge exchange requires all parties involved to collaborate in the spirit of improvement – be that improved outcomes or improved information. A strong sense of shared purpose is therefore key to impactful knowledge exchange.

What is less well developed is a sense of how the process of exchange brings benefit in turn to the academic community. Academic impacts such as new networks, a more dynamic research agenda, as well as financial reward where the activity is linked to a research grant, HEIF or QR funding, are often not given the same profile as benefits to the 'user' community. However, the process of knowledge exchange should bring clear benefit to all parties involved; the impact on academia is discussed in more detail later in the chapter.

Finally, the *diffusion of knowledge into the norms and discourses of particular communities* is a pathway to impact that, although important, is more difficult to measure. It is also an outcome that is most often associated with research that takes place outside the STEM disciplines, a fact to which we return in the final section of this chapter. The absorption of new knowledge is a powerful measure of its resonance and influence within a community and one that can only occur when that community has had the opportunity to invest in the research themselves. Understanding KE as an iterative and participative process increases the impact of that exchange, and therefore the likelihood that it becomes diffused through norms and discourses. The idea of diffusion within a *particular community* is also important, because those parameters give the knowledge a particular resonance and credibility:

> Local and social embeddedness of economic and institutional actors in clusters has been identified as vital for the diffusion of knowledge and particularly of tacit knowledge. (Lillebrygfjeld Halse and Bjarnar 2014, p.104)

Knowledge exchange, then, is not the same thing as impact. It is an activity, or series of activities, that facilitate exchange for the purpose of having impact. KE is the conduit to impact, but not the impact in itself. It may of course be possible to undertake KE and find that it is not impactful – if the collaboration is not well designed, if the partners are not committed – or the impacts may emerge at a much later date. Similarly, excellent and important impacts may come about through many routes that are not based on knowledge exchange – a presentation at an academic conference, the publication of a paper to a community group. An ECR addressing questions of impact should simply be aware of the many ways in which impact may occur, and be willing and able to plan for their desired impacts whilst fostering opportunities for serendipitous impacts too. Knowledge exchange is one of the approaches that enable the researcher to do this.

To summarise, as an established feature of the higher education landscape, knowledge exchange is often conflated with similar, but distinct, processes including knowledge transfer and technology transfer. What sets knowledge exchange apart is its focus on the reciprocal exchange of knowledge between academics and non-academics, and the iterative process of collaboration. These features make it a powerful agent of impact, and we have discussed five of the pathways that contribute to that agency.

Knowledge exchange and the early career researcher

Knowledge exchange, as discussed above, has a number of distinctive properties that set it apart from other areas of academic activity. These properties are mirrored in some of the professional priorities of the early career researcher (ECR), and in this section we consider three in more detail: the role of networks, the opportunities for funding, and research strategy.

One of the greatest imperatives for the ECR is to develop a professional network both inside and outside of academia. A network offers possibilities for mentorship, the discussion of ideas, data and methods, routes to publication, the signposting of opportunities and support with any number of professional challenges which an ECR may be facing for the first time. In their 2017 article, Ylijokia and Henriksson identify five different 'career stories' amongst junior academics and note the importance of networking in these stories. For freelance academics, 'sustaining networks calls for constant alertness and persistence, otherwise one's career is threatened' (2017, p.1303), while even for those who work in a more predictable environment as part of a research group, 'success in fundraising tends to require interdisciplinary collaboration, including partners not only from universities but also from research institutes and the business sector, both at home and abroad' (p.1302). Networking, therefore, is integral to the professional development of ECRs, regardless of the shape of their contract or their disciplinary profile.

It is this emphasis on networks that makes ECRs so well-placed to develop a healthy portfolio of knowledge exchange activities. Knowledge exchange is reliant on networks of different scales in order to build the trust and resilience required for collaboration. One of the difficulties with more narrow, commercially focussed understandings of knowledge exchange is that this disguises the breadth of networks that support successful KE collaboration.

> There is an increasing focus on the role of networks and knowledge exchange in the innovation process. Yet, the policy discourse is often narrowly focussed on areas such as technology transfer and fails to capture the importance of variety, complexity and the role of place and path dependence (Christopherson et al. 2008, p.172).

So it is, in fact, a multiplicity of actors that enable knowledge exchange from not only businesses, but also the public and charitable sectors, as well as members of the wider public and organised communities of interest. Knowledge exchange may involve working with one type of actor or several, on one occasion or many, but the opportunity to undertake projects that offer different scales and scope of networks is 'a necessary and appealing cornerstone to career-building' (Ylijokia & Henriksson 2017, p.1304).

A second property of knowledge exchange is the funding that is associated with it. Here the ECR will find knowledge exchange activities offer useful opportunities to build not only a network, but an area of expertise for which funding represents a marker of professional esteem. The funding for knowledge exchange may be awarded by the non-academic partner, for example by payment for consultancy services, contract research or prototyping. Or funding may be awarded by a third party such as research funding bodies or government departments. In the UK opportunities include knowledge exchange fellowships, follow-on funding and knowledge transfer partnerships. The funding may be awarded at an institutional level – the UK Higher Education Innovation Funding is an example of this – where financial support for knowledge exchange is then devolved to the university and its staff. Or awards may be made to individuals for projects of their own design. There is also funding available to support activities related to knowledge exchange such as public engagement or impact. These varied routes for financial support mean that ECRs are able to supplement the traditional imperatives to apply for competitive research grants with complementary streams of funding. Because these streams of KE funding are more diffuse, they may receive fewer applicants. And as they can be for relatively small sums of money, they are useful as a helpful first step in building a track record of externally funded projects. The fact that they are funded also means that there are associated structures for support within the university and partner organisations, so what may be initially a relatively exploratory or informal programme of exchange could go on to be supported institutionally, building experience in project management, financial management, reporting and regulatory requirements on a scale commensurate with the experience of the ECR. While it is important to note that individual funding schemes change over time, the commitment to funding knowledge exchange in UK Higher Education has only increased over the past 20 years, weathering changes in government and economic circumstance. It is, therefore, safe to assume that it will remain a strong focus for funding for the foreseeable future.

The impetus for ECRs to attract funding is well-documented. In her 2017 study, Sutherland found that 'research productivity' was the most talked about theme in objective career success, and within that theme 'external grant funding' and the 'number of publications and citations' were mentioned most often (p.749). By placing a monetary value on knowledge exchange activities, these activities acquire credibility and recognition in the same way as traditional research grants that are considered a mark of professional esteem. Universities are increasingly including elements of knowledge exchange activity in their promotions criteria, so the rewards for undertaking this activity can bring personal as well as professional benefit. At Bath Spa University, for example, the criteria for promotion to Reader or Professor includes evidence of knowledge exchange activities. Knowledge exchange and impact are also part of the academic framework at Coventry University, and are supported by Strathclyde University through the recruitment of Knowledge Exchange Fellows. While different institutions may attribute different values to knowledge exchange, fluency in KE is undeniably advantageous to an academic's professional profile.

Finally, the iterative process of collaborating on knowledge exchange activities means that the research that sits within it can be refined and made more impactful, leading to a more developed sense of research strategy for the ECR. An ECR may wish to ask themselves: who might benefit from my work and how might my work benefit from their insights? How could I meet with them or offer them access to my network? What support will I need in order to move these relationships forward? How could I sustain these relationships and projects? An effective research strategy will afford the researcher a clear sense of their research agenda: the questions they wish to investigate, the appropriate collaborators and sources of information, the communities they wish to engage with and the relevant sources of mentoring and professional support they require. By incorporating knowledge exchange activities into this port-folio of activities the researcher is able to maximise their efficacy in these areas.

The process of collaborating with non-academic partners can often lead to a snowballing of contacts. This 'gatekeeping' service has been well-established as a methodological tool for data collection in the social sciences, but also offers a more holistic way of connecting to individuals and organisations who may have a stake in the work that the researcher would not previously have considered. At the early stages of career development these contacts have an important currency – both as relationships that may be mutually beneficial to the researcher and partner, but also by placing the researcher and partner as 'nodes' on their respective networks and offering the opportunity for them to be referred to new contacts in turn. By building this network through a process of engagement and referral over the longer term the researcher may find this process builds momentum and their network grows organically with less cultivation.

Furthermore, additional stakeholders introduce new perspectives on the work being undertaken. This can lead to greater challenge of the underlying assump-tions: the research questions, the research design, the interpretation of the results. By making their work visible to non-academic audiences the researcher is encouraged to articulate and justify their approaches in new ways, becoming a more reflective and critically engaged professional in the process. This is an important dimension of knowledge exchange because it underlines the agency of the non-academic partners in the collaboration and their ability to influence and transfer their knowledge (tacit or explicit) into the academic setting.

Lastly, the requirement for effective knowledge exchange to build networks means that researchers are required to build trust and credibility with new sta-keholders. Their work must be communicated clearly to a variety of audiences, made salient and understandable. The ability to build trust and credibility within partnerships is an enormously important skill that transfers through to other areas of academic endeavour – interdisciplinary collaborations or teaching for example. This is an often-overlooked part of research strategy, but one that is central to the successful development of future projects, new collaborations, and to the successful representation of a researcher's work. Similarly, the ability to articulate this work to a variety of audiences in a way that resonates with them is important not only within knowledge exchange, but also related fields such as public engagement. In this way, KE can be seen as a tool that helps to develop the skills necessary for the long-term success of a researcher's strategy.

To conclude, some of the skills necessary to the development of effective knowledge exchange activities intersect with the professional priorities of the ECR. For this reason we can point to three specific reasons that KE is especially well-suited to those at the early stages of developing their research career. Knowledge exchange helps to build networks and to cultivate democratic and pluralistic approaches to research. Secondly, knowledge exchange is increasingly supported by funding on a wide variety of scales and from a wide variety of sources. This diffusion of opportunity means it is easier for ECRs to identify funded projects on a scale that is commensurate with their experience, contributing in turn to a professional track record of attracting and managing projects in a supported environment. Finally, the process of undertaking KE helps to refine particular skillsets of benefit to the ECR. These include understanding the currency of relationships and networks, the ability to use challenge from non-academic partners to refine and reflect on research strategies, and the ability to build trust by listening to collaborators, articulating and adapting arguments to resonate with them.

Knowledge exchange as an agent of change in the university system

While the previous two sections have concentrated on knowledge exchange as an agent of change outside academia, it is important to understand that the democratisation of knowledge is impacting upon the landscape of higher education too. This influence is twofold. First, knowledge exchange, as a means of undertaking impactful research, has an important role to play in a cultural shift within universities towards a more transparent and engaged contribution to social and economic life. Second, knowledge exchange is discipline-agnostic and built on a diversity of networks from business to public to third sectors. Engaging in knowledge exchange is a mechanism by which the whole ecosystem of actors and interests in the university system can be better represented. In this final section we consider these influences in turn.

Knowledge exchange encompasses a range of activities that impact upon different communities in different ways. Hughes and Kitson identify four categories of activity that capture the breadth of potential impacts (2012, p.736):

1. People-based activities that include enterprise education, student placements and curriculum development.
2. Community-based activities that include school projects and public exhibitions.
3. Commercialisation activities that include licensed research and patenting.
4. Problem-solving activities that include external secondment and joint research.

By acknowledging the full range of activities that are associated with knowledge exchange we can begin to identify how 'third mission' activity can create a cycle of influence that feeds back into a whole range of university business, including curriculum development, student and staff training and enterprise education, employability attributes, research agenda development and the role of the university as an 'anchor institution' in its locality. In this way the breadth of KE activities can be mapped against the breadth of university activities and the scope of the impacts upon HE become clearer.

The impacts of KE activity may also be felt by individual researchers. Staley points out that 'the knowledge that researchers gain from…the public often fills gaps in their own knowledge. It reveals what researchers "don't know" or would not otherwise have anticipated. This may subsequently have an impact at any stage of their research' (2017, p.160). These impacts may shape new research questions that the researcher wouldn't otherwise have considered, new approaches to data collection, or access to participants / collaborators that required gatekeeping by non-academic partners. Therefore 'what is often described as an impact on research appears to be underpinned by researchers' learning – enhancing their knowledge and skills, as well as changing their priorities and attitudes' (p.163). For the ECR who is establishing their research agenda, these insights can be especially meaningful. They afford an opportunity to consider their research in new ways, to cultivate an awareness of the different audiences for their research and to customise their activity to maximise impact in these respective areas.

Secondly, by recognising the full diversity of actors and academic disciplines that are represented in KE activity, we have the opportunity to better represent those interests within higher education. In their 2012 study of knowledge exchange and impact in HE, Hughes and Kitson point out that 'the extent and breadth of knowledge exchange beyond the science, technology and mathematics disciplines (STEM) is not prominently acknowledged in much of the academic and policy discourses. These lacunae in part reflect an absence of data on non-STEM interactions and on knowledge exchange beyond the private sector' (p.724). We are faced therefore with the under-representation of KE activity that takes place in the social sciences and arts and humanities, and with partners in the public or third sectors including charities and social enterprises. Similarly, Christopherson, Kitson, and Michie point out that in the UK and US contexts 'the narrow view of university–business interactions—where the focus is on technology transfer increasing local or regional innovation—fails to capture the reality of the complexities and varieties of such interactions and their impacts' (2008, p.169). In this example, it is the international possibilities for the scope of the knowledge exchange that are marginalised, when it is assumed that the impacts of the research take place in geographical proximity to the university partner.

It is important to redress the assumptions that find themselves translated into government and university policy in order to ensure that all of the systemic rewards for undertaking knowledge exchange and impactful research, such as REF-related QR funding, HEIF funding, research grant income and institutional promotions criteria, also reward this 'invisible' dimension of knowledge exchange as richly as that which is commercially focussed. ECRs have an important role to play in redressing this balance by critically evaluating the way in which knowledge exchange is understood as part of their professional practice. Sutherland highlights possibilities of disruptive thinking when she writes:

In the meeting of these two structures – the university's rules, processes, and buildings, and the academics' communities in which their teaching, research, and service practices occur – lies also the agency of the communities and the individual academics. Thus, success in academia is constructed by the institutional rules, expectations and policy manuals, and the ability (and willingness) of individual academics to comply with or resist these structures. (Sutherland 2017, p.746)

Ultimately, it is the responsibility of the academic community to understand the full range of activities and actors represented by knowledge exchange. Undertaking knowledge exchange has the opportunity to shape (and improve) the work of individual researchers, but also to feed back into the development of the university system more broadly through the attributes of its graduates, the development of its curricula, and the behaviours it rewards. Impact may, therefore, be felt outside academia, within universities, but also within the wider policy conversations about impact outside of STEM subjects and businesses.

Conclusion

Knowledge exchange has crystallised as an important dimension of the higher education landscape over the past twenty years. The ability of ECRs to understand the way in which this agenda is evolving through government policy and is being translated into the university environment is crucial in identifying the opportunities that KE represents. The current tensions between the rhetoric of the government who see knowledge exchange as a proxy for commercially beneficial transactions between the science base and business, and the rhetoric of the funding bodies who reward social and environmental benefits, means that ECRs need to critically engage with how they choose to undertake knowledge exchange.

This chapter has offered a starting point for ECRs seeking to understand how knowledge exchange can catalyse impact within their work. It has teased out the distinctiveness of knowledge exchange as an iterative process of two-way exchange for social or economic benefit – setting it apart from related concepts such as technology transfer. The first section explored how this exchange can be an agent of impact, discussing Oancea's five pathways through which this can happen: participation; visibility; use; benefits; and diffusion.

In the second section we discussed the ways in which the practices of effective knowledge exchange intersect with the professional skills required by ECRs. Knowledge exchange is built on the collaboration of non-academic and academic partners, the process of collaboration building a network of mutual benefit. It is precisely this focus that makes it well-suited to ECRs who are at a career stage where building networks is so important. We highlighted the weakness of the commercially focussed interpretation of knowledge exchange, which means non-STEM subjects and non-business partners are often not considered as part of a KE network. By recognising the participation of all disciplines and public and charitable sector partners the scope and potential value of knowledge exchange as a networking tool becomes clear. This approach to networking also has the effect of encouraging a more pluralistic and democratic approach to research. We went on to explore the way in which knowledge exchange activity is increasingly supported by funding. The opportunities for funding in this area are more diffuse than for research, lending themselves to ECRs who are establishing a track record of funding in a way that is commensurate with their experience. By the same token, this funding can be seen as a proxy for professional esteem, ensuring that activity is recognised and rewarded appropriately by HE. Finally, we noted that the process of undertaking KE helps to refine particular skillsets of benefit to the ECR. These include understanding the currency of relationships and networks, the ability to use challenge from non-academic partners to refine and reflect on research strategies, and the ability to build trust by listening to collaborators, articulating and adapting arguments to resonate with them.

In the final section of the chapter, we turned our attention to the impact that knowledge exchange can have on the higher education landscape itself. By recognising the full range of activity beyond the commercial that knowledge exchange encompasses, we can see the multiple ways in which the exchange may be felt on an institutional level as well as an individual level. Influencing curriculum development, graduate attributes, or the role of the university in its locality are examples of this. Critical debates about research impact and the contribution of knowledge exchange also encourage reflection about the role of the social sciences and arts and humanities in the higher education landscape – particularly the financial and reputational rewards that they receive relative to the STEM disciplines. ECRs, as the next generation of academics, have a responsibility to engage in these debates, to pursue impactful research and to shape the relationship between academia and non-academic partners in the process.

Learning points

- KE is an iterative process that brings two-way benefit and is an important agent of impact.
- KE is especially relevant to ECRs because the skills required for success and the opportunities available map well against an early career stage.
- KE can also have an impact on higher education, shaping our understanding of the role of universities and the contributions of particular disciplines.

References

AHRC (2015). *Knowledge exchange and partnerships*. Arts & Humanities Research Council. [Viewed 29 October 2017]. Available from: www.ahrc.ac.uk/innovation/knowledgeexchange/
Christopherson, S., Kitson, M. and Michie, J. (2008). Innovation, networks and knowledge exchange. *Cambridge Journal of Regions, Economy and Society*. 1(2), 165–173.
Cruickshank, L., Whitham, R. and Morris, L. (2012). Innovation through the design of knowledge exchange and the design of knowledge exchange design. International Design

Management Research Conference, August, Boston MA [Viewed 23 August 2018]. Available from: http://imagination.lancs.ac.uk/sites/default/files/outcome_downloads/cruickshank_whitham_morris_paper_copy.pdf

Davenport, J. (2013). Technology transfer, knowledge transfer and knowledge exchange in the historical context of innovation theory and practice. The Knowledge Exchange, An Interactive Conference, September, Lancaster University [Viewed 16 March 2018]. Available from: http://thecreativeexchange.org/sites/default/files/ke_conf_papers/paper_28.pdf

ESRC (2017). *Tips for doing knowledge exchange.* ESRC. [Viewed 29 October 2017]. Available from: www.esrc.ac.uk/research/impact-toolkit/tips-for-doing-knowledge-exchange/

Hagen, S. (2008). From tech transfer to knowledge exchange: European universities in the marketplace. In: L. Engwall, and D. Weave, eds., *The university in the market, vol. 84.* London: Portland Press. pp. 103–117.

HEFCE (2017). *Guide to funding 2017–18.* London: HFCE [Viewed 29 October 2017]. Available from: www.hefce.ac.uk/media/HEFCE,2014/Content/Pubs/2017/201704/HEFCE_Funding_Guide_2017-18_.pdf

Hughes, A. and Kitson, M. (2012). Pathways to impact and the strategic role of universities: new evidence on the breadth and depth of university knowledge exchange in the UK and the factors constraining its development. *Cambridge Journal of Economics.* 36(3), 723–750.

Johnson, J. (2017). *How universities can drive prosperity through deeper engagement.* Gov.UK. [Viewed 29 October 2017]. Available from: www.gov.uk/government/speeches/how-universities-can-drive-prosperity-through-deeper-engagement

Lillebrygfjeld Halse, L. and Bjarnar, O. (2014). Social fields in knowledge flows. In R. Rutten, P. Benneworth, D. Irawati, and F. Boekema, eds., *The Social Dynamics of Innovation Networks.* London: Routledge. pp. 103–120.

Lockett, N., Kerr, R. and Robinson, S. (2008). Multiple perspectives on the challenges for knowledge transfer between higher education institutions and industry. *International Small Business Journal.* 26(6), 661–681.

NERC (2017). *Knowledge exchange fellowships.* NERC. [Viewed 29 October 2017]. Available from: www.nerc.ac.uk/funding/available/schemes/kefellows/

Oancea, A., Djerasimovic, S. and Stamou, E. (2015). *Impact and knowledge exchange.* University of Oxford. [Viewed 29 October 2017]. Available from: www.education.ox.ac.uk/impact-and-knowledge-exchange

Rasool, Z. (2017). Collaborative working practices: imagining better research partnerships. *Research for All.* 1(2), 310–322.

Research Councils UK (RCUK) (2014). *Impact through knowledge exchange: RCUK position and expectations.* RCUK [Viewed 7 March 2019]. Available from: www.ukri.org/files/legacy/innovation/keposition-pdf

Staley, K. (2017) Changing what researchers 'think and do': is this how involvement impacts on research? *Research for All.* 1(1), 158–167.

Sutherland, K. (2017). Constructions of success in academia: an early career perspective. *Studies in Higher Education.* 42(4), 743–759.

Ylijokia, O. and Henriksson, L. (2017). Tribal, proletarian and entrepreneurial career stories: junior academics as a case in point. *Studies in Higher Education.* 42(7), 1292–1308.

REFLECTION

Communicating research to policymakers: The challenge of engagement and the knowledge broker role

Diana Warira

The need for evidence-informed policymaking, an approach to policymaking in which policymakers consider the best available research evidence in the policymaking process (Oxman et al. 2009) is important now more than ever. In the face of shrinking global resources for development assistance, developing countries, particularly in Africa, need to look 'inward' to solve their development challenges, such as high poverty and unemployment levels, low quality and access to education opportunities, frail healthcare systems, corruption and lack of transparency and accountability in the use of public resources, among others. There is a great deal of high quality research that has been undertaken by African scholars, but much of this research does not find its way into policymaking processes. While not all research is relevant for policy-making purposes (Stone et al. 2001), much of it is, and is going to waste. While research generated to address similar problems on other parts of the globe may be useful, it does not have the advantage of local context. Research generated on the continent is, therefore, extremely valuable for the formulation of sustainable solutions to Africa's seemingly intractable development challenges.

In recent years, there has been a growing effort by African experts in the research-to-policy landscape to link policy-relevant research with policymaking processes. In particular, science communication, which is a two-way process of engagement (Nisbet 2009) and communication of scientific evidence to the public for their social, economic, political or intellectual gain (Ren and Zhai 2014), has played a significant role. This essay is a reflection of my observations working in an institution that uses research evidence to engage policymakers in Africa on various development issues.

Politics and policymaking

Playing the communication and knowledge broker role is riddled with challenges. Perhaps the greatest challenge is that **policymaking and politics are not mutually**

exclusive, and the latter often has more influence. In fact, different policies require different political relationships (Bryner 2003). For instance, Kenya's Adolescent Sexual and Reproductive Health Policy of 2015 has suffered major drawbacks in terms of coordinating some of the cross-sectoral policy recommendations (Warira 2017). Specifically, based on evidence, the Ministry of Health (MoH) policy outlines access to sexual and reproductive health information and age-appropriate comprehensive sexuality education for adolescents as key actions to reduce risky sexual behaviour among adolescents, which if not addressed results in high teenage pregnancies, HIV/AIDS infections, and other negative outcomes. However, for in-school adolescents, this policy recommendation can only be effectively implemented by having a harmonised policy provision in Kenya's education curriculum policy under the auspices of the Ministry of Education, Science and Technology, (MoEST). The subject of providing comprehensive sexuality education for Kenya's adolescents has been an emotive issue, facing backlash from religious stakeholders and parents, among others. This has seen the education ministry fail to integrate comprehensive sexuality education in Kenya's National Curriculum Policy of 2015 and the subsequent roll-out of a new curriculum which began in 2017, despite the policy's emphasis that it would promote lifelong learning. Currently, sex education in schools places an emphasis on abstinence, with teachers taking a conservative approach that discusses sex as immoral and harmful, as well as not teaching safe sex practices for those who choose not to abstain (Sidze et al. 2017). While this approach resonates with the cultural and religious views of many key stakeholders, including policymakers, it has not helped reduce the negative sexual and reproductive health outcomes faced by Kenyan adolescents. Evidence shows that an 'abstinence-only' approach does not effectively address negative sexual and reproductive health outcomes among adolescents such as teenage pregnancies, unsafe abortions, and HIV/AIDS infections(Sidze et al. 2017).

This scenario presents a battle between evidence from research and the politics of the day. The reality is that in Kenya if policymakers take unpopular stands on socio-cultural issues, these may have ramifications on their careers. As a result, politics often trumps evidence. The challenge for communication and knowledge brokers, therefore, is how to avoid a battle half-won (by virtue of there being a policy recommendation by the health ministry, but not the education ministry) and foster sustained engagements with the education ministry until the current gaps are plugged. I would say this provides a great learning opportunity for those communicating research and engaging policymakers on this and other controversial development issues. It is critical to step back and look at the situation with an objective lens. It is important to take a moment and let go (temporarily) of the evidence and assess why the evidence is failing to gain traction among education policymakers. Why have health policymakers embraced the evidence, but their education counterparts have not? Did it have to do with the framing of the evidence? Was the framing palatable for some policymakers but not others?

Proper framing of suggested solutions is critical in effectively communicating research to policymakers (Warira 2018). In my view, the fact that the debate on comprehensive sexuality education has attracted the wrath of key groups, and especially religious ones, means that framing is one of the major problems. Perhaps it is useful to mention at this point that religious groups in Kenya are extremely influential and policymakers often avoid being in their cross hairs. The value of age-appropriate comprehensive sexuality education has been lost in the misunderstanding that children (in this case adolescents) are to be taught how to engage in sex. In addition, the dimension that this education shall be 'age-appropriate' has been completely lost, and the use of the term 'comprehensive' does not help the situation either. Experts should therefore engage policymakers and other relevant stakeholders, including the greatest opponents of the policy, and analyse the causes of the failures before re-starting engagements.

Policymaking, an iterative process

Beyond politics, the interaction of research with the policymaking process is not easily discernible, for various reasons. Firstly, **policymaking is an iterative process** with several components that may be pulling in different directions, but have to fit (Bryner 2003). If the goal of communicating research to policymakers is to inform the policymaking process, the research can: set the agenda for a new policy or shape the direction that a new policy should take; bring new information to ongoing policy debates and contribute to policy formulation and / or enactment; stimulate the implementation of a stalled policy; and / or bring new perspectives in the review of existing policies. This means that experts have to continuously engage with the policymaking process and observe if they are succeeding, as opposed to waiting for one big win at the tail end of the policymaking process (the tail does not exist anyway). For instance, in the case of the sexual and reproductive health policy for Kenya discussed above, experts engaging policymakers should conduct retrospective engagements with key stakeholders and use the findings to figure out how to bridge the gaps. This could include reframing the policy recommendations in the sexual and reproductive health policy, taking into account the existing concerns of those opposed to the recommendations. Just as policymaking is not linear, neither is the engagement and knowledge brokering process.

Research and policy, a sea of theoretical models

Secondly, there are **various models** seeking to explain the various ways in which research and policy interact. Some models suggest that research may inform policy, some that policy may influence the research generated, and some that policy and research inform each other in an iterative process. And in some cases, it is suggested that there is no causal relationship between research and policymaking, but that on occasions the two spheres may interact (Boswell and Smith 2017). These diverse models form a great basis for in-depth analysis by scholars and industry experts on the different ways in which research and policy connect and whether each of these scenarios requires nuanced approaches to communicate and engage with policy-makers in order to achieve the intended objectives. It is important to note that, irrespective of the model considered, research by itself does not inform policymaking, rather it is the synthesis of the research and the subsequent communication of how the findings connect to the challenges at hand that is of value to policymakers. In the case of adolescent sexual and reproductive health, if research evidence shows that teenage pregnancies are increasing at an alarming rate, this evidence is not complete without in-depth analysis of what is driving the numbers up, how this challenge interacts with other challenges faced by teenage girls, what is the action required to reduce teenage pregnancies, and what are the implications if no action is taken.

Whose voice counts?

Thirdly, more often than not, policymakers receive policy advice (in addition to research evidence and data) from various agencies within the same window of time. This means that there are **several voices** clamouring for policymakers' attention. As such, without strategic thinking and alignment, different stakeholders working towards similar goals may end up pulling policymakers in different directions. A smart way to ensure coordinated engagement with policymakers on a specific issue is the formation of organised groups. For instance, in Kenya the majority of the stakeholders that have consistently driven the sexual and reproductive health agenda are members of a technical working group convened by the Ministry of Health. This strategic coordination has made it easier to deal with emerging challenges with one voice, for instance figuring out mechanisms to effectively engage with the education ministry.

Not the only variable

Fourthly, research evidence is **not the only variable** that interacts with the policy-making process. Policymakers, whether those in legislative elected positions, those appointed by the government of the day, or the technical experts in government ministries, are influenced by their own personal and political interests, personal beliefs and values, as well as subject to external influences from government and international agencies. All these factors have a huge bearing on the direction public policies take (Broadbent 2012). Furthermore, the reality is that research evidence and data are not the strongest factors that drive policies in a particular direction. This, therefore, demands that experts assess and understand the policy context in which they are working. As I have discussed in a recent research paper, other factors that determine whether experts succeed in their communication and knowledge brokering efforts are the timing of when the research lands at the policymaker's table. Experts often fail to present research to policymakers when they *need* it. Relationships with policymakers can also be extremely important. Policymakers are more inclined to engage with experts whom they trust and have close relationships with. I have engaged with a researcher who spoke of having off-the-record discussions with a policymaker prior to a major policy debate on the existing evidence related to a policy issue, at the request of the policymaker. This is an indication of a high level of trust. I dare say that relationships with policymakers is perhaps the most critical factor in achieving evi-dence-based policy, as without this experts will not even be in the room to know if the timing, framing or the politics (among other factors) are right.

Thoughts for the future

Conversations on the role of evidence in policymaking have evolved significantly in the past decade, and continue to evolve. For experts working in this field, more effort is needed to generate knowledge on what works, for whom, and in what contexts. Policymakers are not a homogenous group and, therefore, what works in Kenya may not necessarily work in neighbouring Uganda. Document-ing challenges and lessons learned is a critical way of preserving knowledge, not just for the purposes of adapting to, but also for understanding, the complex world of policymaking. It is only when we understand the different facets of the research-to-policy ecosystem that we can continue to innovate with solutions that work for better public policies. Ultimately, the goal is to ensure public policies address the real needs of people in the most effective way.

While taking into consideration the existing models of measuring the impact of policy influencing and advocacy efforts (Tsui et al. 2014), there is still a need for more rigorous methods to evaluate how policymakers' perspectives on develop-ment issues shift as a result of their interaction with evidence, and how this shift blends with policymaking processes. It is also critical to bear in mind that changes in policy and policymaking processes take a very long time, and in most cases, those who begin the process (such as policy initiation and definition) are not involved later in the policy cycle. This is especially common in African countries, such as Kenya, where shifts in government often result in new appointments at the top level in government ministries. New election cycles also bring new policymakers in the legislature. Therefore, finding sustainable ways to engage with technical experts in African parliaments and government ministries may increase chances of success. Understanding the processes and practises for communicating research to policymakers is critical. It not only enables us to measure progress, but informs future efforts so that we can better undertake evidence-based policymaking.

References

Boswell, C. and Smith, K. (2017). Rethinking policy 'impact': four models of research-policy relations. *Palgrave Communications* . 3(44), 1–10.

Broadbent, E. (2012). *Politics of research-based evidence in African policy debates: four case studies.* Overseas Development Institute. [Viewed 22 August 2018]. Available from: www.odi.org/publications/8757-politics-research-based-evidence-african-policy-debates-four-case-studies

Bryner, G.C. (2003). Public organizations and public policies. In: B.G. Peters, J. Pierre, eds., *Handbook of public administration.* London: Sage Publications. pp. 300–309.

Nisbet, M.C. (2009). The ethics of framing science. In: B. Nerlich, B. Larson, and R. Elliot, eds., *Communicating biological sciences: ethical and metaphorical dimensions.* London: Ashgate. pp. 51–74.

Oxman, A.D.Lavis, J.N., Lewin, S. and Fretheim, A., (2009). SUPPORT tools for evidence-informed health policymaking (STP) 1: What is evidence-informed policymaking? *Health Research Policy and Systems.* 7(S1), 1–7.

Ren, F. and Zhai, J. (2014). *Communication and popularization of science and technology in China.* Heidelberg: Springer.

Sidze, E.*et al.* (2017). From paper to practice: sexuality education policies and their implementation in Kenya. Guttmacher Institute. [Viewed 24 August 2018]. Available from: www.guttmacher.org/report/sexuality-education-kenya

Stone, D., Maxwell, S. and KeatingM. (2001). *Bridging research and policy.* Proceedings from the International workshop funded by the UK Department for International Development, 16–17 July, Warwick University, UK. [Viewed 26 February 2019]. Available from: https://warwick.ac.uk/fac/soc/pais/research/researchcentres/csgr/research/keytopic/other/bridging.pdf

Tsui, J., Hearn, S. and Young, J. (2014). *Monitoring and evaluation of policy influence and advocacy.* Overseas Development Institute. [Viewed 24 August 2018]. Available from: www.odi.org/publications/8265-monitoring-and-evaluation-policy-influence-and-advocacy

Warira, D. (2017). *Sexuality education for Kenya's youth: when the evidence is on the wall, but politics gets in the way.* U-Report [Viewed 24 August 2018]. Available from: www.standardmedia.co.ke/ureport/story/2001246878/sexuality-education-for-kenya-s-youth-when-the-evidence-is-on-the-wall-but-politics-gets-in-the-way

Warira, D. (2018). *Making the dividend count: bridging research and Africa's policy processes.* Research Paper No. 22. Wilson Centre. [Viewed 26 February 2019]. Available from: www.wilsoncenter.org/sites/default/files/research_paper_-_making_the_dividend_count_bridging_research_and_africas_policy_processes.pdf

5

EXPERIMENTING WITH INTERDISCIPLINARITY

Researcher development and the production of impact potentials

Robert Meckin and Sandrine Soubes

Entanglement of impact and interdisciplinarity

Ideas on impact and interdisciplinary research (IDR) circulate through the UK higher education sector. These concepts have emerged alongside changes in knowledge production towards more collaborative forms of research orientated towards applied problem-solving (Gibbons et al. 1994; Nowotny et al. 2001). Important forms of research activities include: anticipating future impacts, engaging citizens and stakeholders, and integrating disciplines across natural and social sciences (Barben et al. 2008). In the UK, the 'impact' of academic research has been defined as 'research influence beyond academia' (Penfield et al. 2014, p. 21). On the other hand, there are many different definitions of IDR and they include various forms such as inter-, cross-, multi- or trans-disciplinary collaborations (Barry & Born 2013; Bruce et al. 2004). These shades of disciplinarity can be described at the same time as 'boundary transgression' (Barry et al. 2008, p. 21) or boundary crossing (Blackwell et al. 2010). There are at least three rationales for IDR, including: increasing the accountability and relevance of academic research to non-academic audiences, benefiting markets and economies, and challenging assumptions in conventional knowledge production (Barry & Born 2013; Barry et al. 2008). These 'logics of interdisciplinarity' – accountability, innovation and ontology – can be seen as an entangling of impact with IDR, since they each shape the purposes, assessment criteria and organisation of research.

In the current funding landscape of large international interdisciplinary research collaborations, and the incorporation of *impact* requirements into research grants and research evaluation mechanisms at national levels (e.g. Research Excellence Framework in the UK), early career researchers (ECRs) can find themselves in unchartered territory in attempting to respond to such agendas. ECR is a term which is often ill-defined, sometimes including postdoctoral researchers, research fellows and early career academics (Soubes 2017). For ECRs still in the process of establishing themselves as experts in specific (often single-discipline) research niches, the prospect of considering interdisciplinary practice, broad collaborative approaches and the concern that their research may need to connect to wider societal agendas, may be problematic. While disciplines are dominant in universities, through faculty structure, organisation, teaching and career progression, there is a paucity of understanding of how to nurture talent within these interdisciplinary frameworks (Lyall & Meagher 2012). Research sponsors can play an important role in building IDR capacity and ensuring sustainability by explicitly funding IDR schemes (Lyall et al. 2013), but it can remain challenging for ECRs to see the value of engaging with development opportunities.

The analysis in this chapter arose from the evaluation of a researcher development programme, called the Crucible, which provided interdisciplinary experience for ECRs and aimed to develop *outward-facing researchers*. We aim to provide insights into the ways IDR and research impact influence one another and to encourage ECRs to consider how embedding interdisciplinary collaborative practices and an openness towards external engagements could transform their perceptions of impact and approach to research. This may motivate other ECRs to identify pockets of opportunities within their own institutions and research networks, or request provision of such developmental support. We want to tempt ECRs to take time out to experiment with such approaches.

We draw on the work of Barry et al. (2008) and Barry and Born (2013) on logics and modes of interdisciplinarity to discuss the effects of the Crucible programme. We propose that the conditions set up through the Crucible, such as fostering small-scale interdisciplinary projects and affording time, space and risk-taking, enabled particular forms of collaborative organisation that opened up the possibilities for a wide range of impact potentials. We argue that the participants and facilitators in the Crucible enacted a 'mode of suspension' for interdisciplinary research training. This allowed researchers to experiment with project designs and with their own roles. To greater or lesser degrees, they suspended their disciplinary affiliations and experienced other areas of research, either 'living' them as novices or collaborating closely with others. We suggest that this produced *impact potentials*, which may not have been realised within the Crucible programme timeframe, but which have the prospect to be realised as researchers continue in their careers.

Context of the Sheffield Crucible programme

Programme ambition and structure

The Crucible programme was originally developed by NESTA (National Endowment for Science, Technology and Arts) in 2007 as a programme aiming to provide ECR participants with an entry point to consider their research practice in the context of an enhanced drive towards interdisciplinary working environments, a wider view of research and its potential to impact society, and the creation of wider research networks (NESTA 2018). The NESTA Crucible programme was originally run at national level, though only a few programmes took place (Blackwell et al. 2010; Pharoah 2009). The programme was later continued and further developed, and has been running for a number of years across institutions in Scotland and Wales (Scottish Crucible 2018; Welsh Crucible 2017).

One of the authors, Dr Sandrine Soubes (working as a researcher developer) ran two Crucible programmes (in 2012/13 and 2014/15) at The University of Sheffield (TUoS) (Soubes 2015). The drive for her to introduce this programme within the institution reflected the ambient policy discourse and discursive assumption that innovation requires an environment fostering connections and communities between academics from different disciplinary backgrounds and diverse external stakeholders. Whilst interdisciplinary working, industry partnerships, policy and public engagement appear to have become expected norms for academics' professional practice (e.g. Research Councils UK 2013; Vitae 2018), the space and time to explore such ways of working remain limited. Therefore, providing structured opportunities and experiential learning for ECRs to encounter such approaches ought to be considered a priority in researchers' professional development. This could offer scope for unpicking policy agendas and allow a space to redefine them. If institutions are to provide researchers with the necessary support to become the interdisciplinary innovators of the knowledge economy, attention needs to be paid to effective ways of delivering such a grand ambition (Lyall & Meagher 2012). Although attempts have been made in the UK to construct interdisciplinary enculturation via cohort training of Research Councils-funded PhD programmes, the role of such programmes in shaping the interdisciplinary research approach of ECRs has remained underexplored. Furthermore, a great proportion of the research workforce in the UK comes from overseas (41%) (Khattab & Fenton 2015). It is difficult to assess whether researchers joining the UK workforce as ECRs have been exposed to much interdisciplinary training and working. Hence, within such contexts, Dr Soubes perceived the running of a Crucible programme as a priority for researcher development.

Like the NESTA version, the Sheffield Crucible programme pictured itself as an initiative that aimed to challenge researchers to consider their outward-facing research practices. It played a 'facilitative role' as a 'broker[s] of collaborations' (Walsh & Kahn 2009, p. 83). The overall ambition of the Sheffield Crucible programme, as communicated to the local research community, was to provide an environment rich in opportunities to nurture new and *unexpected interdisciplinary collaborations* between *talented and ambitious* researchers who may not normally meet and interact. The Crucible intended to promote conversations amongst ECRs across all faculties, creating a local network of peers within the research community to fuel potential interdisciplinary working and provide the foundation of career-long networking skills and relationships. It challenged researchers to consider all aspects of knowledge exchange, social and economic implications of research, and to develop a wider view of the world of research. The aim of the programme was also to make researchers more aware of the skills and attitudes of innovators, whilst considering approaches to enhance grant-capture opportunities. In reflecting on why she had initiated an interdisciplinary professional development programme such as Crucible in her institution, Dr Soubes perceived it as an ambition: to give people a space to think, to give young researchers the pleasure of being in each other's company, to give you the challenge of each other's different views about the world, to give you the freedom to be (Soubes 2014).

This was about creating a space of exploration focused on the process of experimenting with diverse research approaches and less concerned with the delivery of formal research output; the intention was able to cultivate a certain openness of engagement that may contribute towards non-trivial and less cynical versions of the concepts of impact and interdisciplinary collaborations. The ethos was also about fostering local campus researcher communities, attempting to reduce the often perceived ECR experience of departmental and institutional isolation, despite the promotion of national and international networks. This was also about addressing the potential dimension of parochial collaborative networks within a globalised research context.

Given the various logics for IDR – accountability, innovation, ontology – this raises the question of what is *actually being promoted* through professional development programmes in terms of interdisciplinary collaborative practices. Different versions of impact and interdisciplinarity are expressed in different contexts by institutional agents (from programme manager to programme participants). In some ways, all institutional agents are aware of the multiple discourses about innovation, interdisciplinarity and impact, and whilst divergent meanings may be enacted in practice, Crucible is an attempt to create spaces for meaningful interactions and opportunities. A programme such as Crucible has the potential to provide a platform where researchers' needs for progressing their academic career come face-to-face with institutional needs to maintain grant capture competitiveness. In this context, ECRs can explore their individual and institutional needs and shift towards a more nuanced understanding of the research landscape, their position and their opportunities within those spaces. After running the programmes, Dr Soubes realised that, in some institutional documents about the programme, she had presented the aims for the institution and those for researchers as separate entities and, while some of these aims overlapped, the term *impact* itself was initially used mostly for the institutional aims. The term became much more dominant during the running of the second programme, illustrating a step change in the position of *impact* within the institutional discourse. This observation could also indicate that the term *impact* may have become part of a rhetorical device used by diverse institutional actors, who do not necessarily have the same agenda.

What actually took place: Labs and funded projects

The Crucible programme involved selecting early career researchers / academics from five faculties to attend three two-day residential training courses, called 'Labs'. Potential participants formally applied to the scheme in writing. A panel reviewed the applications and assembled the cohorts with an ethos of constructing balanced groups of peers with diverse experiences, interests and disciplinary backgrounds.

Selection criteria involved the applicant demonstrating an excellence in research, applicants' interest and / or experience in interdisciplinary research, their interest in creative thinking, their desire or experiences of other collaborations and their commitment to the broader role of research in society. The main factor that shaped selection, however, was a concern with demonstrating motivation and commitment towards exploring new ways of working. In terms of advertising the programme, it was difficult to assess whether there is an optimal career stage for ECRs to experience IDR professional development – the complexities of research careers mean that it is problematic to create comparative longitudinal evaluations. However, offering this opportunity to ECRs at various stages of their careers aimed to signal an important commitment to respecting researchers' agency towards their own professional development.

Each Lab gave opportunities for researchers to communicate their own research, network with one another and learn about other aspects of developing influential research such as possible approaches to interdisciplinary working, informing public policy, commercialisation, research dissemination, and social enterprise. During the Labs, the researchers were encouraged to form collaborations and submit project proposals for up to £5,000 or £10,000. There was an 'incubation' period after the Labs during which groups developed and refined their proposals before submission. Following a panel review, funds were awarded to researchers to carry out their collaborative projects. Researchers were encouraged to get involved in multiple projects. Overall, 59 ECRs participated, 30 researchers led a project application, whilst 49 supported proposals as co-investigators. Over the course of the two Crucible programmes, participants proposed 38 projects, 18 of which were funded. After the award, the groups had a period of 10 months to carry out their work and participants reconvened for a fourth Lab to review the experience of engaging in these projects.

Embedding engagement as a core principle

The concept of *impact* has been intrinsically linked to considerations of how researchers may contribute and engage within the *public sphere*. Models of public engagement have shifted (Burchell 2015), moving from public understanding towards propositions of communication as a three-level approach (transmit, receive, collaborate) proposed by a previous government department (BIS 2010a, 2010b), 'dialogue' models (e.g. Bhattachary et al. 2010; Stilgoe 2007), 'patient and public involvement' approaches fostered in areas of medically related research and, more recently, a framework for 'Responsible Research and Innovation' (Engineering and Physical Sciences Research Council 2015).

As a space for exploration, Crucible embedded engagement as a core principle in the application process for the seed-funding. Following attendance at the three residential workshops and prior to the submission deadline of applications for seed-funding, each group of collaborative applicants were required, as part of the application process, to deliver a public engagement activity at the Festival of the

Mind (Festival of the Mind Group 2018). During this local festival (itself a collaborative endeavour between the city council, creative communities and the university), researchers were tasked with pitching their potential interdisciplinary collaborative projects to festival-goers. The event was held in a spiegeltent, which is a traditional circus structure set up for the festival right in the heart of the city. Project teams set up their stalls in the small booths within this unusual and intricately decorated space, made of wood and coloured glass. Members of the public were given a list with all the projects in competition for funding (with a title and a very short summary) and asked to choose the five projects you find the most interesting and worthwhile of an investment. The combined public vote was used as one vote in the university grant-selection panel. In this situation, researchers were tasked with talking about projects which had not yet been funded and were compelled to articulate to non-specialists the worth of public investment into their projects.

Experiencing public engagement prior to undertaking research triggered a realisation for some researchers that engagement may be something quite different from what they may have done before:

> One of the things that… for me was quite an eye opener was when we were thinking about public engagement… Maybe, actually it should be a bit of a two-way conversation and maybe you should actually be listening to what people want and things like that… that had quite a big impact on me because I had not really thought of it like that, I thought I was doing public engagement quite well but actually I was just going and telling people, 'Oh, I do this and this is this,' and actually you want a bit of a conversation. [C2 P15 Interview]

Following the festival, we shared the comments made by members of the public at the time of voting with project applicants and also asked researchers to reflect on the experience of this interaction with the public within the seed-funding application itself. The intention here was to lead researchers to consider the *voice* of the public within the research process. What could it mean for them to engage upward at the point of initiation of a project?

Questions remained about where and when to engage, which role this might play and what it really means to deliver impact. In this case, impact is articulated through the diversity of the conversations, from conversations with researchers from other disciplines, towards being open to the potential impact of broader conversations that are enablers within the research process. It was not straightforward to evaluate the role played by these public conversations in the shaping of the seed-funding applications. In a report, an ECR described discussions with the festival participants as follows:

> [They] asked us questions or made observations that proved of paramount importance in the clarification of our final proposal for funding…some members of the public…questioned the concept of our project and the artistic reasoning at the basis of it. These questions proved to be extremely

useful not only because by responding to them we clarified even more the conceptual framework of our project but also by providing constructive feedback they alerted us to issues that we had not considered before. (anonymised participants 2014)

Project report

It is challenging to address whether such reflection within a funding application represents a genuine observation or constitutes a performative artefact of what the applicants expected the review panel to want to see.

For some researchers, the Festival of the Mind public engagement experience shifted their thinking towards integrating engagement as a core component of the research process, supporting our intention of remodeling the cynicism that may be associated with notions of impact:

> ... thinking about how you design a project, how you build users in, how you build in public engagement into what you're doing really had an impact on how I thought about the Future Leaders [programme] when I was proposing it. Doing the Crucible made me really sceptical of that kind of add-on, 'I'm just going to disseminate my findings by having a public around when I stand up and talk at people.' ... Whereas actually building in processes... so there are different people there... the public are integrated so it's going to be far more collaborative and hopefully have more impact. [C2 P26 Interview]

Thus, the researcher noted a distinct change in their approach to engagement. For them, engagement became intimately entangled with creating knowledge projects, and they saw value in establishing formative connections early in designing a project. Throughout, then, Crucible worked towards establishing engagement as an integral part of project design and crucial in the production of influential research.

Evaluating the contributions of the Crucible programme

An analysis of participants' experiences in the programme, initially collected via observations in the Labs and reading the project reports, revealed many had engaged in a range of new academic activities. Some of this data, demographic information, approaches and issues in recruitment procedures, as well as practicalities with programme delivery, have been reported elsewhere (Soubes 2015). However, in order to inform institutional practices, we undertook a more formal evaluation of the Sheffield Crucible programme in 2016. The evaluation was conducted by one of the authors (Dr Meckin) who had not been involved in the development and delivery of the programme. The focus of the evaluation was to assess whether the Crucible programme had achieved its aims, to consider whether it should be run again and if so, which recommendations should be made for future organisers of similar programmes. The evaluation intended to capture participants' perceptions and experiences of this initiative.

The evaluation study took the form of an online survey (64% completion across the two programmes), semi-structured interviews (n=11) and document analyses (participants' application forms, project proposals, project reports and other documents from project outputs). A thematic analysis was performed on interview transcripts and documents, to understand and describe how such a programme contributed towards researcher development. Interviewed respondents came from across all faculties, at different career stages and having experienced Crucible from different viewpoints (funded Crucible project lead, funded Crucible co-investigator and one interviewee with an unfunded project). Because of the short-term nature of some researchers' employment, a number of researchers had already left the institution by the time the evaluation took place. This meant that some participants could not be recruited to the evaluation. Equivalent numbers of survey respondents and interviewees came from the two programme cohorts. Whilst such analysis remains small scale and does not intend to propose a general perspective on all professional development programmes of this sort, such a case study approach can 'produce grounded understanding' (Clark 2008, p. 549) to illuminate how institutional initiatives contribute to enacting interdisciplinarity and impact. We draw on these experiences of managing, facilitating and evaluating the Crucible in the rest of the chapter.

Theoretical framework: Producing 'suspension'

There are a range of arguments or motivations for conducting IDR. These can be divided roughly into instrumental and critical forms, where the focus is to achieve particular (sometimes disciplinary) outcomes or challenge the epistemological status quo, respectively (Klein 2010, pp. 22–24). Three possible rationales, or 'logics', for interdisciplinarity are accountability, innovation and ontology (Barry & Born 2013; Barry et al. 2008). *Accountability* (Barry & Born 2013, pp. 13–17; Barry et al. 2008, pp. 31–33) is about researchers becoming increasingly answerable to other stakeholders, societal actors or publics (Nowotny 2003). *Innovation* is where actors aim to produce novelties, usually for markets (e.g. by connecting users and designers in the IT industry) (Barry & Born 2013, pp. 13–17; Barry et al. 2008, pp. 31–33). *A logic of ontology* which, for arts-science collaborations, can be about:

> …long-standing concerns to shift the ontological grounds of what art is or can be, evident in recent decades in diverse practices that probe the relations between both art and technology and art and the social (Barry et al. 2008, p. 38).

These interconnected but distinct rationales are identifiable in different collaborative projects. In addition, Barry et al. (2008) suggest at least three 'modes' of knowledge production in IDR, which include:

1   Synthetic-integrative, where disciplinary knowledge practices are combined.
2   Domination / service, where a hierarchy of contributions is established.

3 Agonist-antagonist, where there is a reflexive challenge to existing knowledge structures and assumptions. (Barry & Born 2013, pp. 10–13; Barry et al. 2008, pp. 26–31)

These categories were established particularly for IDR involving social and natural science researchers. Our use of this framework in analysing these ECR projects thus comes with a caveat: while participants were invited to engage in 'wild collaborations', around half of the projects funded by the Crucible did not include a social or humanities researcher, but we have still applied the analysis to those projects.

Furthermore, projects funded through researcher development initiatives are not necessarily subject to the same kinds of logics and constraints as publicly sponsored research. So, through our analysis, we have suggested an additional mode of interdisciplinarity, which may be particular to researcher development, called the 'mode of suspension'. We have chosen this term because suspension implies an interval or hiatus as well as a support of something (perhaps, a vehicle, to enable it to move over rougher ground). We see suspension in IDR as a pausing of what is *known*, in terms of disciplinary backgrounds, and this facilitates an experimental, creative dynamic. We contrast this to recent sociological literature on trust (Brownlie & Howson 2005; Frederiksen 2012; Mollering 2001), where 'suspension' is a key concept to explore how people 'reach a point where our interpretations are accepted and our awareness of the unknown, unknowable and unresolved is suspended' (Mollering 2001 p. 414). A mode of suspension, we think, is where researchers interrupt their disciplinary attachments, step out of their current roles, and enter unfamiliar disciplinary areas where they can behave more like novices. Indeed, collaboration does not necessarily mean that researchers contribute in consistent ways in collaborative projects; what constitutes a profound input can be tricky to ascertain (Lee & Bozeman 2005). Some projects in Crucible could be called agnostic towards the disciplinary structures since participants moved out of their areas of expertise into new disciplinary areas, but this was not usually done to challenge the existing epistemological or ontological structures. Instead, suspension seemed to be a way that participants could develop a wider perspective on research and research influence by 'living' in another (inter)discipline. We put this down to the experimental nature of Crucible and the establishment of a 'safe space' for ECRs to take risks that facilitated small-scale yet ambitious projects. Where ECRs have prioritised developing collaborative and societally relevant research, exploring experiences outside of their disciplinary expertise can lead to imaginative and innovative approaches to future research.

We also draw on a broader debate happening in the field of science and technology studies, as well as other disciplines. The discussions centre on ways to conceptualise how realities are constructed and sustained, and circle around ideas of performance and action. From these debates we borrow the notion of 'enactment' (e.g. Law 2002; Mol 2002) to describe how interdisciplinarity and impact are done. The notion of enacting emphasises the generative nature of practices in the constitution of reality (Woolgar & Lezaun 2013). By moving to 'enactment' we want to emphasise the way that modes of knowledge production in IDR are brought into being through practices of researcher development and experimental project design. We find this notion useful because it conceives of realities as always needing work, that they are contingent and that, without repetition, particular realities disappear (Law & Mol 2008). The Crucible, through the practices of recruitment, facilitating Labs, funding projects and so on, enacts interdisciplinarity and impact simultaneously. They are performed alongside one another. The forms of *impact potentials*, the latent possibilities created through Crucible, emerge in particular ways as they are brought into being in new contexts. In the next sections, we give an overview of the projects and then describe the generation of these impact potentialities in three Crucible projects, explaining the different ways each was enacted in a new context.

Types of projects

The participants came from all five faculties at TUoS. However, the size of the collaborations that successfully submitted project proposals ranged from two to eight participants. These reflected a range of cross-faculty partnerships. While we suggest that Crucible attempted to facilitate 'wild' collaborations in projects, this was not necessarily the dominant mode in some of the projects. Thus, one way of categorising the projects was by those that contained at least one arts, humanities or social researcher, and those which contained only natural scientists, engineers or medical researchers. This produced a fairly even split across the two cohorts in terms of the numbers of funded projects, where eight projects involved science, engineering and medicine researchers (see Table 5.1), and ten projects involved at least one researcher with a disciplinary affiliation in the arts, humanities or social sciences (Table 5.2).

The projects without arts, humanities or social researcher involvement tended to operate around certain logics and modes of IDR and be orientated towards

TABLE 5.1 IDR project groups consisting of scientists and engineers

Project name	Main logics	Dominant mode	Potential impact domain
Blindfold	Innovation	Service	Medicine
Osteolytica	Innovation	Service	Medicine
Magnetic beads	Innovation	Service	Medicine
Migraine app	Innovation, ontology	Service	Medicine
Parkinson's disease app	Innovation	Service	Medicine
Cancer software	Innovation	Service	Medicine
Brain imaging	Innovation	Service	Medicine
University inventors	Innovation	Suspension	Local research community

TABLE 5.2 IDR project groups consisting of scientists, engineers, and arts, humanities or social science researchers

Project name	Main logics	Dominant modes	Potential impact domain
Life with stroke	Accountability	Suspension	Health care
River robot	Innovation	Service	Environmental
No picnic	Ontology	Suspension	Academic communities
Condoms of tomorrow	Innovation, ontology, accountability	Integrative	Social / health
Phoenix	Accountability	Integrative, suspension	Health care
Giant's bone	Innovation, account-ability, ontology	Integrative, suspension	Education / health
Tales of river	Ontology	Integrative	Environmental
Kindergarten safari	Ontology	Integrative	Health
Better to know	Innovation	Service	Law / health
Where are the women?	Innovation	Suspension	Employment

addressing medical problems (see Table 5.1). The one project that was not aimed at medicine proposed to explore ECR commercialisation experiences at the university and planned to use social science research methods to address issues of awareness and provision for entrepreneurship and innovation, such as patenting and spin out arrangements. The medically oriented projects did not always contain medical researchers, but they tended to combine in various ways physics, chemistry, computer science, cell biology, and medical knowledge. Five projects were targeted towards better diagnostics, sufferers or medical professionals, and two projects were aimed at potential therapies that could interrupt different cancers.

In terms of logics, the projects were mostly organised around innovation – producing new technologies that the teams envisaged entering medical markets. The organisation of the projects tended to be around the service model, where one discipline had identified a problem and needed the expertise of other disciplines to approach novel solutions. An example of this type of organisation, done by five teams, involved using computer scientists' expertise to collate, analyse and visualise medical data in novel ways to make knowledge accessible to particular audiences. Thus, the project configurations and orientations enacted impact as tangible technological innovations in particular kinds of health contexts. This suggests that, in Crucible, project teams with members from only the science, engineering and medical faculties conceived of impact and interdisciplinary structures in conservative ways – the understanding of impact was one of a material intervention with a health imperative, perhaps reflecting wider ideas of grand social challenges and what counts as impact.

Looking at Table 5.2, half of the projects that included arts, humanities and social researchers were organised around a logic of ontology, which can be a feature of collaborations involving both natural science and engineering scholars along with arts and social researchers (Barry et al. 2008). These projects explicitly challenged existing ontologies of central objects, such as rivers and city spaces, and explored collaborative methodologies for knowledge production. There was also greater diversity in the structure of the collaborations, with projects tending to be organised in synthetic-integrative modes. The funded projects that included arts, humanities and social researchers demonstrated a wider variety of IDR in terms of the logics they deployed, the modes they enacted and the scope of impact domains.

What is significant here is that we were able to identify 'suspension' as a dominant mode of IDR in a number of projects, mostly in Table 5.2. In the next section, we take three projects from Table 5.2 that we describe in more detail, and discuss how IDR and impact potentials were enacted. We have selected these projects as each of them offers a different way in which the mode of suspension enabled researchers to develop their projects, and what this has meant for their potential for socially influential research.

Influencing future proposals

Here, we want to describe how a mode of suspension in the IDR experience appears to give researchers time and space to develop and how some researchers articulate the effect this has had on their approach to collaborations and grant applications. One project aimed at bringing together qualitative observational data collection with statistical analyses to attempt to explore and better understand disease transmission between young children in group situations. In this project, researchers brought their expertise together in an integrative way, as there was explicit recognition in the proposal that the different epistemological approaches could benefit one another.

The participants had regular discussions during their project. These involved recognising their different disciplinary backgrounds and what that meant they needed to do to accommodate one another. For example, the participants developed an insight into how ethics and knowledge production were entangled in different disciplines.

> A key moment of clarity came for us when we realised that [we] were both driven to these approaches by ethics, just different conceptualisations of ethics. In [a] biomedical tradition, it is not considered ethical to embark on active research without a clear protocol, goals and reasonable assurance that research questions can be answered. In [an] ethnographic tradition, it is felt ethical to avoid unnecessary pre-specification and allow participants to shape the direction of research. (anonymised participants 2015)

Project report 2015

In their project report, the researchers were able to reflect on the difficulties of collaboration and identify a key difference between their approaches to ethics. In a later interview, one researcher went on to describe how their Crucible project experience changed their approach to their career and future collaborations:

> I think Crucible has changed my approach to my career a bit for the better... I've tried to be a bit more proactive and entrepreneurial about it. I think in particular the sort of thinking about a scientific career is a bit like a start up and trying to be entrepreneurial about it... I think a higher sense of importance around the importance of communication and wider value to society and, in all honesty, a slightly more cautious appreciation of the difficulties of ... working across disciplines where the conception of knowledge and the approaches are very different. I think that's harder than I appreciated before I did Crucible. [Interview with C2 P12]

There are two main points to pick up on from this quotation. The first is a perceived overall change in attitude towards their career. The researcher describes wanting to be more entrepreneurial, which tends towards the common sense ideas of setting up a company – taking risks and 'getting out there' to market and advertise one's research, and a generalised normative notion that research should be relevant to society. The second point is that their experiences on the project have made them aware of the potential difficulties of working across different disciplines, particularly where knowledge is understood and produced in different ways.

The apparently contrasting attitude to risk seems to connote an acknowledgement that researchers are becoming more active in finding collaborations and communicating research on the one hand, but that Crucible also facilitated experiences of some of the challenges involved in outward-facing, collaborative research. Interestingly, given these points, researchers from the project were involved in the preparation of a larger interdisciplinary proposal that aimed to combine a greater number of disciplines to explore pathogens in schools. A project of this kind, submitted to Research Councils UK, addresses a range of social, educational and health issues. Thus, the *potential* for impactful researchers appears to be increased as they had a greater appreciation of the challenges for collaborative work, but enacted the value of IDR by creating a more ambitious follow-up project.

Establishing an engaged career niche

In this section, we describe how the development of an IDR project can generate potential impact by helping establish a research career through provision of a research space insulated from expected academic project success criteria. In this case, the project centred on contraceptive and safe sex technologies and aimed to use social research methods to explore the possibilities of different materials for condoms and other female-led contraceptives. The aim was to explore user perceptions of contraceptives and use these to inform the selection and testing of other potential materials. The researchers wanted to challenge an orthodoxy they identified that cultural arguments (e.g. religious beliefs) are a dominant way of explaining the lower than hoped use of contraception (anonymised participants 2012a). The project can be understood as innovative because of the desire to produce marketable products, but it was organised around an onto-logical challenge, in the sense that the relationships between subjects and objects were being reconfigured through the project design. The idea was that users of contraceptives may be able to inform the technical specifications of the design, and may thus reshape explanations of success and failure for contra-ceptive devices, rather than being seen as passive end-users.

In terms of impact, the project imagined audiences such as UK sex workers and African communities. A future possibility for the research (given follow on funding) was to 'improve the user experience and increase uptake of the devices'. However, the researchers positioned this as a pilot project that would use digital and social media to raise awareness of the project and the related issues, with the hope of creating a platform that could be used to carry it on. Thus, the idea of achieving social change was embedded in the project, and the impacts arose from particular disciplines and the particular approach the researchers wanted to take. While this was a profound and well-designed proposal, the career and personal contexts for the academics meant the project progressed slowly. At the time of the evaluation, several years after the funding was awarded, the project had not begun in earnest, but the researchers remained in contact and still planned to conduct the research.

Despite this state of affairs, one of the researchers felt their Crucible experience had transformed their career, both in terms of clarifying their own position towards research, and also helping to clarify their own research career.

> ...[Crucible] was the best thing I did. Because I think it's got me my jobs, it's got me on a permanent post... and it's given me a range of projects to work on, and I suppose it's helped me establish that I do research into [health]... I'm now in the health faculty... so that's interdisciplinary... the woman I spoke to this morning, I probably wouldn't have spoken to her if I was just doing work on [the] sex industry because she's a nurse and she's interested in health even if she's in aging. She's interested in the sexual health and the sexuality side, and the other people who I've been in touch with about the Condoms Project I wouldn't really, well, I wouldn't have got in touch with them. [Interview with C1 P30]

Thus, although the project suffered a number of setbacks, the participant describes how their experiences informed their current research practices. C1 P30 has a permanent post in an interdisciplinary health faculty and engages a set of actors and publics that they would not otherwise have been in contact with. Thus, the researcher enacts *potential impacts* generated through their Crucible work in other contexts after the end of the project. This suggests that suspension allowed a researcher to develop experience that informs their creative, innovative and socially relevant research practices.

Playing beyond disciplines

The final story illustrates a particularly radical approach to interdisciplinary working. The collaborative project at the centre of this argument was called 'Tract', which meant to signal both a short publication of writing and a section of land. The project aimed to develop 'innovative and experimental collaborations between Crucible researchers and established artists to transform cities and address urban problems' (anonymised participants 2012b). The original framing of the project was antagonistic to knowledge structures as it aimed to challenge the perceived local hegemony of architecture, landscape and town planning departments over the way cities were interrogated. Thus, by bringing together a diverse range of non-experts from science (psychology, animal and plant science, human communication), chemical engineering, material sciences, English and geography, in collaboration with artists, the project aimed to reconceptualise urban issues (in this case, a piece of derelict land). The team set up meetings and the project progressed but, due to some setbacks with their planned public engagement strategy, focused more on the relations between artists and researchers.

In conducting the research, the team acted as much as lay investigators as disciplinary experts. This appears to be a hybrid form of interdisciplinarity, where researchers more or less completely suspended their disciplinary training to walk, photograph and sense the tract of land in person, as well as write reflective accounts of their experiences: 'we practiced forgetting what we had learned' (Beck et al. 2014).

However, these exercises were done alongside regular team meetings. Below is a quotation from a participant reflecting on their experience in Tract:

> … I sort of felt I'd already made a transition into another space and I really enjoyed that, so I thought the chance to talk to people from other disciplines is interesting because engineers think about things [in] fundamentally different ways to biochemists… so learning how to talk to someone else from another department in a way that they could understand what you're doing and see it as accessible, that was something that I really learnt through the Crucible. I can't say I've done lots, but I've definitely done things and looked for opportunities to do them [public engagement]. As part of my job, I interact with other departments and things, so already had to do quite a lot of that, but it's quite nice to look outside the university. I'd want to do something that I just wouldn't get the chance through normal funding channels to do. And, okay, that might make it difficult to then follow it up because it's not the normal kind of thing to do, but it's an opportunity to just explore what that's like. [Interview with C1 P7]

The researcher describes some of the benefits of participation, including communicating and thinking, but also gaining a wider experience of what it might be like to live a different life in research. This allowed them to suspend their own background and sample academic research in an (inter)discipline. Through this mechanism, Tract (and other funded projects) developed researchers' experiences of academic disciplines and broadened their concepts of public engagement, possible routes to impact and what impact might be. Thus, participants in the surveys and interviews reported on considering how IDR and society might inform their project designs. These are what we called *impact potentials*. This was made possible because Crucible facilitated a safe space to play and take risks.

Another example of *impact potentials* was realised during the launch of the book *No Picnic* (Beck et al. 2014) that came out of the project. With the view of making the process accessible, as well as sharing the challenges that such interdisciplinary open interactions represented, the group worked together to develop a book that documented the process of such conversations. The book was sent to a number of staff and students across the institution. They were invited to react to it during the launch hosted within the space where these conversations had taken place and a series of 'reaction pieces' were presented.

A striking point from this part of the project was how different individuals reacted to the book across the institution. Many readers felt puzzled about what the project was really about, challenged about what these interactions between researchers from different disciplinary perspectives and artists really meant. A contributor picked on the emotional transitions described by researchers in the book: 'collision of feelings, from guilt to pleasure, from dissolution to reimagination'; the guilt of being involved in such an unusual project eventually left space for 'enjoyment and personal satisfaction' to emerge (Rodriguez-Falcon 2014). One of the historian contributors to the launch drew a link to her research on socio-political conversations in the 16th to 17th centuries and the role played by dialogue in liminal spaces; like other contributors she pointed to a certain form of resistance exhibited through the project: 'you've resisted institutional / sector pressures…you've realized that process can be more important than product; and – in forming your community – you've celebrated the role of communing: of sharing, eating, talking' (Shrank 2014). The diversity and dimensions of the commentaries illustrated how such a project represented a way of shaking vigorously at the core of the purpose of being researchers / academics. It captured with powerful narratives the whole ethos of the Crucible programme, beyond the confines of a single project. One of the Crucible participants talked about 'instrumentalism' and 'failures', as he dropped out of one of the projects when he felt that he needed to prioritise 'the need for results – which structured my time. So I decided I couldn't afford to be involved'. He referred to some texts of the Czech dissident Vaclav Havel that reminded him of the need to resist. The book helped to remind him of 'the importance of spaces outside of the narrow instrumentalism that rules so much of [my] life' (Stafford 2014). Impact was realised through Crucible in reigniting meanings about the role of research and higher education, and shows that impact can be imaginatively defined in ways beyond material health-related interventions.

Conclusion

What we have tried to show is that interdisciplinary research and impact are entangled and that by engaging in IDR development ECRs can produce a wide range of possibilities for impact. While projects are orientated towards future possibilities, and inform the design of projects, forms of interdisciplinarity take shape in the present. We focused on describing a *mode of suspension* as a way to understand how a particular interdisciplinary researcher development programme enabled researchers to gain experience of developing impact potentials. Crucible offered a *safe* space where risky research collaborations were encouraged, by providing a bubble of time and by endearing researchers to the development of playful collaborations. Thus, participants suspended their disciplinary training and temporarily lived different research lives, or were partly insulated from academic success criteria for the Crucible projects. In so doing, they gained a broader perspective on research influence, types of audiences and routes to impact, and we have described how some participants continued in their research careers with an enriched appreciation of impact. We suggest that ECRs may wish to experiment with working in modes of suspension to develop their own practices, which may involve seeking out development programmes, adapting their own engagements with other existing programmes, lobbying for institutional support or creating their own IDR networks.

Our analysis identified that research projects, which included participants from both natural and social sciences, produced a greater diversity of logics, modes and potential domains for impact. Thus, when ECRs engage with IDR development programmes and practices, they might consider the possible objectives of such programmes, and that research creativity appears to be linked to greater disciplinary diversity, particularly among projects with natural science alongside social science and the humanities (as observed in the cases we have presented). We suggest that the explorative ethos of the Crucible enabled ECRs to construct IDR experiences that allowed them to experiment with alternative forms of research organisation and impact potentials. These ambitious projects were not always successful on their own terms, but researchers developed confidence and experience that allowed them to articulate and evidence interdisciplinarity and impact in other contexts, including funding applications and job proposals. By engaging in IDR development, rather than seeing impact as an afterthought or bolt-on, participants enacted a less sceptical version that influenced their subsequent research practices which resulted in ECRs developing more congruent, imaginative and integrated impact strategies. These findings may well encourage other ECRs to find ways to suspend their disciplinary backgrounds and engage with diverse actors to creatively develop influential research.

Learning points

- Engaging with interdisciplinary training can give researchers experience of designing and organising projects with diverse possibilities for impact.

- Suspending one's background and experiencing other research traditions, particularly across the social-natural science divide, is a way to inspire creative approaches in future collaborations.
- Early career experiences of interdisciplinarity can support researchers to recognise their own position and potential for contributions within the larger landscape of academia.

References

anonymised participants (2012a). *Crucible project report*. [Unpublished internal University of Sheffield report].

anonymised participants (2012b). *Crucible project report*. [Unpublished internal University of Sheffield report].

anonymised participants (2014). *Crucible project report*. [Unpublished internal University of Sheffield report].

anonymised participants (2015). *Crucible project report*. [Unpublished internal University of Sheffield report].

Barben, D., Fisher, E., Selin, C., and Guston, D.H. (2008). Anticipatory governance of nanotechnology: foresight, engagement, and integration. In: E.J. Hackett, O. Amsterdamska, M. Lynch, and J. Wajcman, eds., *The handbook of science and technology studies*. Cambridge, MA: The MIT Press. pp. 979–1000.

Barry, A. and Born, G. (2013). *Interdisciplinarity: reconfigurations of the social and natural sciences*. London: Routledge.

Barry, A., Born, G. and Weszkalnys, G. (2008). Logics of interdisciplinarity. *Economy and Society*. 37(1), 20–49.

Beck, A., Cheeseman, M., Evans, C., Levene, B., Paragreen, J., Reeve, H., Schroder, A. and Spencer, S. (2014). *No picnic: explorations in art and research*. Sheffield: University of Sheffield.

Bhattachary, D., Calitz, J.P. and Hunter, A. (2010). *Synthetic biology dialogue*. London: TNS-BMRB.

BIS (2010a). *Science for all reporting and supporting document*. BIS. [Viewed 22 August 2018]. Available from: http://webarchive.nationalarchives.gov.uk/20120708131556/http://interactive.bis.gov.uk/scienceandsociety/site/all/2010/02/09/science-for-all-report-and-supporting-documents/

BIS (2010b). *Science for all public engagement conversational tool*. BIS. [Viewed 22 August 2018]. Available from: http://webarchive.nationalarchives.gov.uk/20120708131542/http://interactive.bis.gov.uk/scienceandsociety/site/all/2010/09/23/public-engagement-for-science-and-society-a-conversational-tool/

Blackwell, A., Wilson, L., Boulton, C. and Knell, J. (2010). *Creating value across boundaries: NESTA report*. London: NESTA.

Brownlie, J. and Howson, A. (2005). Leaps of faith and MMR: an empirical study of trust. *Sociology*. 39(2), 221–239.

Bruce, A., Lyall, C., Tait, J. and Williams, R. (2004). Interdisciplinary integration in Europe: the case of the Fifth Framework programme. *Futures*. 36(4), 457–470.

Burchell, K. (2015). *Factors affecting public engagement by researchers: literature review*. London: Policy Studies Institute.

Clark, B.R. (2008). *On higher education: selected writings 1956–2006*. Baltimore: The Johns Hopkins University Press.

Engineering and Physical Sciences Research Council (2015). *Framework for responsible innovation.* EPSRC. [Viewed 23 November 2018]. Available from: www.epsrc.ac.uk/research/framework/

Festival of the Mind Group (2018). *About a unique collaboration.* University of Sheffield. [Viewed 12 March 2018]. Available from: http://festivalofthemind.group.shef.ac.uk/about/

Frederiksen, M. (2012). Dimensions of trust: an empirical revisit to Simmel's formal sociology of intersubjective trust. *Current Sociology.* 60(6), 733–750.

Gibbons, M., Limoges, C., Nowotny, H., Schwartzman, S., Scott, P. and Trow, M. (1994). *The new production of knowledge: the dynamics of science and research in contemporary societies.* London: Sage.

Khattab, N. and Fenton, S. (2015). Globalisation of researcher mobility within the UK higher education: explaining the presence of overseas academics in the UK academia. *Globalisation, Societies and Education.* 14(4), 528–542.

Klein, J.T. (2010). A taxonomy of interdisciplinarity. In: R. Frodeman, J.T. Klein, and C. Mitcham, eds., *The Oxford handbook of interdisciplinarity.* Oxford: Oxford University Press. pp. 15–30

Law, J. (2002). *Aircraft stories: decentering the object in technoscience.* Durham, NC: Duke University Press.

Law, J. and Mol, A. (2008). The actor-enacted: Cumbrian sheep in 2001. In: C. Knappett, and L. Malafouris, eds., *Material agency.* Boston: Springer. pp. 57–77.

Lee, S. and Bozeman, B. (2005). The impact of research collaboration on scientific productivity. *Social Studies of Science.* 35(5), 673–702.

Lyall, C. and Meagher, L.R. (2012). A masterclass in interdisciplinarity: research into practice in training the next generation of interdisciplinary researchers. *Futures.* 44(6), 608–617.

Lyall, C., Bruce, A., Marsden, W. and Meagher, L. (2013). The role of funding agencies in creating interdisciplinary knowledge. *Science and Public Policy.* 40(1), 62–71.

Mol, A. (2002). *The body multiple: ontology in medical practice.* Durham, NC: Duke University Press.

Mollering, G. (2001). The nature of trust: from Georg Simmel to a theory of expectation, interpretation and suspension. *Sociology.* 35(2), 403–420.

NESTA (2018). *Welcome to Crucible in a box.* NESTA. [Viewed 12 March 2018]. Available from: http://crucibleinabox.nesta.org.uk

Nowotny, H. (2003). Science in search of its audience. *Nova Acta Leopoldina, NF.* 87(325), 211–215.

Nowotny, H., Scott, P., Gibbons, M., and Scott, P.B. (2001). *Re-thinking science: knowledge and the public in an age of uncertainty.* Buenos Aires: SciELO Argentina.

Penfield, T., Baker, M.J., Scoble, R. and Wykes, M.C. (2014). Assessment, evaluations, and definitions of research impact: a review. *Research Evaluation.* 23(1), 21–32.

Pharoah, R. (2009). *Crucible 2007: impact assessment.* London: ESRO Ltd.

Research Councils UK (2013). *Concordat for engaging the public with research.* [Viewed 12 March 2018]. Available from: www.ukri.org/files/legacy/scisoc/concordatforengagingthepublicwithresearch-pdf/

Rodriguez-Falcon, E. (2014). [Untitled contribution]. In: M. Cheeseman, ed., *Supplement to 'No picnic: explorations in art and research'.* Sheffield: NATCECT. p. 6.

Scottish Crucible (2018). *Scottish Crucible.* [Viewed 12 March 2018]. Available from: https://scottishcrucible.org.uk

Shrank, C. (2014). [Untitled contribution]. In: M. Cheeseman, ed., *Supplement to 'No picnic: explorations in art and research'.* Sheffield: NATCECT. p. 7–8.

Soubes, S. (2014). [Untitled contribution]. In: M. Cheeseman, ed., *Supplement to 'No picnic: explorations in art and research'.* Sheffield: NATCECT. p. 3.

Soubes, S. (2015). Cultivating interdisciplinary researcher communities: the Crucible effect. In: T. Bromley, ed., *Vitae Researcher Development International Conference, September 2015, Manchester*. Cambridge: The Careers Research and Advisory Centre (CRAC) Limited. pp. 23–32

Soubes, S. (2017). *Postdoctoral researcher development in the sciences: a Bourdieusian analysis*. EdD thesis, University of Sheffield. [Viewed 24 August 2018]. Available from: http://etheses.whiterose.ac.uk/18296/

Stafford, T. (2014). [Untitled contribution]. In: M. Cheeseman, ed., *Supplement to 'No picnic: explorations in art and research'*. Sheffield: NATCECT. p. 4.

Stilgoe, J. (2007). *Nanodialogues: experiments in public engagement with science*. London: Demos.

Vitae (2018). *About the Vitae researcher development framework*. Vitae. [Viewed 12 March 2018]. Available from: www.vitae.ac.uk/researchers-professional-development/about-the-vitae-researcher-development-framework

Walsh, L. and Kahn, P. (2009). *Collaborative working in higher education: the social academy*. New York: Routledge.

Welsh Crucible (2017). *Welsh Crucible (Crwsibl Cymru)*. [Viewed 12 March 2018]. Available at: www.welshcrucible.org.uk/

Woolgar, S. and Lezaun, J. (2013). The wrong bin bag: a turn to ontology in science and technology studies? *Social Studies of Science*. 43(3), 321–340.

REFLECTION

Research impacts of engineering for society, *with* society

Anh L. H. Tran

Introduction

With significant academic freedom, early career researchers (ECRs) are in a privileged position to pursue research agendas that they are passionate about. I have actively pursued opportunities in *humanitarian engineering research*, in which innovation and technological advances are utilised to meet human beings' basic needs (such as food, water, energy, sanitation, shelter and medicines), particularly among low-income and vulnerable populations such as refugees. My research motivation stems from my history. In the early 1980s, my family fled Vietnam to escape political persecution after the fall of South Vietnam. My parents and sister were lucky to survive the perilous boat journey to a little island in Malaysia; unfortunately some of my other family members were not so lucky. My mother became pregnant with me in the refugee camp and our resettlement was expedited. My family was resettled in Australia and I grew up with all the privileges that come with being born in a developed country. My drive to help others therefore relates to my appreciation of being helped by others. The story of coming to Australia with only the 'shirts on our backs' would be told by my parents countless times during my childhood. In addition to this history, I have a strong personality that enjoys challenging stereotypes. I am a woman in the male-dominated discipline of engineering, a member of an ethnic minority in the UK working abroad as an international ECR, and so essentially I have a feeling of being the 'other' most of time, although I am comfortable with that position. It is with this background that I share my experience of research impact.

Being the daughter of refugees, it resonates deeply with me that there are more than 65 million refugees and internally displaced people in the world today – to put that into perspective that is 1 in every 115 people living, a figure higher than any time reported previously. Issues of migration, vulnerability of people crossing borders, people drowning at sea, these are all things that are happening today and are of considerable global importance and consciousness, especially as refugees are fleeing to Europe and the UK and have now become a very sensitive issue in the political agenda.

Research agendas (and hence funding) are driven by collective needs. The emergence of 'science for society' as a research priority in the European Commission's Science in Society programme and the £1.5 billion investment for the UK's Global Challenges Research Fund (GCRF) from 2016–2020 have resulted in a shift in the number of research projects conducted in the international development sector. I have entered the world of academic research at a heady time, in which significant funding (and hence value) is being allocated to scientific and technological advances *for* society.

One such project is energy access for cooking, lighting and electrification for refugee camps in Rwanda. The challenge of combining engineering innovations, such as improved cooking stoves and household renewable energy systems, with understanding and sensitivities towards vulnerable communities, whilst incorporating sustainable business models, is not easy. However, I attempt below to unpick these challenges and highlight three key reflections about my work on this meaningful research project: working as part of a team; engaging with people; and the ethics of working abroad in sensitive contexts.

Working as part of a team and working abroad

One might say that engineering research with vulnerable communities could be considered easier than traditional social science, as the subject of the research is not the community itself, but the infrastructure, products or services, such as a renewable energy or clean drinking water systems. From my experience, the technology is the easy part – it is *people* that lie at the heart of development issues. Therefore, it is critically important to be able to assess the assets and needs of communities that take into consideration all the different voices – and this requires rigour and experience from a social science perspective. During a research trip to the refugee camps in Rwanda to understand the energy assets and needs of refugees and their host communities, a team made up of engineers, social scientists, business entrepreneurs, international development specialists and local experts was brought together. The diversity of perspectives, gender, experience and background challenged my 'engineering' point of view and enabled me to critically analyse the research objectives. In the field, I partnered up with our lead in-country staff member who was of a similar age to me. We established a good working rapport very early on based on trust and mutual respect. While in the field, she felt no shyness in explaining why some of my actions appeared 'strange' to refugees. Equally, I emphasised that I was there to learn. In one instance of this, I was talking with refugee women about their issues on cooking with wood fuel. I asked to take pictures of cooking pots covered in soot stains and was handed a well-scrubbed shiny cooking pot. I asked why it was cleaned and my counterpart explained to me, that the refugee women were ashamed of the 'dirty pots' – it was a matter of pride and dignity. I then explained that I wanted to understand how cooking with firewood was laborious not only during the cooking process but also for additional tasks such as cleaning pots and clothes. I was then given a pile of dirty pots to photograph. In another instance, we passed a group of young men and they said something in Kinyarwanda, which I did not understand. My counterpart shared with me after we passed them a little way further down the hill, that they were saying we were responsible for the 25% cut in their monthly allowance given by UNHCR. We then together back tracked and had an open conversation with the group about our project on energy access in refugee camps and ended up having a long discussion about engineering and the UK. Without an open, trust-based relationship between myself and our local partners, there could have been miscommunication with the refugee community with a potentially negative effect on the project and its impact. What's more, it gave me a richer understanding and experience of the realities of refugees' lives, instead of a 'shiny' version I would have obtained if it wasn't for these and many other conversations. In light of this, my first piece of advice for ECRs is that if tackling complex global challenges such as energy access in a refugee context, make sure you involve a multidisciplinary team of local and overseas researchers and ensure you maintain an awareness of biases and conflicting needs. Working with experienced local staff who know and understands the language and cultural context is a must in these international projects – personally, I would never work on a project unless I have an experienced local community partner on board as part of the research team.

Difficulties and pleasures of engaging with people in sensitive environments

Field work with community stakeholders is probably my favourite part of undertaking research. Here, I am able to interact with people, work to understand their needs and aspirations and then to co-develop solutions with them. Surveys within communities, especially in sensitive environments like refugee camps, require trained local staff who speak the language and who have an understanding of what is appropriate. In addition, field work can be demanding. In Rwanda, we visited three camps in a week, with long days of travelling by road in between to reach our destinations. This confinement in the car provided us with the perfect bubble to share, argue, understand and reflect on the research that we were undertaking, and we always debriefed after each day. This leads me to recommend to ECRs doing field work to allow yourself some mental time to be reflective but also have an open space to learn from others. This reminds me of one of my favourite quotes, the origin of which is unclear. It is frequently attributed to Dalai Lama XIV, but the earliest text-based source is by J.P. McEvoy: 'when you talk, you are only repeating what you already know. But if you listen, you may learn something new' (McEvoy 1945, p. 11).

One example of when I learnt something new, which had the impact of changing my perspective on the research project, was when I talked to the refugee committees. The committee members available for the interview were made up of a President (male) and three other committee role-holders (all women). They were asked what they thought was the most important energy service. The male President highlighted electricity as his priority whereas the women all prioritised cooking. This interaction emphasised to me that energy access can be a very gender specific issue, and that taking in a range of perspectives is important to understand the real needs of the communities and who we need to be interacting with to make sure we successfully implement the research project. I also learnt that you need to build room within your project proposal to conduct rigorous needs analysis within the funding remit to take into account community voices. Even better would be to co-design the research proposal with the communities you intend to work with (though this is difficult to accomplish without spending time with the community, which is rarely funded). However, there are opportunities for preplanning projects such as networking grants and seed funding for pilot projects. My second piece of advice is that you always write the proposal in a way that emphasises a *range of solutions*, and that is broad enough to allow flexibility in the research outcomes, so that the needs of the research team, the community and the funders can all be met.

Ethics of working abroad and in sensitive environments

In engineering, like many other disciplines, research ethics has become a tick-box exercise relating to informed consent, data protection and occupational health and safety. However, it is very important for ECRs to undertake deep self-critical reflection to understand the research goals and balance this with risk to oneself and others. Research work on global development projects is fraught with ethical dilemmas. It is important not to promise anything you cannot deliver and be clear with the communities about your intentions from the outset (e.g. discussions about energy may not necessary lead to every person in the camp receiving improved cooking stoves or solar panels for their households). Another ethical consideration is the vulnerability of people involved in the research project and how they are represented through research outputs. I learnt from our social scientist involved on the project that perceptions of refugees are very important in trying to eliminate the moral high ground researchers may have of 'helping others'. This attitude in reality just perpetuates existing power imbalances that say that developed countries know what is best. This attitude has informed our writing. The original project proposal stated:

> Ultimately, the project hopes to create a paradigm shift in the way refugees see themselves, instead of 'beneficiaries' dependent on handouts, they will be able to 'HELP' themselves and become agents able to choose, produce, consume and take part in the running of their own communities. (Guara 2017)

However, for the final project publication (currently being written), this text has been amended to:

> Ultimately, the project hopes to create a paradigm shift in the way refugees see themselves **and are seen by others, including humanitarian and development organisations: rather than being perceived as** 'beneficiaries' dependent on handouts, refugees and other displaced people will be able to 'HELP' themselves and become agents able to choose, produce, consume and take part in the running of their own communities. (emphasis added)

These minor nuances in text highlight how we as researchers can consciously influence sensitive political agendas such as how refugees are perceived by the broader community through what we publish. My third piece of advice for ECRs is therefore that you should be conscious of how your own biases may perpetuate existing power imbalances through your words and actions. Ultimately, the value of our work is its service to society through unbiased evidence-based research.

Conclusion

The impact of humanitarian engineering research for society, particularly in low-income and vulnerable communities, should be undertaken by multidisciplinary teams that are aware of the challenges and pitfalls of working overseas in a sensitive context. Researchers should understand their limitations, in terms of cultural understanding, language barriers and prejudices they carry, and consider how, as researchers, they can build the capacity of local staff to undertake research. My main take-home message is that even though this type of research is complex, it should not deter ECRs from embarking on this journey of mutual benefit for both the communities and the researcher.

So what is research impact from the perspective of an ECR? For me, it means conducting research with a mutual understanding of the values, needs and potential of the people you are working with. It requires a humane and dignified approach. It requires that research be translated for decision-makers so that they can make evidence-based choices and policies that improve the provision of services and products, for and **with** others. Then, who knows? Maybe a future publication could incorporate the voices of a new generation of ECRs /refugees writing their own story of how research has real impact.

References

Guara, E.G. (2017). *Humanitarian, Engineering and Energy for Displacement (HEED)* [EPSRC Funding Proposal]. [Viewed 18 March 2019]. Available from: https://gow.epsrc.ukri.org/NGBOViewGrant.aspx?GrantRef=EP/P029531/1

McEvoy, J.P. (1945). Passing the hot potato. *The Rotarian.* 70(5), 11–12.

6

CONNECTING EPISTEMOLOGIES AND THE EARLY CAREER RESEARCHER

Helen Graham, Katie Hill, Peter Matthews, Dave O'Brien and Mark Taylor

Introduction

Early career researchers (ECRs) are a vital part of the Higher Education landscape. However, their experiences are often underrepresented in discussions of Higher Education, for example the UK's recent Stern Review (Stern 2016). ECRs occupy an uncertain position: not securely settled into an academic position, nor having completed their academic training, while being essential to the on-going success of the UK Higher Education system of teaching and research. They are especially important to one-off, competitively funded research projects, such as those supported by national research councils, and are at the forefront of the delivery of a new era of academic research projects shaped by the impact agenda.

The context for considering the ECR experience is set out by Enright and Facer (2017). They identify three key trends radically reshaping the situation for the ECR community, which manifest in three interlinked ways. The nature of collaborations between universities and external partners; whether communities, businesses, organisations, or the state, have been altered by policy interventions; and changes in academic disciplinary norms. This is particularly because of the new requirement for academic research to demonstrate its impact on the wider world. In turn, disciplines themselves have seen changes in the orientations towards knowledge production, particularly with the rise of co-production as a mode of making knowledge that is seen as legitimate within academic disciplines (Campbell & Vanderhoven 2016; Flinders et al. 2016). In addition there is the shift in patterns of employment, from the tenured and secure route for academics, to a more precarious pattern of shorter term contracts (Enright & Facer 2017).

With these broader trends in mind, this chapter considers the experience of one group of ECRs, funded by the UK's Arts and Humanities Research Council's (AHRC) *Connected Communities* programme. Here we draw on one project within this programme, *Connecting Epistemologies*. This project sought to explore both the methods and the experiences of ECRs within *Connected Communities*. The programme itself is rooted in the impact agenda and therefore the experiences of ECRs working within *Connected Communities* are fundamentally shaped by the requirement for generating provable benefits of research beyond the academy. The chapter presents findings from the project, showing how ECRs understand their working conditions, their research practices, and their sense of themselves as academics, in the context of a new, emerging, form of academic identity against a backdrop of a changing academy that is repositioning itself in relation to other institutions and society.

Note: as a group of committed collaborative researchers who are all experienced either in applied research or in the co-production of research working with people rather than doing research on people, making a distinction between the 'university' and the 'real world' is uncomfortable. We are all part of the real world (mrs kinpaisby 2008). However the language of impact implies a separation between someone creating impact, and someone being impacted upon. In order to be succinct in our analysis we have distinguished in our writing between the university or academy and others – the wider world, society, the real world. In the projects that we are drawing from this distinction was often blurred, and we want the reader to be mindful that where we have written about the university and the 'other', however we have described them, it is an uncomfortable separation for us because breaking down that separation is at the heart of what we do.

Background: Connected communities

Connected Communities was a British research council funded programme 'designed to help us understand the changing nature of communities in their historical and cultural contexts and the role of communities in sustaining and enhancing our quality of life' (AHRC 2017). This understanding ranged across seven themes, including health and wellbeing; the creative economy; community heritage; and work, occupation and enterprise. The nature of the themes and focus on communities created a close and natural fit for research impact – easily identifiable beneficiaries beyond the university and beyond disciplinary academic debates.

At its start *Connected Communities* was embroiled in wider debates about education policy and the financing of universities. The first iteration of the programme was controversial due to references to the UK Government's policies of localism and 'the big society' in AHRC's Strategic Plan. This linked *Connected Communities* to these policies which were associated with the austerity and public sector cuts begun by the coalition government in 2010. Whilst there had been little opposition to references to government policy in previous UK research council strategies, such as the Economic and Social Research Council's focus on social exclusion, or the Engineering and Physical Sciences Research Council's funding of work on the digital economy, *Connected Communities* raised issues of policy and public relevance in a way that was uncomfortable for many arts and humanities scholars. There was a cynicism about the programme because it was linked to the introduction of measuring research impact on the wider world and there was an anxiety about proving the worth of the arts and humanities in a way that had not previously been required (O'Brien 2015).

This broader controversy regarding the instrumental push for higher education institutions to support government policy (Slater 2012) provides a broad framing for our discussion of the experience of ECRs (Enright & Facer 2017). Debates about the plight of ECRs have often been articulated through anxieties about how the academy is organised and how academic subjects are appropriated for that organisation. Yet the political trajectories articulated by *Connected Communities* are much more complex than a simplistic critique suggest. The programme was, in its most straightforward articulation, interested in supporting research conducted 'with' (rather than 'about' or 'on') communities. In using this language, *Connected Communities* drew on 30 years of participatory research that sought to see knowledge as best produced equitably and collaboratively, often with radical political change as an aim (O'Brien & Matthews 2015; Enright & Facer 2017).

The focus on work 'with' communities raises questions about the relationship between the academy and society. As such, *Connected Communities* was both a product of the introduction of the requirement to evidence impact, and at the same time an opportunity to critique the nature of the fundamental relationship between the academy and society. These questions manifested themselves in debates around the appropriate methods for delivering the aims of *Connected Communities*. Research methods are the key mechanism for brokering the relationship between researcher and research subject (a distinction which itself becomes blurred within co-produced research). Because of this, attention needs to be given to the nature of the academic who will employ such methods. Thus *Connected Communities* was about what it means to be an academic, as much as it was about community research.

These questions of what it means to be an academic working in the arts and humanities through *Connected Communities* can be linked to more general on-going crises in the arts and humanities around their public role, as compared with the social or hard sciences (Bate 2010). The shifts towards 'research impact' and linking the value of arts and humanities not solely to contribute to disciplinary debates but to 'wider society', coupled with increasing pressure to deliver employment skills to students, has substantially challenged the ways universities have previously operated. Far from being wholly negative, this pulling apart has also made other kinds of spaces, to rethink knowledge, research and teaching, possible (Pain et al. 2011).

There have been two critical tendencies in theorizing of institutions that have persisted in the debates that surround academic careers and the contemporary university. Drawing on theories of power associated with the Frankfurt school, the first is to see institutions as sites for top-down flows of hegemonic power, always carrying the potential to co-opt any radical initiative. The second is its mirror, to see the academic practice as constantly needing to battle so it might be a site of unbound critique that speaks truth to power, something Bourdieu (2000, p. 41) has termed the 'unrealistic radicality' of academics.

Yet *Connected Communities*, as with most day-to-day life in UK universities today, demands a more careful and nuanced reading of power and change. *Connected Communities* opened up spaces for collaborative research within universities as those methods and those approaches have been accompanied with research council funding.

Connecting epistemologies: Project background and methods

Connecting Epistemologies was funded as part of the middle rounds of *Connected Communities*, following a research development workshop in Edinburgh during the summer of 2013. The project had three main aims: firstly, to raise awareness of the differing methods and methodological traditions within the *Connected Communities* programme; secondly, to understand the experiences of ECRs' use of these different methods and methodological traditions; and lastly, to critically explore how these experiences and traditions intersect.

These aims and objectives reflected three core areas of inquiry that are linked to the broader structures and debates above. In the first instance they sought to explore the *Connected Communities* programme's aims 'to understand the changing nature of communities' and to 'inform the development of more effective ways to support and catalyse community cultures and behaviours'. Second, the use of participatory methods and their potential limits were explored, albeit in a limited manner. This happened in the way participants shaped their role in the data collection. It was also attempted in a workshop on data analysis by the core research team. Lastly, they sought to open out and unsettle the presumptions and the critiques of the 'impact' agenda.

The rationale for a focus on methods and methodologies within the project came from the recognition that the *Connected Communities* programme was designed to be methodologically eclectic and innovative, reflecting both the range of approaches found in the various disciplines constituting the arts and humanities, as well as the interdisciplinary, cross-research-council basis for the funded projects. Importantly, focusing on methods allowed us to focus on the impact the programme was aiming to produce with a shift from research *on* communities to research *with* communities. Methodological eclecticism can be an obvious strength, offering the possibility of synthesising a range of approaches, generating diverse forms of data and answering complex questions which cut across traditional academic disciplines. However, there are risks with this approach for researchers (Flinders, Wood & Cunningham 2016), risks that are grounded in the uneven distribution of power and expertise within academic research projects. *Connecting Epistemologies* explored these risks in two ways, in co-operation with a specific community – that of ECRs.

ECRs are a community defined and created by the funding council(s) and universities, giving the research a clearly bounded group to work with that has two important characteristics. They make up a quasi-elite community in the sense that ECRs as qualified and skilled but also – due to short term contracts – peripheral and precarious. Second, ECRs working on *Connected Communities* projects were often at the front line of trying to navigate the different disciplinary logics within community collaboration. The peripheral, but quasi-elite nature of the ECR community offered an opportunity to explore and to challenge the assumptions underpinning the *Connected Communities* programme. The programme was designed to be co-produced, and this project raised questions about both co-production and collaboration, as it focused on and was developed with an elite community, academics, who are embedded in methodological traditions that give greater or lesser status to collaboration.

The research team of five ECRs (three men and two women), comprised of four researchers in full time academic posts at universities – two of which were fixed term – and one community partner whose portfolio career included part time employment within universities as well as independent research and community work through third sector organisations. Three of the team had completed PhDs and two were working on PhDs at the time. All of the research team had worked on multiple *Connected Communities* projects, with various on-going working relationships within the team. The community partnership represents a recognition that contemporary ECR career paths are increasingly complex and ECRs from the *Connected Communities* programme have roles outside of traditional academic institutions. This point was important in how participants in *Connecting Epistemologies* understood their academic identities as part of the *Connected Communities* programme.

Connecting Epistemologies began with an event for ECRs in May 2014. In advance of this workshop, a call for participants was circulated where the purpose of the project was explained. The workshop provided an opportunity for the participants to network, share experiences of their working lives, and hear from presenters on issues of the precariousness of contemporary labour. Participants, and non-participants who had expressed an interest, were then invited to submit an expression of interest. From these a group of 11 ECRs were recruited to take part in a three-month reflective data collection exercise. The sample size was such that each researcher was paired with two to three ECRs.

The 11 participants were chosen to represent a broad spread of discipline, tenure, geographical location and professional role. The range of disciplines was identified by the hosting department or institution. A broad range across arts and humanities subjects was chosen. It should be noted that several participants stated in their applications that they were working on multidisciplinary projects or that they had worked across different disciplines. There was a mix of full time and part time employment and studentships, and all were on, or had been on, fixed term contracts. Participants were located across the UK. Some participants had worked on several research projects, while others had more limited experience. Most members of the group were women, reflecting the gender balance of the applications received.

Co-production of the research happened over the summer and autumn. Participants were invited to make three further contributions, and were open to decide upon an appropriate format for completing the reflexive data collection exercise that fitted with their own research practice. The researchers met with the ECRs to discuss each of their contributions and further reflect on what their contributions meant. At the end of this period, the various contributions were analysed and pulled together into a final report. The original workshop participants were invited back to a further workshop where the report was presented and there was further opportunity for reflection, discussion and networking.

Recognising the ethical implications of doing co-produced research, participants were provided with stipends to cover their time, and workshop participants could ask for their travel to be reimbursed (Banks & Manners 2012; Beebeejaun et al. 2015). For many, the paying of participants is a vital part of coproduced research, especially as it can enable low-income groups to participate when otherwise they would be excluded. We do recognise that this can be ethically problematic in the way it puts research participants into a contractual agreement with the researchers (Banks et al. 2017). However, given the precarious situation of the ECRs participating in the project – and why we wished to engage them as participants – it was felt that providing compensation for time spent on the project was appropriate.

The participants' contributions were then analysed by the *Connecting Epistemologies* team at a workshop in September 2014. The analysis also drew on the team's reflections of their roles on the project, including conversations with participants and their struggles over data collection, as well as their own experiences as ECRs. These reflections gave clues to the larger issues analysed in this chapter. For example, unfinished contributions, deadlines moved and meetings missed or rescheduled due to other work commitments were common occurrences in the data collection period.

Setting the scene: Little Habermasians?

Much of the writing on the position of early career academics is positioned within a broader field of critiques of global neoliberalism. This body of research sees ECRs as being at the whim and mercy of the modern, global multiversity (Shore 2010). The 'empowerment' through flexibility that ECRs 'enjoy' through short term project working recreates them as subjects of neoliberal power (Cruikshank 1999). In this understanding, their desire to create portfolio careers with a range of skills is actually misrecognition of their exploitation in insecure employment without the terms and conditions of a permanent employee.

However, looking across the contributions of our participants we can see a much more nuanced subjectivity – an honest and open excitement about the opportunities brought by working on *Connected Communities* projects, tempered with a concern that they are in an insecure position.

While our participants could be considered the 'reflexive subjects' of modernity in a Giddens' tradition, more accurately they could be described as 'little Habermasians' (Barnett et al. 2008). The participants have a number of moral truth claims with which they are engaging: that *Connected Communities* projects are doing positive work with diverse communities; that the skills they require for a successful career and self-fulfilment are varied; that they are disempowered by the short term contracts and poor terms and conditions of their employment; that they recognise the moral and intellectual value of research produced by the academy for wider society; and that the academy is increasingly being debased by global neoliberalism.

In their submissions, our participants play these moral judgements off each other. In one case, this took the form of an actual report of a Habermasian-style discourse – an edited account of a number of discussions with colleagues on these issues. As with all Habermasian discussion, the morality is ambivalent 'in the gray areas in between' (Habermas 1996: 120). This is not just a work on the self, as suggested in Foucauldian critiques of subjectivities of neoliberalism, this is clearly our subjects working to understand society and thus the morality of their actions and the actions of others, including complicit institutions such as universities.

The role of the university is related to the role of the academic disciplines that frame the ECR participants' working lives. As universities and funding councils look for research to become trans or interdisciplinary, their internal organisation is still based around a disciplinary perspective. The work of Abbott (2001), although drawn from the American experience, is useful for situating the discussion of ECRs and questions of trans, cross or interdisciplinary work. It also helps to contextualise many of the anxieties and forms of precariousness that are manifest in the discussion of the themes raised in the data provided by the ECRs. For Abbott (2001) 'fractal distinctions' are one of the key ways in which differences emerge and develop within disciplines, nonetheless reinforcing distinctions between them. The relevance of the fractal in fractal distinctions is that, at each stage of development, the same internal struggles are taking place. That this situation came to pass is partly a consequence of how disciplines work, itself a function of how higher education and universities themselves work. The kinds of departments that exist in the social sciences and humanities in a university now are more or less the same as 100 years ago. Part of this is down to administrative reasons, both pedagogical and professional. This leads to a path dependency where interdisciplinarity is more highly regarded in principle than in execution. This is a vitally important contextual idea for *Connected Communities* researchers that do not have established, or in the case of ECRs, permanent and secure, academic positions. Challenging the path dependency of academic organisation thus presents significant challenges and risks (Barry et al. 2008; Flinders et al. 2016).

Precariousness

One such risk is captured by the experience of precarity in academic labour. This precariousness is related to wider social and economic changes in both the professions and also in work itself. For some it is part of a change to more fluid and flexible labour markets, with more choice over aspects of career. For others it reflects deskilling and the decline of associated forms of work security, such as pensions.

For some participants this simply continued experiences of precariousness from previous sectors they had worked in – the creative and cultural industries that the *Connected Communities* programme are aligned to are notoriously precarious. One participant spoke of someone they had met in their professional sector who was approaching retirement and had never had an employment contract lasting more than six months. Another participant found themselves in a *Connected Communities* programme after being made redundant from previous arts-based employment following cuts in local government spending. However, it is vital to stress that the root of precariousness for all of the participants was the issue of whether and how they would get a full time, permanent job. Even for those participants who did not desire a traditional academic career, the fear that this might be closed to them was an important way of structuring their experience as an ECR.

Our participants experienced and framed precariousness in differing ways, stressing the reality of the uncertainty generated by not having a permanent job, whilst also describing the forms of freedom they encountered. This freedom could come in the manner of their working practices:

> I work on trains quite a bit (which I think most people do) but it also keeps things interesting. I don't get stuck in a rut and it's hard to get bored, which I like.

or in project work, the most common form of ECR contract. These working practices gave them the freedom and autonomy they wanted. Already it was felt that 'the odd range of skills that I'd collected through a range of short term contracts ... made me suitable for this job' and a particular project 'gives me enormous freedom, allowing me breaks for personal or professional development'. Indeed, one participant, from a design background, did not use the language of precariousness, and in conversations around the matter framed work in keeping with a discipline that is project, rather than permanent contract, based. The insecurity offered by project working was framed very positively. The 'positives of precariousness' were seen as a 'lifestyle choice' that 'gives me freedom and I don't feel tied down'. However, this was tempered with awareness that 'we're all on short term contracts, we're all looking for the next job within three months of starting the new one'.

Getting the jobs was the core site for the expression of precariousness, with many of the participants identifying their presence on *Connected Communities* projects as random or lucky, see in the repetition of the phrase 'right place at the right time':

> The first appointment was, it must be admitted, largely a question of being in the right place at the right time. The result, however, has been to initiate an unplanned but so far successful career path that utilises my unusual skills, and which fits the department's current research enthusiasms.

The element of precariousness underpinning their current roles came through very strongly for those working across more than one project, especially where the participant had a peripheral relationship to a specific department:

> I have a building I go to each day but no actual desk, or computer, or phone. There's something a little unsettling about not having a proper workspace of your own.

Even for the full time, longer term, post-doctoral or doctoral ECRs who participated in the research there were experiences that were profoundly negative, tied to the lack of permanence of their positions:

> I don't want a job which makes me feel stressed or consumed when I am away from work.

However, even within the nuanced recognition of the ECR position, there was still a residual core uncertainty. This uncertainty was usefully solicited through visual and material culture methods, including discussions of visual representations of ECR activities during the data-gathering period. These visual representations crystallised in ECRs' production of cultural artefacts to represent these issues, such as Figure 6.1.

This 'cultural' production was an aspect encouraged by the research team as a way of reflecting the intersection of visual methods, such as GIS mapping or social network analysis, employed by the ECRs in their research work, along with the art and design background of several of the participants. These cultural products, of which the above was one, sit alongside a discussion of specific objects as metaphors for the ECR experience:

> This is my wheelie case which gets dragged around with me, each week. I bought it less than six months ago but it's already falling apart from the amount of travelling I do for work, as well as delivering papers based on my own research. It's also a bit of a cheesy metaphor for what it's like as an ECR; it looks perfectly fine on the outside but underneath it's knackered.

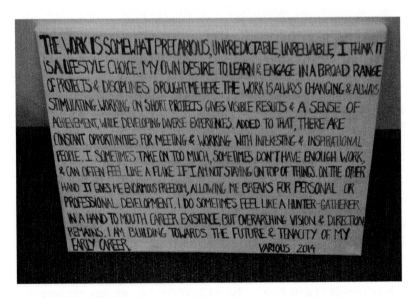

FIGURE 6.1 ECR art work

These types of metaphors were linked to broader questions of how to balance work and life. This was especially important for those of the participants with families:

> My personal circumstances (I have a family and live an hour from the university) result in me popping into the office to see everyone but I have not invested enough time to develop any relationships beyond the office.

Networks were seen as important markers of quality of working life and for developing a career. However issues of work / life balance were clear for all 11 contributors, whether in comments about balancing moving house, responding to a partner's expectations or just in terms of not having enough time to live and complete the tasks expected in work. One participant was blunt about where the experience had left them:

> it came from a desire to have more time at home, with family and less time working, or thinking about work when at home. It also came from a political belief that... we shouldn't be working at the expense of our families, our health or our community.

And another spoke openly about the perception that compromising over family life or leisure time would be necessary to succeed in an academic career:

> survival in academia...requires making sacrifices to be able to make any meaningful progression.

A final aspect of precariousness is tied to career development, which is intimately linked with getting a permanent job. This is explored in more detail in the sections below, but it is worth picking up on one ECRs comment that stands as a useful aggregation for many of the discussions with the project participants. This focuses on how career development works for an ECR:

> Career development is apparently a significant part of my role as an ECR... The phrase, however, cannot be found in my contract of employment, and a clear idea of what constitutes career development is hard to ascertain. Helpfully, perhaps, the AHRC are vague about what constitutes 'leadership and / or career development support', meaning that I and my PI can make it up as we go along.

The issue raised by this comment indicates that although the framework for the ECR is one that recognises their need for support and career development it is often unstructured. In many ways this reflects the impossibility of creating a detailed framework for dealing with individuals and disciplines that are so diverse, even within the broader umbrella of arts and humanities. However it also points to the individualisation of the risks associated with building an academic identity, particularly with regard to getting a 'good' manager or supervisor of a project. One important question for research is the extent to which this happens – all of the 11 contributors spoke of how they'd had predominantly (although not entirely) good experiences of support on their projects. But there is no way, without a more systematic approach to this issue, to know if this reflects a well-functioning academy or simply luck on the part of the participants in *Connecting Epistemologies*.

Academic identity

The discussion of precariousness concluded with a comment on career development. This is as much to do with the socialisation of the academic personality as it is to do with having the right CV for a job. In previous years the academic identity had a close relationship to discourses of academic freedom, tied to permanence of tenure. As has been touched upon above, this has been eroded in several ways in the UK, but it has gone hand in hand with other changes within the academy and the growth of roles such as delivering impact through one's research (see, for example: Bastow et al. 2014). The following discussion of the role of academic identity develops this idea, exploring both the specific identities of the participants, as well as interrogating the potential emergence of a new form of academic identity, formed by the *Connected Communities* programme and its specific alignment to 'impact' agendas.

The peculiarities and contradictions of academic identity were common to those participants who discussed it:

> The long working hours but continued suggestion that we have so much autonomy and flexibility.

Along with

> The pressure individuals put on themselves in academia and how it appeared a very individualised career – you have to make sure you write your own papers and develop your own portfolio if you want to stay in academia and move up the career ladder.

This individualisation was often at odds with the researchers' status as part of project teams:

> It is interesting working within a multi-disciplinary team with a range of methodology, this can be good experience at this stage of my academic career but I'm not sure where this will take me in the future.

The emergence of a new form of academic identity came through much of the discussions and the submissions because of the difference (and distance) between researchers' practices on projects and their perceptions of academic identity. This is linked to the final section's discussions of research practices, but in the context of academic identity it is worth noting how the abilities that were most valuable to the research work they were conducting were often not those they associated with traditional academia. Those skills were specifically those we might perceive as being vital to delivering 'impactful' research: organising meetings; translating between academics and communities; hanging out with participants in a range of situations; or other mundane activities that were essential to the projects' successes but were hard to characterise as 'academic'. This was contrasted with formal 'academic' practices, such as writing papers, which was seen as a core activity by many participants. For example:

> In my current academic role I use some of these skills but others I have had to develop (somewhat reluctantly). These include writing – I have never been bad at writing but I struggle with the language and format required for an academic journal. I find I am not able to be as creative as I would like in these situations. I also lack confidence in my knowledge and ability to argue a point feeling perhaps that I don't have the necessary academic context and rigor.

But the varied 'non-academic' practices also:

> Challenge me in many ways that more traditional academic work does not.

The potential tension between writing and other aspects of academic work reflects the emergence of newer forms of identity, discussed in more detail below. At this point it is worth focusing on the perception, voiced by many of the participants, of the relationship between being an academic and the activity of writing. This was important both to post-docs and doctoral researchers questioning their suitability for an academic career:

> I'm proud to be a doctor but not sure if sitting in a university office writing every day is me.

And also to how descriptions of time were narrated by participants. The issue of time, linked to precariousness, meant ECRs were often doing two jobs: working on delivering projects, and struggling with the process of academic writing.

> I will need evidence of publications to continue as funding for this post comes to an end in two years. I will need something on my CV beyond a thesis to apply for other posts.

For post-doctoral participants there was a clear need to balance their new projects with the more academic (in their view) expertise they had developed as part of their PhDs:

> I am currently revising two manuscripts from my PhD that have been invited for resubmission. These are not related to my current work and I feel that this

needs to be done in my own time. I would like to get these and one other paper from my PhD published so that I can focus on publications within my current role. It feels as if I need to shed this skin to enable developing a new identity within my current role.

Changing identities was closely related to participants' narratives of hopefulness for careers, which was in turn part of an emerging role for universities as public institutions with the need to deliver impact as part of their core mission:

> it's not to say I don't have a career plan…but what I'm seeing more and more is the type of person universities are looking for is someone quite interdisciplinary and creative… I don't know. I'll find out.

The type of academic described above is at the core of much of the methodological and practice-based innovation within the *Connected Communities* programme. However, reflecting the ambivalence in the discussion of precariousness and the interdisciplinary status of their roles as researchers, the idea of a 'new' academic gave rise to fears for future employment and the extent to which they were really fulfilling the purpose of *Connected Communities*:

> Is the pursuit of the interdisciplinary really working? Maybe the question should be: is the pursuit of the interdisciplinary within the academy really working? I ask this because I can see that my CV…looks intriguing, and it ticks that interdisciplinary box. But will it forward my career? ….I'm not so sure. The fact is that the majority of academic positions demand a specialist in one field or another, not a jack-of-all-trades. The impression therefore is that I am using an ECR's unique and flexible position to achieve a CV and skill set for employment outside the academy – and that feels like something of a betrayal of the AHRC's support, primarily financial, but also ideological.

Yet others took an approach that embraced the fluidity of where academic research fits within their lives and careers:

> I think I am keeping my options open about what to do after this PhD experience. I love the interdisciplinarity of *Connected Communities* but I have no idea how I would slot into a discipline afterwards! I think I would enjoy teaching and intend to investigate whether I could get involved in this in my 3rd year, I also enjoy my work outside of academia in events and festivals, so would be reluctant to give that up completely.

It is perhaps those people who have a strong sense of their own political or creative trajectory, which might criss-cross inside and outside academia, which *Connected Communities* has most effectively supported.

The role of the academy

A fear of creating a 'non-academic' CV, or having skills that were undervalued by a wider performance management regime focusing on writing papers or individual academic achievements, provides a bridge to the consideration of the specificity of *Connected Communities* work. *Connected Communities* research projects were about finding ways to develop research with communities in a context that commonly had not been subject to academic consideration, or working on issues that had seen potential partners alienated from universities and academics. The discussion of *Connected Communities* at the beginning of this chapter gives a flavour of the context for these issues. How did they play out for *Connecting Epistemologies* participants?

Ideas about new forms of academic identity and practice were emerging within *Connected Communities* projects, particularly as the link between community and university:

> I feel like the link between 'the academics' and the community. It is really important that I establish good relationships with partners who have been working in the community before we offer the groups as they can open doors by raising awareness and sharing information. Once…I had established good partnerships with community partners the referrals came in and this can only be achieved by gaining their trust and being present as a reminder of what we are trying to achieve.

However, the role of broker was a difficult one and not just because of well-rehearsed ethical challenges with participatory research (Banks & Manners 2012). In the case of one participant's narrative, represented in the form of email communications, the community participants put 'community' literally in inverted commas and concluded that 'it just doesn't seem worth spending 2–3 more days taking part in the [research] project to answer the sort of research questions you are asking'. A great deal of the contribution of another participant focused on this process of relationship forming and developing, with events recorded such as an intimate conversation with a community partner in a car after an event where the community partner revealed a momentous career decision.

The role of broker was also that of translator, moving between different forms of academic expertise on large projects, or between languages of community and university (see also: Connelly et al. 2015). This was experienced as a useful skill that might lead to employment:

> I am fortunate that the CC project I am on provides the flexibility of activities and diversity of connections to allow this experience to appeal to a much wider group of people when I begin to apply for other jobs.

And also, in the case of another participants' narrative, as a form of moral responsibility that adds another layer to the identity of the *Connected Communities* academic:

> I feel a great sense of duty towards communicating and disseminating our work to a wide range of audiences, and in particular community groups who I feel could benefit from the different things we are learning from the research.

This was clearly aligned to many of the broader challenges identified in delivering impact through research in an ethical, engaged way, rather than viewing it as a broadcast activity (Beebeejaun et al. 2015; Campbell & Vanderhoven 2016).

There was also a sense of *Connected Communities* transforming individual ECRs' approaches to research in a fundamental way. This sense of new identity was not unproblematic. Previous sections have touched on the issues of establishing oneself in a disciplinary or departmental context. Participants also described having difficulty in drawing *Connected Communities* ways of working into other academic contexts:

> For me, it illustrates the sharp edge that you run into when the sensibility that is supported by the programme carries over into other contexts. This sharp edge was deeply embodied, anger, fear, threat arising throughout the day. It divided me from colleagues that I like a great deal and have a lot of respect for. And has made me wonder how much I have changed and what other situations I'll find myself not fitting in to.

While in some cases this shift was expressed positively as underpinning a political and epistemic challenge to the academy, in others there was the sense of a threat to expertise and professional status that is potentially expressed in co-production or participatory forms of research, whereby new methods may 'devalue the professional skills and training that we have'. This echoes the experiences of other *Connected Communities* projects, where the varying engagement with 'applied' research associated with academics' disciplinary identities affected the relationship of individual academics to research practice (Matthews et al. 2017).

There may be, then, the emergence of an academic identity shaped by participants' experiences of *Connected Communities*, one that is at the locus of a complex intersection of interdisciplinary research practices and new ways of 'doing' academic research through co-produced methods to deliver wider impact. However it is one that, like the more traditional academic identity and the position of the ECR within the academy, requires support if it is not to be merely precarious and then fleeting.

What is research for the new academic?

Connecting Epistemologies was keen to understand how research methods were being developed and how methods were related to personal academic identity and particular methodological approaches. These questions were captured in the analysis under the umbrella question of 'what is research?' This question allowed the analysis to link together questions of identity, precariousness and the experience of being involved in *Connected Communities*.

It is worth repeating, as a caveat to these points, the sheer diversity of methods and approaches captured by the arts and humanities. This is not just a matter of the disciplines to which participants were related, but also of what counts as knowledge. For example, one participant, when doing qualitative analysis of interview data, approached this spatially and visually, as opposed to working just on the text or using software. This diversity, even for standard research practices, was typical of the 11 participants.

There are, of course, commonalities. The most notable of these is the way research is not the research of the scholar, but is rather a set of practices that are as much to do with professional project support, development and management as to do with the ideal type of the scholar. Much of the working life of the participants was fairly routine, reflected in the nature of the contributions themselves: notes of meetings and email chains both featured. This is similar to research project management and similar level roles with the economy more broadly – supporting larger tasks and activities through providing administrative support. Indeed it was part of their identity as researchers:

> It is difficult to identify these events and the process of organising them, documenting them and building on the findings and discussion from them as a methodology. However, they do form a key part of the project and they produce insight which we will theorise, analyse, build on and write about.

Albeit one that needed to be negotiated as it disconnected them from their academic background:

> My academic background is quite different from the literature I use today and I don't have experience working within Arts and Humanities, I have very little practice working with communities.

That notwithstanding, some were able to adapt their disciplinary approach to the administrative tasks of their research project:

> I have also been very involved in the organisation of the final events, but mainly from a practice point of view in terms of how everything is presented. For me it is very important to have something to show at the end of a project that is concrete and exists in the real world rather than remaining an abstract notion or a list of recommendations (which so often is the case).

For some this experience was disconcerting and made them feel they had moved away from how their doctoral research had trained and developed their expertise, leading them to describe their research roles as a 'hybrid of life experience rather than training'. Even where there was continuity between doctoral and post-doctoral research, the difference was that participants felt that only a tiny proportion of their time was spent doing 'research' and that most time was spent managing relationships with community partners, taking part in meetings and organising events. Again, these are activities that can clearly be seen as those which deliver wider impact from research activities. Yet while some ECRs did interpret these types of activities as 'not research', others were clear that it was in these type of activities – how the tea was to be made, who made the cakes, building relationships – that productive 'knowing 'and 'insight' took place. For some this was clearly different from 'doing research':

> I moved from a desk based researcher more interested in theory to doing fieldwork, it was unexpected, I felt lost as a person.

But also was part of the emerging form of academic identity discussed previously:

> The revelation for me has been that project management and research 'proper' are not necessarily two unrelated things.

The positive space for reshaping academic identities – becoming known for pioneering new forms of academic meetings or for specific projects – was perhaps most clear for those ECRs taking higher-status roles as project leaders and principal investigators (PIs).

Yet, as one ECR PI notes, following the flurries of bids in the wake of two annual *Connected Communities* summits came the experience of juggling being PIs and co-investigators on multiple projects and a certain amount of project-fatigue:

> Around the time that the applications for this year's projects were due I was having a conversation with a colleague who wondered why I was thinking of applying when I had recently received a [prestigious fellowship]. She had to remind me that I was already being funded to do almost 100% research, so why was I applying for more? It was really strange that I hadn't actually noticed this myself, I was so caught up in the CC [*Connected Communities*] world I couldn't see where I actually was. So that shift in perspective was also really critical to my current involvement (or drastically reduced involvement).

It's worth closing with two of the more pessimistic, but revealing, quotes. Ultimately ECRs face many challenges, even as they love the work they do and are utterly committed to it, on the level of their sense of identity through to their methodological practices. However this is tempered by the reality of struggling with university systems, academic disciplines and the assumptions of what an academic is:

> I'd love to have my own, consistent space to work in, which came with some equipment. It would make me feel like I actually had a 'proper' job. It can be embarrassing admitting to family and friends outside of academia that I don't have these things. It's not what they imagine working at a university to be like.

The challenges ECRs face are alleviated by some elements of *Connected Communities*, but as that programme itself has faced criticism, it can be hard for an individual ECR to have problems of interdisciplinarity, new methods, or the struggle for legitimation of academic practices added to their quest for an academic post:

> It's difficult to maintain confidence when you are challenging the way that things are being done.

Conclusion

Connecting Epistemologies aimed to explore the ECR experience of *Connected Communities*, along with questions of methods and methodologies. In doing so it has raised a range of issues, both from the data presented above and from the experiences of the five members of the *Connecting Epistemologies* project team. The ECR experience is diverse, even within a sample of only 11! For those who have a clear disciplinary home and desire for an academic career, *Connected Communities* causes anxieties, as Enright and Facer (2017) have also argued, given the methods, practices and identities best suited to the forms of research foregrounded in the programme. For those who have a reflexive sense of personal trajectory or sense of political purpose, which might flow in and out of a traditional academic trajectory, the programme has created a relatively high-status, funded space for collaborative research and broader collaborative work.

The above point is especially pronounced in those cases where an ECR had taken a leadership role. In particular, the explicit support for ECRs as principal investigators and project leads enabled some people to become recognised for their work through fellowships and through gaining positions in prestigious institutions. Yet this is not a universal experience and feelings of being cut adrift without a clear 'home' were expressed especially by those in research assistant and doctoral positions who did not have a professional or practice background to inform their work.

In relation to this concern is the emerging picture of an interdisciplinary, multi-skilled professional who draws on more than a doctoral or post-doctoral path, underpinned by experiences from beyond the academy. This professional is essential to the new world of the impact agenda and for a university's connection to communities. However it is clear that the usual form of academic training, the PhD, is not providing fully the necessary skills to fulfil this role. Equally the training available to staff at most HEI's is not yet supporting these new skill sets. Training in community engagement, communication and project management should become as common as training in literature searching and teaching skills.

The new identity described in contributions shows a tension between the traditional individualised researcher and the connected, communicative research broker emerging in *Connected Communities* roles. For some, their roles on projects were about forging new modes of knowing and they welcomed the challenges to academic ways of being that attended it. Yet beneath the theoretical questions raised lurked a practical problem of what the career path looks like for this type of researcher. And whether working towards a transformed academy was likely to fit with a permanent job that included the associated support and benefits, such as a pension. This paralleled the growth of the 'impact' agenda within research, and the related tensions between doing research using traditional methodologies and working with communities, or research end-users, to drive methodological innovation (Pain et al. 2011; Slater 2012; Flinders et al. 2016).

Here our case study returns to the broader questions of this book, not only around how best to support and nurture ECRs, but also how best to win the struggle for more progressive political academic interventions in the contemporary university. If research funders and universities want to take impact seriously then they need to look at how they can attract and keep professionals with this new academic identity and the varied skills it requires. Connected Communities has been an ideal training ground for people who want to build and maintain links between the university and other organisations. If career opportunities are not provided by institutions, then this expertise will dissipate. One of the benefits of more varied career paths where people move in and out of university employment is that there is more understanding of the academic world embedded in other organisations, but the danger is in the current environment of funding cuts, wage stagnation, erosion of employment rights and managerialism that more people will leave academia in favour of a working environment where these skills are more highly valued.

This chapter has presented our research findings and a narrative about change in higher education driven by impact through four themes: 'Precariousness', 'Academic identity', 'The role of the academy', and 'What is research for the new academic?'. Here are our ideas on how to develop sustainable opportunities for ECRs to thrive in an impact-focussed HEI landscape:

Precariousness: Very obviously projects like those funded through *Connected Communities* are about doing research that has direct impact in the wider world, but the current funding structure for those projects promotes precarious employment practices. Universities are not alone in having high levels of short term part time contracts; it is common in other sectors too. However, we can see from our participants that tensions are created by the juxtaposition of temporary contracts and very secure permanent contracts which creates a power imbalance. The risk is that as a sector we develop this new expertise but don't have the infrastructure in place to keep and nurture it. This is a sector-wide issue that needs a strategic intervention and also needs individual institutions and project leaders to take action. The next three themes are suggestions for how universities can better support the career development of people on the front line of real world connections between the universities and other institutions.

Academic identity: This research evidences the emergence of a significantly different set of skills to those traditionally associated with 'the academic' that are being developed through this project-based collaborative research work. Demand for these skills is starting to appear in job descriptions: this needs to happen more, but also needs to be embedded in the development of new researchers through research training and the PhD. It then needs to be recognised in the grading of academic posts with equivalence to other skills in job descriptions (i.e. don't just make posts that require community engagement skills a lower grade, therefore lower paid).

The role of the academy: This programme was shaped by the introduction of the impact agenda into the academy. It can be viewed positively as underpinning a political and epistemic challenge to the academy in a way that supports rigour in rethinking the relationships between the university and others, and prompting the demonstration of value to society. On the other hand, it can generate a sense of a threat to expertise and professional status whereby new methods may 'devalue the professional skills and training that we have'. Going back to theories of power and change, the debates around these types of projects and impact can make an important contribution to the nuanced understanding of power and change both within the academy and between the academy and those on the other side of 'impact'. This debate needs to continue.

What is research for the new academic? This research documents a fundamental shift in the practice of research, in what a researcher does and therefore what we can understand research to be. As this programme is born out of a strategic response in arts and humanities to the requirement to demonstrate impact, we argue that this shift in understanding of 'what is research' is also fundamental to achieving impact. Research practice progresses through the documentation of precedents for new approaches to research, the publication of descriptions of research methods, and the development of methodologies and their philosophical underpinnings. This calls for individual researchers to document and publish this new research practice to create the literature that can enable new researchers to adopt these approaches in their PhD research. The academy can then formalise this way of working through inclusion of these skills and competencies in job descriptions and training opportunities and therefore improve the career opportunities of ECRs working in this way.

Learning points

- Be proactive in speaking out about the impact of precarious employment as you experience it and seek broader support from other colleagues in less precarious positions.
- In your own institutions demand training, development opportunities, mentoring and coaching to meet the requirements of project-based collaborative research.
- Document and publish this new research practice to create the literature that can enable other new researchers to adopt these approaches.

References

Abbott, A. (2001) *Chaos of Disciplines*. Chicago: University of Chicago Press.
AHRC (2017) *The Connected Communities Programme*. Available from: www.ahrc.ac.uk/research/fundedthemesandprogrammes/crosscouncilprogrammes/connectedcommunities/ (accessed 22/11/2017).

Banks, S., Herrington, T. and Carter, K. (2017) Pathways to co-impact: action research and community organising. *Educational Action Research* 25: 541–559.

Banks, S. and Manners, P. (2012) *Community-based Participatory Research: A Guide to Ethical Principles and Practice*. Durham: Centre for Social Justice and Community Action.

Barnett, C., Clarke, N., *et al.* (2008). The elusive subjects of neo-liberalism. *Cultural Studies* 22(5): 624–653.

Barry, A., Born, G. and Weszkalnys, G. (2008). Logics of interdisciplinarity. *Economy and Society* 37(1): 20–49.

Bastow, S., Dunleavy, P. and Tinkler, J. (2014). *The Impact of the Social Sciences: How Academics and their Research Make a Difference*. London: Sage.

Bate, J. (2010) *The Public Value of the Humanities*. London: Bloomsbury.

Beebeejaun, Y., Durose, C., Rees, J., *et al.* (2015) Public harm or public value? Towards coproduction in research with communities. *Environment and Planning C: Government and Policy* 33: 552–565.

Bourdieu, P. (2000) *Pascalian Meditations*. Stanford: Stanford University Press.

Campbell, H. and Vanderhoven, D. (2016). *N8/ESRC Research Programme – Knowledge That Matters: Realising the Potential of Co-Production*. Manchester: N8 Research Partnership. Available from: www.n8research.org.uk/research-focus/urban-and-community-transformation/co-production/ (accessed 27/02/19).

Connelly, S., Durose, C., Richardson, L., Vanderhoven, D., Matthews, P., and Rutherfoord, R. (2015). Translation across borders: exploring the use, relevance and impact of academic research in the policy process. In P. Matthews and D. O'Brien (eds.), *After Urban Regeneration: Communities, Policy and Place* (pp. 181–198). Bristol: Policy Press.

Cruikshank, B. (1999). *The Will to Empower: Democratic Citizens and Other Subjects*. London: Cornell University Press.

Enright, B. and Facer, K. (2017) Developing reflexive identities through collaborative, interdisciplinary and precarious work: the experience of early career researchers. *Globalisation, Societies and Education* 15(5): 621–634

Flinders, M., Wood, M., and Cunningham, M. (2016). The politics of co-production: risks, limits and pollution. *Evidence & Policy: A Journal of Research, Debate and Practice* 12(2), 261–279.

Habermas, J. (1996). What is universal pragmatics? In: W. Outhwaite (ed.), *The Habermas Reader* (pp. 118–131). Cambridge: Polity Press.

Matthews, P., Connelly, S., Durose, C., Richardson, L., Vanderhoven, D., and Rutherfoord, R. (2017). Everyday stories of impact: interpreting knowledge exchange in the contemporary university. *Evidence & Policy* 14(4), 665–682.

mrs kinpaisby (2008). Taking stock of participatory geographies: envisioning the communiversity. *Transactions of the Institute of British Geographers* 33(3), 292–299.

O'Brien, D. (2015) Cultural value, measurement, and policy making. *Art and Humanities in Higher Education* 14(1): 79–94

O'Brien, D. and Matthews, P. (2015) *After Urban Regeneration*. Bristol: Policy Press.

Pain, R., Kesby, M., and Askins, K. (2011). Geographies of impact: power, participation and potential. *Area* 43(2): 183–188.

Shore, C. (2010). Beyond the multiversity: neoliberalism and the rise of the schizophrenic university. *Social Anthropology* 18(1): 15–29.

Slater, T. (2012). Impacted geographers: a response to Pain, Kesby and Askins. *Area* 44(1), 117–119.

Stern, N. (2016) *Building on Success and Learning from Experience: An Independent Review of the Research Excellence Framework*. Available from: www.bisa.ac.uk/files/Consultations/ind-16-9-ref-stern-review.pdf (accessed 21/11/2017).

REFLECTION

Collaborative work of early career researchers: How the impact agenda transcends across contexts

Anna Mary Cooper-Ryan, Alex M. Clarke-Cornwell and Jenna Condie

In this reflection, we draw upon our experiences of being early career researchers (ECRs) who work together across countries (UK and Australia) in the context of both constraints and autonomies such as time, funding, and varying levels of encouragement from our institutional systems, which frame and measure our 'success' as researchers. We should note that we (the authors) met as PhD students at the same university and joined the same department for our first academic positions. While we all remain within academia, one of us (Jenna) now works in Australia, and two of us (Anna and Alex) remain working in the UK (at least for the time being!). We are still considered ECRs in each of the countries (where definitions are not standardised). Through email, Skype, and occasional visits, we jump time zones to figure out how to be academics and how to be the kind of academics we want to be, as well as the kind we are expected to be. The strength of our postgraduate foundations and friendships established during that time, when we indeed had the time to build our relationships, have influenced how we have moved from working together in the UK to a continued international collaboration.

The aim of this reflection is to explore the impact (i.e. the contribution that our research (and teaching) has on society, and also within our own academic fields) of being ECRs navigating the current business and politics of academia, while doing scholarship in new ways that can often go unrecognised or unrewarded within traditional academic metrics (e.g. the Research Excellence Framework in the UK and Excellence in Research Australia). To illustrate our balancing acts in academic practice, we examine our collaborative work across two continents with examples of projects we have worked on together.

Learning to juggle academic requirements: Balancing teaching and research

At the start of an academic career, there is an onslaught of acronyms, agendas and expectations that ECRs need to manage. There is also a realisation that the business of academia is to publish, to have impact, and to generate income: this can create a tension between teaching duties and scholarly ambitions as researchers (Cadez, Dimovski & Zaman Groff, 2017). In the increasingly competitive global marketplace of academia, published research is one key measure of academic impact (Carpenter, Cone & Sarli, 2014); it is regularly assessed through personal development reviews, research evaluation assessments such as Excellence in Research Australia (Australian Research Council, 2017) and the Research Excellence Framework in the UK (REF2021, 2017), workload allocation systems, as well as 'presence' and 'reach' on professional and academic social networking platforms (i.e. LinkedIn, ResearchGate, Google Scholar). To firmly place a foothold on the academic career ladder and successfully progress into an independent researcher with a clear, strategic research agenda, ECRs have to contend with an increasingly individualistic culture of competition (Bazeley, 2003; Laudel & Gläser, 2008).

Our question as ECRs is whether this 'business' of academia is helping us to flourish and succeed. The growing complexities of academia and the role and support for ECRs can vary depending on individual pressures (i.e. research, teaching and administration loads); given this, we explore whether universities are able to provide the supportive environment needed for ECRs to succeed. Each academic year, we find ourselves working towards our metric requirements, but also trying to maintain and grow our international collaborations and joint publications in the contexts of significant responsibilities (both internal and external, e.g. module evaluations and the UK's emerging Teaching Excellence Framework) linked to teaching and learning. For the three of us there is no doubt that the fact we are collaborating between two countries that often have similar policies and education systems has supported our ability to work together. It's easier due to Australian-UK links and similarities in systems but perhaps this ease is not present for others from non-western countries, and more creative methods and approaches may be needed. Within academia and higher education there is an increasing amount of our work that is measured (i.e. publications, income, teaching quality), ranked and monitored; a reflection of the growing marketisation and privatisation of higher education, the desire to rank academics and institutions externally but also changes to the political agenda and what constitutes impact (Peseta, Barrie & McLean, 2017). However, as ECRs we also need to ensure we are not afraid to push boundaries and look at new ways of working that may be more to the intended output (e.g. a blog, an exhibition or a podcast) rather than feeling we need to stick to traditional outputs measured by more traditional metrics.

In recent times, academics have been required to work digitally to collaborate beyond geographical boundaries, which is likely beneficial to many ECRs whose work resonates at international levels. We feel cross-country work should be both encouraged and recognised as an important aspect of an ECR's development and potential. Across academia, there is a growing recognition that the 24/7, easy access culture of communication helps promote and disseminate research activity (Nicholas et al., 2017). The plethora of digital platforms available to academics supports collaboration between ECRs regardless of place and time (e.g. this reflection was written initially on Google Docs and has since gone back and forth via email and Facebook Messenger, and no doubt will be shared on Twitter and Academia.edu when it is published). We argue that traditional measures of success, such as citation-based metrics, align to more established, less digitally mediated ways of working; while the development of alternative metrics (i.e. Altmetrics and PlumX) that measure social media engagement are more likely to be embraced by digitally literate ECRs (Weller, 2015). With a growing recognition of the impact of digital scholarship on academic practices, the impact and measurement agenda needs to better capture less traditional and more collegiate outputs and participatory networked practices.

Doing work that 'doesn't count' (but actually does): ECRs performing new ways of scholarship

Working collaboratively across countries is beneficial for us in terms of fostering innovative and creative ideas, sharing knowledge, building and maintaining our international profiles, and deepening our understandings of the role of research in international policy contexts. We think, write, produce and apply for funding together, which all takes time, effort and commitment to one another's work and wellbeing. So far, the products of our labour that 'count' in terms of traditional metrics of research success are through publishing journal articles. Our collaborations on outputs that do not 'count' in traditional metrics go beyond the traditional boundaries of peer-reviewed publications but have impact in other ways and lead to more projects. For example, commissioned reports gain local impact and web-based research outputs gain digital impact.

To give a more specific example, in 2015, we crowdsourced, produced and self-published a 'Book of Blogs' on sustainable urbanisation and the transitions towards living in urban contexts (Condie & Cooper, 2015). We each submitted chapters about our research (Condie, 2015; Cooper & Clarke-Cornwell, 2015), which contributed to a large chapter collection of work from a diverse range of scholars from across the globe with varied employment status (students, casual and tenured academics, independent researchers). Overall there were 70 chapter collections of work from 83 authors located in the UK and Europe, North America and Canada, New Zealand, Pakistan, Mexico, South Africa, Nigeria, India, the Philippines, Israel, Brazil, Australia, China, and Taiwan. We did not set out to ensure equality of authors in terms of gender or career attainment, but we also chose not to refer to authors by their titles, thus removing any hierarchical preconceptions this may have for readers. We gained a significant number of contributions from women, ECRs and post-graduate researchers, perhaps due to the accessibility of the type of publication or the inclusive nature of the call for contributions via social media (Cooper & Condie, 2016).

The 'Book of Blogs' has a wide potential reach and promoted author inclusivity, mitigating in some ways the fact that the project would not be counted as substantive academic output using traditional research metrics (e.g. research excellence, citation rates, impact). However, those traditional academic metrics do not capture the digital impact and international reach of this piece of work. Collaborating on the 'Book of Blogs' represents one of our most meaningful academic contributions and epitomises the kind of researchers we want to be –collegiate, inclusive, networked and open (Cooper & Condie, 2016). This project is freely available online but not indexed on formal systems such as Scopus and Web of Science; in turn, the time, effort and respect gained from this project is not captured in our workloads and assessment of our research impact. It is difficult to strike the balance between doing work that matters to you as an academic and doing work that 'counts' for your job. We also recognise that we are speaking from the perspective of ECRs in tenure-track positions and acknowledge the security that this provides us to work on non-traditional and unconventional projects and publications. The 'Book of Blogs' exists: it is a tangible output, available online and open access. If as academics we consider the concept of impact in a similar way to that of 'evidence' (as 'socially constructed, i.e. what counts as evidence, rules and criteria for assessing evidence and whether evidence is valued at all are negotiated phenomena' Rychetnik & Wise, 2004, p. 248), metrics could adapt to new ways of working to allow us to engage in the participatory networked practices that digitalisation affords to ensure our efforts 'count'.

Through more inclusive digital scholarship (e.g. books of blogs), we can seek to readdress Western dominance within scholarly outputs and what could be seen as a global system of knowledge inequality. By contributing to more democratic outputs and processes, ECRs can support participatory / emancipatory methods, gain impact in terms of collaborations and reach but also challenge the gendered practices of knowing and doing that are privileged by the current system of impact. With a growing number of platforms supporting the production of crowdsourced publications, ECRs should continue to push boundaries of the topics being covered and published in a collective manner.

All we need is time: Institutional support for ECRs

There is an abundance of literature examining the role of the institution in managing and supporting ECR scholarship (Gordon, 2005; Laudel & Gläser, 2008; Hemmings, 2012). Within this literature, there is an emergent consensus as to what constitutes good practice (e.g. Mann et al., 2007; Rayner, 2016) but a plethora of institutional challenges are also documented. A large cross-institutional project undertaken by the Universities and Colleges Employers Association (UCEA) of the UK, the European Federation of Education Employers (EFEE) and the European Trade Union Committee for Education (ETUCE) (2015) identified a number of challenges ECRs face such as the increased use of fixed-term contracts, the prevalence of job insecurity, high workloads, unrealistic ECR expectations, poor or absent mentoring programmes, and unclear line management. The report recommends improving line management, addressing barriers to progression for women ECRs and improving the status and recognition of ECRs within the workplace.

Funding councils and research metrics often have sections that refer to ECRs, which include definitions of who and what constitutes an ECR (e.g. REF), but a more supportive approach is often taken by universities and departments. For example, Locke, Freeman & Rose (2018) reported a number of inconsistencies in relation to the definition of an ECR both in the literature and in practice. They found that the definitions of an ECR went up to 10 years post doctorate (range 5–10 years). One of the authors (Anna) is currently the co-chair of an ECR group as part of one of the university research centres. This group takes a very open view of who constitutes an ECR and invites people who self-identify as being at the start of their research journey, and those coming back to research after time out of academia or coming to research from more teaching-focused roles. Furthermore, an ECR is not defined by a doctorate. The decision to be inclusive and not ask people to articulate why they are an ECR allows the group to support both academic and contract staff, and particularly women who have had a career break or disruption. In this sense, the group not only creates space for support but it also helps highlight the work and needs of ECRs within the wider research environment.

Tightly definitional boundaries around ECR status can be restrictive and problematic, where being outside a specific time period post-PhD or not yet having a PhD can impact on where people are seen to fit or feel they fit within academia. It could also lead to challenges accessing resources targeting ECRs (e.g. funding, mentoring, or time for professional and research development within workloads). A number of models have been produced that seek to demonstrate the variety and diversity within ECR journeys. For example, Lauder & Gläser (2008) outlined three aspects of ECR academic careers, and how particular variables can impact the career transition: organisational career (e.g. scholarship and contract types; variables – time, autonomy and expectations); cognitive career (e.g. PhD project and subsequent projects; variables – collaborators, breadth and continuity); and community career (e.g. mentored and independent contribution to knowledge; variables – publications, plans and citations).

There are a number of push and pull factors that shape the relationship between institution and ECR as academics, and how they transition from early career to established researchers and academics. All three of the authors in this reflection have a number of leadership roles and mentoring related activities, but still themselves seek out and use mentors and leaders to support their development. This symbiotic relationship works both ways in that mentors can learn as much as mentees do: ECRs often push the boundaries in terms of research, publications and practices with more experienced staff helping guide them in line with the traditional academic models of metrics and measurements. Sometimes those mentors and leaders are not from our own academic institutions, nor indeed working in the same country. This collegiate, cross-university, cross-country work is important and deserves formal recognition and support.

Conclusion

We argue that collaborating (international, nationally and within your institution) with other ECRs can help with progression (e.g. as an important metric for CVs and promotions) and support (particularly women ECRs), through the collegiality of working with others at a similar career point (e.g. in terms of being in similar research spaces and levels of collaborate working). Each of us have benefited from strong mentors who have taken on a number of roles as we have needed them, supporting us to progress by creating the space for us to pursue our interests and secure permanent work. However, despite this support we cannot escape the growing academic requirements and pressures on our time. The transition from PhD student to ECR is a big learning curve, which is hard, at times frustrating, and we are still figuring out what we are expected to do. Finding support from ECRs, mentors and leads in a department can be crucial to ensure you make the most of being an ECR.

Throughout this reflection we have tried to reflect on how academia can help us to build impact and succeed as ECRs by considering support through collaboration, the impact of digital scholarship alongside traditional metrics, and our representation in terms of equality and diversity. We propose that ECR culture in higher education institutions needs to change direction, not only to foster research impact, but also to make a real impact on the lives of ECRs. Could this be through encouraging representation via ECR networks, providing access to mentors and role-models and making realistic expectations for research output? For us in the present, being a collective of ECR women working together at an international level enables us to grow together, locate our research at different scales (e.g. local, global), and apply for funding that fosters our international research endeavours (albeit with no success at this point). Our comfort with one another also enables us to take risks and do work that does not easily fit within the current standards of measuring academic success. Going forward we suggest that:

- ECRs should be encouraged to carry out scholarship in new ways alongside traditional outputs. This is likely to improve impact using traditional metrics through increased opportunity to collaborate by developing relationships (nationally and internationally) and through developing communication skills for more diverse audiences.
- Although there is a need to balance teaching and research workloads, ECRs should also be given the time to foster and continue collaboration that embraces digital methods of working and publishing. Impact can be more than just metrics, and the use of alternative metrics may change how we recognise scholarship.
- Universities and staff that work closely with ECRs need to reflect upon how they support them. This could be by allowing time for development in teaching and research, as well as considering how to recognise the impact of less traditional scholarship activity.

- The journey into academia and the continuing path for women ECRs can take a number of routes and interruptions. With greater acknowledgement of the impact of gender and other social markers of difference, ECRs are more likely to thrive for a better future of academia.

References

Australian Research Council (2017). *Excellence in research for Australia*. Australian Government: Australian Research Council. [Viewed 24 August 2018]. Available from: www.arc. gov.au/excellence-research-australia

Bazeley, P. (2003). Defining 'early career' in research. *Higher Education*. 45(3), 257–279.

Cadez, S., Dimovski, V. and Zaman Groff, M. (2017). Research, teaching and performance evaluation in academia: the salience of quality. *Studies in Higher Education*. 42(8), 1455–1473.

Carpenter, C.R., Cone, D.C., and Sarli, C.C. (2014). Using publication metrics to highlight academic productivity and research impact. *Academic Emergency Medicine*. 21(10), 1160–1172.

Condie, J.M. (2015). Social media for social housing in the UK and Australia. In: J. Condie, and A.M. Cooper, eds., *Dialogues of Sustainable Urbanisation: Social Science Research and Transitions to Urban Contexts*, pp. 310–313. [Viewed 24 August 2018]. Available from http s://researchdirect.westernsydney.edu.au/islandora/object/uws:30908

Condie, J.M. and Cooper, A.M. (2015). *Dialogues of sustainable urbanisation: social science research and transitions to urban contexts*. Sydney: University of Western Sydney. Available from: https://isscbookofblogs.pressbooks.com/

Cooper, A.M., & Clarke-Cornwell, A.M. (2015). The built environment, active design and public health: the impact of office design on activity. In: J. Condie, & A.M. Cooper, eds., *Dialogues of sustainable urbanisation: social science research and transitions to urban contexts*. pp. 148–152. [Viewed 24 August 2018]. Available from: https://researchdirect.wester nsydney.edu.au/islandora/object/uws:30908

Cooper, A.M. and Condie, J. (2016). Bakhtin, digital scholarship and new publishing practices as carnival. *Journal of Applied Social Theory*. 1(1), 26–43.

Gordon, G. (2005). The human dimensions of the research agenda: supporting the development of researchers throughout the career life cycle. *Higher Education Quarterly*. 59(1), 40–55.

Hemmings, B. (2012). Sources of research confidence for early career academics: a qualitative study. *Higher Education Research & Development*. 31(2), 171–184.

Laudel, G. and Gläser, J. (2008). From apprentice to colleague: The metamorphosis of early career researchers. *Higher Education*. 55(3), 387–406.

Locke, W., Freeman, R. and Rose, A. (2018). *Early career social science researchers: experiences and support needs*. London: Centre for Global Higher Education. [Viewed 24 August 2018]. Available from: www.researchcghe.org/perch/resources/publications/ecrreport-1.pdf

Mann, K., Moyle, K., Reupert, A., Wilkinson, J. and Woolley, G. (2007). When two universities meet: fostering research capacity among early career researchers. Paper presented at the AARE Focus Conference, Canberra, 13–14 June. Available from: www.aare.edu. au/data/publications/2007/man0713x.pdf

Nicholas, D.*et al.* (2017). Early career researchers and their publishing and authorship practices. *Learned Publishing*. 30(3), 205–217.

Peseta, T., Barrie, S. and McLean, J. (2017). Academic life in the measured university: pleasures, paradoxes and politics. *Higher Education Research & Development*. 36(3), 453–457.

Rayner, M. (2016). The journey from interested spectator to active researcher: a practice-based case study on the development and support of early career researchers at the University of the Highlands and Islands. *Education in the North.* 23(2), 98–127.

Research Excellence Framework 2021 (2017). *Research excellence framework.* REF2021. [Viewed 24 August 2018]. Available from: www.ref.ac.uk/

Rychetnik, L. and Wise, M. (2004). Advocating evidence-based health promotion: reflections and a way forward. *Health Promotion International.* 19(2), 247–257.

Universities and Colleges Employers Association (UCEA) of the UK, the European Federation of Education Employers (EFEE), and the European Trade Union Committee for Education (ETUCE) (2015). *Supporting early career researchers in higher education in Europe: the role of employers and trade unions (final report).* [Viewed 24 August 2018]. Available from: www.ucea. ac.uk/download.cfm/docid/28D087A3-D55F-4CAA-94AD22E3CAC68E08

Weller, K. (2015). Social media and altmetrics: an overview of current alternative approaches to measuring scholarly impact. In: I.M. Welpe, J. Wollersheim, S. Ringelhan, M. Osterloh, eds., *Incentives and Performance.* pp. 261–276. [Viewed 24 August 2018]. Available from: http s://link.springer.com/chapter/10.1007/978-3-319-09785-5_16

PART III

Research impact systems and structures

7

PROPELLED FOR TAKE-OFF?

The case of early career social science researchers in South Africa

Ke Yu, Ian Edelstein and Balungile Shandu

This chapter explores the extent to which doctoral programmes in the social sciences in South Africa propel their graduates to make an impact. Through the lens of *capability, motivation* and *opportunity* (Michie et al. 2011), we examine how selected doctoral programmes in South Africa conceptualise and articulate impact and survey the perspectives of ECRs. We find that doctoral programmes in South Africa tend to narrowly focus on the academic pursuit of thesis completion and knowledge advancement, with little direct reference to or support for impact. However, our ECR participants demonstrate a wider range of objectives and ambitions for their research and this includes social impact. Our research highlights the need for government policy, higher education institutions, and also doctoral supervisors to pay greater attention to the interests (*motivation*) already exhibited by ECRs and to nurture this interest more deliberately and effectively to better support the latter's professional development.

Introduction

There has been a surge of interest in research impact in recent decades, especially in research evaluation. Although definitions and understandings of research impact vary, numerous funding and research evaluation bodies have incorporated impact elements into their research assessment frameworks. The UK's Research Excellence Framework (REF) has included an impact component since 2014. In Australia, Excellence in Research for Australia (ERA) piloted an engagement and impact component in 2017 and expects to incorporate this as part of its nationwide research assessment exercise.

Research impact is often discussed in relation to the global shift towards a managerial and audit culture and resultant increased pressure to demonstrate 'the value of science for society' (Martin 2011, cited in Bornmann 2012, p. 674), as opposed to the earlier paradigm of automatic trust in the intrinsic value of research warranting public funding. This has resulted in increased demand for accountability, particularly from entities and activities supported through public funding (Federation for the Humanities and Social Sciences 2014). The interest in research impact is also considered in conjunction with the shift of knowledge production models: from Mode 1, characterised by disciplinary boundaries and scientific criteria, to Mode 2, which is more oriented towards collaboration, user relevance and values (Bornmann 2012).

The importance of research impact is also evident in emerging approaches to research training, particularly doctoral training. For ECRs who are generally regarded as novices both within the academic hierarchy and beyond academia, and who often need to be inducted into the world of work from 'their abstract theoretically oriented training' (Samuel 2016, p. 14), we, the authors, argue that doctoral training on research impact can influence the understanding, expectations and capabilities of doctoral researchers more broadly. In this chapter, we examine the aims and designs of current doctoral programmes in South Africa to determine how they shape ECRs' perspectives on research impact.

Our interest in and approach to this topic are informed by the major deficiencies Wolhuter (2011) identifies in the literature on doctoral education, both internationally and in South Africa. According to Wolhuter, there is 'the lack of any empirical validation of the claimed social rates of return to doctoral education, an absence of the empirical reach or scholarly contribution / impact of doctoral education, and the inadequacies of the paradigms employed to research doctoral education' (p. 126). Our aim here is to provide empirical evidence on how selected doctoral programmes in South Africa conceptualise and articulate impact and how ECRs in South Africa perceive and understand research impact. Our primary interest lies in the social sciences, where a societal link is implied in the name of this broad discipline, but is, in reality, often less straightforward, especially in comparison to the natural sciences. While basic research in the natural sciences can struggle to demonstrate relevance and direct utility compared to more applied research fields such as IT, engineering, innovation and technology (Salter & Martin 2001), we argue that the lack of concrete products and fuzzier research utilisation patterns (often more conceptual rather than instrumental (Weiss 1980)) does contribute to greater difficulties in evidencing impact from the social sciences disciplines.

The central question guiding our investigation is how do doctoral programmes in the social sciences in South Africa prepare their graduates to make an impact? This chapter first presents an overview of the various aims and purposes of the doctoral training in South Africa and internationally, then explores the different training models to achieve these aims and purposes. It then explains the theoretical framework that informed our focus and approach. This is followed by a brief outline of the South African context and the methodology used to obtain our data. The main body of the chapter is devoted to an analysis of *impact*, as articulated by the selected programmes and the perspectives of recent doctoral graduates, as well as through a comparison between the two. The chapter concludes with a summary of our main findings.

The various aims / purposes of the doctorates

Traditionally, doctoral training was aimed at producing 'the next generation of academics' (Samuel 2016, p. 3) to be absorbed back into academia to train future academics, forming a virtuous circle of knowledge production (Enders 2002; Samuel 2016). However, amid the recent economic downturn and resulting pressure on accountability of public funds (university funding included), the notion that doctoral training needs to be 'more relevant for [a] broader variety of other careers outside higher education' (Enders 2002, p. 494) has gained momentum. This trend is uneven among countries: for example, in South Africa the majority (57%) of social sciences doctoral graduates are employed within higher education (ASSAf 2010), whereas in Germany, 60% are employed outside of higher education (Enders 2002). In the UK, a 2005 report on social science doctoral graduates' employment (Purcell et al. 2005) states that 'between a third and half... obtain employment in other sectors' (p. 1). More recent UK data (Vitae 2013) indicate that 58% of social sciences doctoral graduates are employed in higher education (14% in research, 44% in teaching), higher than the average HE employment ratio among doctoral graduates across all disciplines (38% overall, comprising 17% in research and 21% in teaching).

It is important to note that in South Africa many doctoral candidates study part time while working; over 50% do so (ASSAf 2010). While the percentage of those studying and working part time in the UK is smaller, there has been a notable increase in recent years with 11.9% studying part time in 2008 compared to 14.8% in 2010 (Vitae 2013).

With the belief that a highly educated labour force directly contributes to the growth of a knowledge-based economy, discourse on the economic – and, more recently, social – value of doctoral training has emerged (Scott et al. 2004). As university degrees increasingly become 'a commodity to be bargained in the marketplace' (Samuel 2016, p. 4), both potential employers and many graduates themselves have begun to expect that 'a doctorate might be more about generating the appropriate visa into the world of work rather than into challenging the normative existing body of knowledge' (Samuel 2016, p. 3). Considering the German experience, Enders concludes that 'direct links...between doctoral training and employment in public service and the professions were viewed as normal, whereas links to the private economy – apart from R&D and leadership positions – or to the informal sector are viewed as alien' (2002, p. 496). However, 'the increasing complexification of the workplace, the rapid expansion of technological interventions to support practice, and the rapidly changing and expanding knowledge environment' (Samuel 2016, p. 14) have driven the growth of the doctorate and its expected contribution to the economy.

In addition to responding to employment needs outside of academia, scholars have also begun to question the social relevance and potential of a doctoral degree. Again, this interest in social relevance is not new. During the medieval period, the earliest university education 'was largely "considered to be socially useful" with the "twelfth-century committed scholar [pursuing his research] within the exciting and expanding orbit of urban life". It was the Humboldt reforms of the nineteenth century leading to the development of the modern PhD that promoted "a search for a form of universal truth that set [universities] apart from society'" (Wildy et al. 2015, p. 764). As the Humboldt model is the foundation of the modern PhD, its emphasis on the separation of academia from social relevance is notable and influential in how many PhD programmes have since been conceptualised.

In South Africa, the potential of doctoral training, in terms of 'both working towards realising the capacities and capabilities of the wider society system' (Samuel 2016, p. 6), has also been raised as a potential antidote to the social woes and developmental challenges the country faces. Doctoral and masters programmes are seen as 'a way of educating scientific and technical innovators…[who can] bring innovative changes to their workplaces' (ASSAf 2010, p. 36), pioneering novel ideas and generating scientific and social innovations, as well as providing leadership and responsiveness to contextualised social challenges. Writing specifically on the value and purpose of a PhD, Samuel asks whether doctoral education in South Africa has been 'geared to embrace these social issues' (2016, p. 6), and whether the doctoral graduates have emerged 'with responsiveness to contexts that are appropriate, relevant and feasible to offset our crimes of humanity [referring to apartheid]' (2016, p. 6).

Doctorate training models

Since the 1990s, the topic of doctoral training has sparked great interest around the globe. Foci of these discussions include: how to increase the number of graduates (Louw & Muller 2014); how to increase completion / throughput rates (Hockey 1995; McWilliam et al. 2002, cited in Wildy et al. 2015); how to better match the skills required in the workplace (Louw & Muller 2014); and the aims and effectiveness of the various training models. Due to the features of doctoral training in South Africa as well as our sampling limitations (explained in the next section), we focus primarily on the traditional apprenticeship model of doctoral education. The professional and cohort models are also briefly discussed for their potential relevance.

The apprenticeship model is rooted in the 19th century Humboldt model that privileged disciplinary knowledge progression and research as the main means of knowledge production over professional training. It aims at advancing knowledge and developing theoretical insight and abstract knowledge, often requiring the doctoral candidate to produce a fairly substantial thesis under the guidance of a supervisor within an apprenticeship-type arrangement. This training is elite in nature (Louw & Muller 2014) and this elitism may have led to inefficiencies with the arrival of increased doctorate enrolment and the overall massification of higher education. In South Africa, although massification of higher education remains more aspiration than reality, the colonial influence, particularly from the UK, remains evident in the higher learning establishment and tradition. This includes early specialisation and the dominance of the traditional models in South African universities.

According to an influential consensus study from the country's science advisory body (ASSAf 2010), the production of doctoral graduates in South Africa is still on an upward trajectory. However, 'demands for satisfactory performance coupled with increased productivity [to efficiently produce more doctoral graduates], as well as an effective reduction in staff numbers because of the economic downturn, have made the traditional model increasingly unsustainable' (Louw & Muller 2014, p. 19). This shift has, arguably, sparked interest, both in policy and academic circles, to discuss and experiment with alternative models.

First appearing in the 1980s (Scott et al. 2004), the professional doctorate has emerged as the strongest contender to the traditional model (Wildy et al. 2015). It is seen as better aligned to the needs of the modern workplace, particularly as a form of professional development, therefore more economically and socially relevant. The doctoral topics often centre on professional, practice-related, and other applied issues. The thesis is usually shorter. In recent years, the cohort model has also emerged to supplement the traditional model of doctoral study and is sometimes used in conjunction with the professional doctorate. The cohort model is group-based, often in terms of candidate intake and the incorporation of group training components. A thesis typically remains the sole requirement / output of the degree. It is relatively new to the social sciences and seeks to encourage a collaborative spirit aligned with Mode 2 knowledge co-production, shifting away from the traditional, individualistic nature of social sciences research.

The South African context

Since 2010, doctoral graduation in South Africa has seen relative growth in the natural sciences and humanities (close to 40% in 2014 / 2015) and a relative decline in the social sciences (to just below 30%, see Figure 7.1). South African doctoral graduates in the social sciences are approximately 45 years of age after spending an average of five years as doctoral candidates.

The fact that over half of South Africa's doctoral candidates study part time, and that two thirds of these part time candidates stay with their employers after graduation, can theoretically lead to the assumption 'that an employed person pursuing a doctoral degree would have some level of expectation that such a qualification would have an impact on their working environment' (ASSAf 2010, p. 72). However, a large number of these part time students are actually lecturers already employed in universities, therefore, their employment is not in professions beyond academia. In addition, 45% of those who were not working during their studies went on to university employment, with only 17% of graduates migrating to other employment sectors (ASSAf 2010). Among those who migrate out of academic employment, most 'felt that their doctoral qualification was still better suited to a career in higher education' (ASSAf 2010, p. 89). The proportion of those employed in academia is higher in the social sciences than in other disciplines (53% average across all disciplines). Of these social sciences doctoral graduates, 51% claim their qualification has helped considerably or was crucial to obtain their current job, and 72% use the skills obtained in the training very frequently.

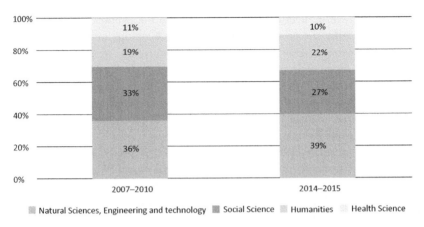

FIGURE 7.1 Percentage of South African doctoral graduates by the different disciplines
Source: Calculated from ASSAf 2010 and 2014 / 2015 HEMIS data (CHET 2012)

Both PhDs and professional doctorates are recognised in official higher education legislation in South Africa. However, because of the historic influence from
the UK, a division between vocational and academic oriented institutions, and
prejudicial privilege for the PhD (Samuel 2016), the PhD and its associated traditional apprenticeship model still prevail in South Africa. Similarly, although training
for an academic career and profession outside of academia are both recognised as
purposes of doctoral training (ASSAf 2010), the doctorate as training for academia
remains the dominant paradigm, particularly within the social sciences (Louw &
Godsell 2015).

The ASSAf report recognises the limitations of the traditional doctoral model, both in
terms of its efficiency and also in terms of the growing 'demand from users of research
for integrated learning and skill development to serve a wider range of workforce needs'
(ASSAf 2010, p. 40). However, most social sciences departments remain interested only
in 'strengthening or improving that process [of the traditional model]… [while] moving
toward coursework of some kind' (Louw & Godsell 2015, p. 137), instead of exploring
alternative models more explicitly. Overall, the professional doctorate is resisted, rejected, and, ultimately, rarely implemented in South African universities.

Methodology

For this study, the disciplines of sociology and education were identified as those
producing the greatest number of doctoral graduates in the social sciences in South
Africa, according to the latest available HEMIS data for 2015 (CHET 2012). An
additional consideration in the selection of disciplines was the variance between
more profession- / policy-oriented and more academic-oriented disciplines with
regard to their potential consideration of non-academic impact.

As doctorate production in South Africa is highly skewed (the top nine universities in South Africa produced 80% of all doctorate graduates in 2015, (ASSAf 2010)), we ranked relevant universities according to their numbers of doctoral graduates. South Africa has three types of universities: traditional universities (often research oriented: 15 in total); universities of technology (formerly technikons: 6 in total), and comprehensive universities (often a merger of the two: 4 in total). One comprehensive university is dedicated to distance learning (and often produces more graduates than any other individual university). In turn, we ranked according to these three types. We found that traditional universities and, to some extent, comprehensive universities dominate the production of doctoral graduates, while technical universities produce far fewer doctoral graduates. We then selected, for each discipline, the top three from among the traditional universities, between one and three from the top comprehensive universities, and one from the universities of technology. When our first priority institutions could not be reached or failed to respond, we moved on to the next in the ranking.

We considered the variation of PhD vs. professional doctorate, but found that for sociology, all traditional and comprehensive universities only offer a PhD degree or PhD equivalent (DPhil or DLitt et Phil). None of the universities of technology offer sociology doctoral programmes. For education, all traditional universities only offer the PhD, the top two comprehensive universities primarily offer the PhD, along with a DEd in education psychology. The top university of technology only offers the DEd, although its administration indicated that it is considering offering the PhD as well.

To review the aims and purposes of the doctoral programmes as well as the training and additional support offered by each university, we first reviewed web pages and public documents for each university / discipline combination, then made contact with the programme administrators to request further details. We also requested a list of recent doctoral graduates (from 2013–2017) to support our qualitative research. In addition to the graduate lists obtained from some universities, we also searched for graduation records online, through university websites (e.g. published graduation lists, or through academic staff contacts) and the online platform LinkedIn.

Historically, white students have accounted for a disproportionate share of the doctoral graduates in South Africa. However, this has changed over the years, with a substantial increase in Africans from other African countries who enrol and graduate from South African universities (see Figure 7.2).

One alleged reason for the comparatively low level of doctoral enrolment by Black South Africans is that educated / skilled Black South Africans are in high demand in the labour market and many are absorbed into industry, government or other sectors before they reach doctoral level as a result of South Africa's redress policies. Due to these considerations, we purposively sampled White South Africans, Black / Coloured / Indian South Africans, Africans from other African countries, and others from outside the continent.

For all successful leads, we contacted these recent graduates by email or phone to proceed with informed consent and a questionnaire through either email attachment or an online survey link. The research protocol was approved by the Human Sciences

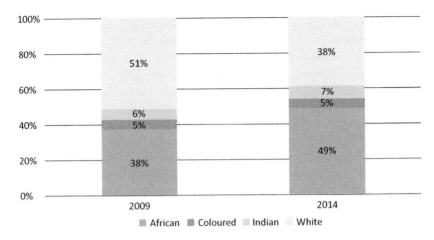

FIGURE 7.2 Racial profiling of doctoral graduates in South Africa
Source: Calculated from Council for Higher Education Vital Stats (Council for Higher Education 2014)

Research Council Research Ethics Committee. Altogether, 20 respondents completed the questionnaire. Tables 7.1 and 7.2 show the universities and sub-discipline combination included in our sampling as well as the demographic profile of participants.

The responses were analysed thematically through content analysis. We substantiated our investigation mainly through the lenses of *capacity*, *opportunity* and *motivation* (Michie et al. 2011). More specifically, in terms of *capacity* and

TABLE 7.1 Sample universities and sub-discipline combination

	Sociology	*Education*
Traditional	University of Kwa-Zulu Natal (UKZN)	UKZN / University of the Free State (UFS. Note: Our original choice was UKZN, but the respondents we accessed were not recent graduates. Further searches through LinkedIn led to one respondent from UFS.)
	University of the Witwatersrand (Wits)	University of Pretoria (UP)
	University of Cape Town (UCT)	UCT
Comprehensive	University of South Africa (Unisa)	Unisa
	University of Johannesburg (UJ)	UJ
	Nelson Mandela University (NMU)	
University of technology	None	Tshwane University of Technology (TUT)

TABLE 7.2 Demographic profile of participants

		Sociology	*Education*
Racial distribution	White South African	2	3
	Black / Coloured / Indian South African	5	4
	From other African countries	1	2
	Other	2	1
Gender distribution	Female	5	5
	Male	4	5
	Chose not to identify	1	
Current employment	Academia (universities, research organisations, including post-docs), both on permanent and contract base	7	9
	Outside academia (industry, government, NGO...)	1	
	Others	2	1
Age profile	Below 30	1	
	31–40	3	5
	41–50	3	3
	51–60	2	2
	Above 61	1	
University profile	Traditional university	8	6
	Comprehensive university	2	2
	University of technology	0	2
Degree	PhD	10	7
	Professional doctorate		3
Total		10	10

opportunity, we examined the doctoral training models and structure, funding and other opportunities offered / accessed; for *motivation*, we examined aims and objectives of the doctoral programmes as well as the reasons why early career researchers (ECRs) apply / enrol for the degree.

Select quotations were identified that exemplified frequent or illuminating responses. In some cases, the absence of data (on programmes, or expected responses from participants) also became a subject of analysis.

Results

Impact as outlined in doctoral programmes

Sociology doctoral programmes in South Africa all require completion of a thesis with the general aim that it 'shall make a distinct contribution to the knowledge or understanding of the subject and afford evidence of originality shown either by the discovery of new facts and / or by the exercise of independent critical power' (UKZN, n.d.). This is applicable to all departments in the humanities faculty, sociology included. The statement from a comprehensive university (University of Johannesburg 2017) is similar: 'On completion of their research, students must submit both a thesis that makes an original contribution to their subject and an academic article that is ready for publication. Finally, candidates must sit in an oral exam [oral defence of the thesis], where knowledge of their field will be tested'.

In terms of structure, these programmes are apprenticeship-based, many on an individual basis, although at University of Cape Town (UCT), there are additional platforms where 'students work in research groups led by one of the professors or lecturers in the department, or linked to research centres such as the Centre for Social Science Research' (University of Cape Town 2018). Some universities offer research-related workshops / seminars (e.g. how to complete a proposal or conduct data analysis) but attendance is voluntary (UKZN); others require certain compulsory elements (e.g. presentation at two seminars, UJ). UJ also promotes that doctoral candidates are expected to undertake the department's advanced course on social research methodology, while at UCT, students are referred to masters or honours courses if they lack certain skills. Some programmes require proof of academic article submission to a journal as part of the degree requirement (UKZN, UJ). Conference attendance is sometimes funded; support is sometimes coordinated through financial aid and scholarship offices (University of the Witwatersrand, Wits); others primarily depend on the resources of the student, supervisor, or project leaders (UKZN, UCT).

Many of the observations above are also applicable to education, despite its more applied orientation. The UCT guide for students and supervisors (Ng'ambi 2018) states that 'the aims and objectives of a PhD in education are to prepare students to become independent scholars in education. The evidence that this objective has been realised is in the preparing of a cohesive, substantial piece of original research that makes a new contribution to knowledge in the field of education'.

We find little difference between the DEd and PhD in terms of their stated aims: the 'objective [of a DEd] is for the candidates to demonstrate high level research competence and to make a significant and original contribution to the frontiers of education' (TUT, personal email). According to UJ which offers a DEd in education psychology, the main difference (according to the programme administrator) lies in the nature of the candidates, where the 'DEd is registered by candidates who hold an MEd in educational psychology and are mostly registered psychologists, and the PhD is registered by other candidates who hold an MEd in other fields' (personal email).

Most of the education doctoral programmes also follow the apprenticeship-based model. However, there have been experiments with variations of the traditional model: the UKZN education faculty has experimented with a collaborative cohort model since 1999 and produces the largest number of PhD education graduates in the country. The cohort structure employed by this faculty is varied and often rather elaborate: including cohorts targeting three different phases of study (proposal, fieldwork and analysis), cohorts grouped by disciplinary interests, or by supervisor. UJ, on the other hand, is waiting for approval to offer a coursework-based, professional DEd in educational psychology, intended to begin in 2019.

Research workshops or seminars are common in education: UJ offers seminars on research-related topics during the first six months while students prepare their proposals; University of Pretoria (UP) has 20 compulsory research support session days during the first year of doctoral study, primarily on quantitative and qualitative methodologies.

Overall, the official documents for the doctoral programmes make little direct mention of *research impact* as either an expected outcome or process. As discussed by other South African scholars and broadly aligned with the ASSAf report, these programmes usually follow the traditional model of apprenticeship-based training. They are often centred on one research project chosen by the doctoral candidate, with the thesis as the sole output and the subject of examination. In addition, the emphasis of the thesis is usually on making an original contribution to the advancement of knowledge.

ECRs' perspectives

Similar to ASSAF's (2010) finding on the reasons candidates pursue doctoral studies, our ECR respondents also cite natural progression (from the masters degree); career considerations (often an expectation or requirement for those already working in academia), and personal curiosity / interest as motivations to apply for the doctoral degree. These reasons are not mutually exclusive. However, practical considerations (career requirements, career advancement and availability of funding opportunities) appear to be more prevalent than knowledge-related objectives.

No significant change was detected when respondents were asked whether their outlook on the purpose of the doctorate changed after being awarded the degree. However, when asked about benefits derived from obtaining the degree, many answers swung back to practical / material benefits (employment, promotion), while several also mentioned the acquisition of skills, knowledge, and experience, as well as confidence, prestige (respect from others), and self-understanding (what one is, or is not, good at). It is also noteworthy that the knowledge objective, as a motivation to pursue the doctorate, was more frequently cited in our education sample than the sociology sample. However, education graduates were as likely (if not more) to defer to practical / material considerations when assessing the benefits of the degree.

All of our respondents were supervised using the apprenticeship model. Several discussed the role of their supervisors, but few beyond the common thesis completion-related aspects, including engagement on methodological issues, providing feedback on the thesis, and so on. Among those who did, some mentioned their supervisors' assistance in facilitating interaction with peers, recommending job opportunities, and one who 'regularly organised critical seminars with leading intellectuals in the field...and with others whom he felt would enhance my intellectual development'. However, one respondent described a supervisor who was unsupportive in mentorship and opposed her faculty appointment over the supervisor's choice.

Three participants (across both disciplines) claimed that they did not participate in any workshops or seminars. All other respondents identified participation in some form of research literacy-focused training or workshops, including on methodology, data analysis tools, how to write a proposal, how to use the library, how to conduct a literature review, how to make academic presentations, and writing skills. One UCT participant talked about a writers' circle run by the Centre for Higher Education Development at the university, which also covered 'how to navigate institutional red tape and writing job applications'. Another University of South Africa (Unisa) participant discussed attending a workshop on 'communication and the art of research' using creative media outputs (including opinion pieces in newspapers).

The majority of these training / workshops were organised by the department / faculty / university. There does not seem to be any systematic difference between types of universities or between the two disciplines, possibly because most training sessions were organised at university (and not faculty) level. The training / workshops were often not formalised and were 'structured but not formal or compulsory'. They varied in frequency, occurring weekly to quarterly to some with no set frequency. Some featured presentations from local, national and international scholars.

Additionally, some participants accessed training / workshops through their earlier academic courses (at honours or masters level). There were also opportunities organised by entities outside the universities. For example, three education participants from different universities (both PhD and DEd candidates) attended a winter school organised by The Southern African Association Dedicated to the Advancement of Research in Mathematics, Science and Technology Education (SAARMSTE). This annual three to four day gathering drew approximately 40–60 doctoral students 'at different stages of completion... from various participating universities', where participants 'shared research [with peers], getting input in all aspects of doing a PhD from experts in the field'. Another respondent also participated in several national meetings as 'part of the 20 PhD students, mainly in Maths and Science Education... [funded] by the Sasol Inzalo Foundation'. Self-organised support groups were also prevalent, particularly reading and writing groups. There were also post-graduate student fora; 'regular seminars and an annual symposium where students could present their work'; and 'study buddy' or email groups 'where we would drop questions, concept papers...and critique each other'. One Wits sociology participant described the 'Post-grad carrels' as central to her doctoral experience, 'we wrote there, read there, lots of tempers there, almost killed each other there, supported each other there. The CARRELS were EVERYTHING [original emphasis]'.

Most respondents felt that the training / workshops were valuable. They gained new knowledge, were supported in 'seeing things differently', learned about 'other areas of study or content' besides one's own discipline, gained 'new perspectives on literature, methodologies and ways of coming at data differently', and discussed, shared ideas and received feedback from their colleagues. Besides knowledge, they also gained emotional support, 'meeting fellow students who echoed [the] same challenges and problems and we would even assist each other in moving forward in our studies'. Many respondents, though, expressed their desire for more workshops that were more structured and that had a clearer direction. The only exception was one participant who thought 'the theoretical seminars were irrelevant for the diverse groups of interest and people who were pursuing their various degrees'.

Most participants reported positive interaction with their peers in the various platforms mentioned above. Participants also mentioned other informal opportunities 'over tea and lunch' or within shared offices. There was only one participant who reported few regular interactions with peers outside the department. Besides trainings / workshops, many of our participants also mentioned conference attendance, often with financial or motivational assistance from their research unit / department / faculty / university / supervisor, and sometimes through their employment as lecturers. Two participants used external funding opportunities attached to their doctoral projects to attend conferences and two used their own funds. Two participants mentioned funding opportunities from their respective universities for other study-related costs (e.g. language editing).

For many, the external opportunities were valuable for networking and 'helpful to understanding how my work fits in to broader academic debates and work'. Several others also sought networking opportunities with 'people from outside the university who attended our departmental and institute seminars'.

Our respondents' definitions of *research impact* first pointed to knowledge advancement with related academic criteria such as journal publications and citations. Some suggested the need to include other academic indicators such as conference presentations and working papers, because otherwise 'it locks our research into a small elite and has no mass appeal'. However, 'publishing is really tough [with high competition and rejection rates]' and 'other forms of communicating or creating impact are not incentivised or accounted for in research funding or grants' which led to diminished prioritisation of the latter. Two participants suggested that the topic of the doctorate could make a difference to achieving research impact and one specifically suggested that projects needed to be 'designed with the needs of people in mind, rather than arbitrary or highly theoretical projects with no real world application'. Four respondents primarily talked about their own growth and development as evidence of research impact.

Many participants, including older and younger graduates across both disciplines, also discussed non-academic impact extensively. Respondents offered their observations that 'social science doctorates in South Africa do not integrate enough experience / training focus on work that is not purely based in academia, particularly in communicating application or impact of the research' and that a 'PhD in

Education without non-academic impact is largely worthless'. Many pointed to the need to make their academic outputs available and accessible to non-academic audiences, including policy makers, the public, and also their research participants. Some also discussed modification of the academic outputs (e.g. into theatre and radio plays, op-eds, online publications), engagement through different platforms (e.g. public fora, radio shows, meeting with policy makers, Research Gate, etc.), as well as the role of networking with other influencers / esteemed scholars. In one example, a conference organiser had enthusiastically promoted one of the respondent's research. In another, an education participant identified the curriculum change in her current university department as a potential impact from her PhD. However, when asked about disseminating their doctoral theses, the most prevalent channels included: the universities' online repositories, conference / symposia presentations, and article / book publications. Some sent their theses / articles to colleagues, relevant organisations, research participants, or 'anyone who asked for it'. Although few engaged in direct and proactive engagement with non-academic audiences, one respondent (aged 51–55) made it her goal to write in a language accessible to non-academics and subsequently shared the research within the relevant industry, initiating a Facebook group and forum (currently with 17,000 members) where diverse contributors offer related news and opinions. She also used these platforms to 'share my research knowledge by posting and making comments to other groups'.

Overall, *research impact*, for our participants, lies in 'advances in knowledge / understanding / theory, profession, practice and methodology', 'making a difference in society', 'sparking meaningful conversations', 'making an impression, changing attitudes / mindsets about established ways of viewing the world and / or creating possibilities for change and transformation at both a personal and social level', and 'can be the foundation of policy-making, capacity development, can impact beliefs and attitudes among non-academics in a major way'. Research impact 'speaks to social relevance of research…it must add value to the world and the people it is researching.'

Two respondents specifically emphasised the quality of the research work and related recommendations [the message itself] as foundational to impact. However, many more participants pointed to engagement as the key to initiating impact. The trainings / workshops seem to have improved research quality, some said, but 'my doctoral training focused on *completing the thesis*—not on dissemination at all [original emphasis]', 'we were not taught how to present our research so that it is available to the public'. There was only one incident where the participant was encouraged by the media relations office at her university to write an opinion piece based on her PhD. This gap between what research can achieve and what it often does led one participant to suggest that 'the doctorate itself does not necessarily have an "impact" factor'. For another participant, upon completing the doctorate, he found that it 'was [only] the beginning'. 'Although the PhD itself did not bring about this change [improving science education, in another participant's case]', the impact lies in the *potential*.

Discussions and limitations

Similar to Neumann (2009) who finds that the structure of the traditional and professional doctorates is often indistinguishable, with the professional doctorate not necessarily exhibiting adequate involvement from the industries or professions themselves. We also did not detect notable differences between the professional doctorate and the PhD in terms of their aims, structures, or student experiences. However, because we primarily relied on the internet to search for and access our participants, our sample of professional doctorate holders and those employed outside of academia was extremely small. Therefore, we cannot draw firm conclusions on the differences. Nor did we detect notable differences of perspective on research impact across race or nationality, or between sociology and education, despite our expectations. We acknowledge the bias in our sample towards graduates from more prestigious institutions because of their larger doctorate production. We would not expect significant shifts in perspective on impact, however, although the discussion on interactions / collaboration might have differed if participants from the UKZN cohort model were included. Although we cannot draw conclusions on any distinctive differences between the traditional and professional doctorate from our sample, it seems that the full potential of the professional doctorate, especially in terms of its direct relevance and impact on practice (sector-specific or within broader society) is yet to be realised in South Africa. Similarly, the potential of a cohort doctorate model, especially in the world of increasing recognition of the need for collaboration, also seems to still be in its infancy in South Africa. We believe that both models are worthy of further study, experimentation and deliberate consideration by universities.

In summary, our analysis shows that the official aims and purposes of doctoral programmes included in this study tend to primarily centre on knowledge advancement with little direct reference to impact outside of the knowledge realm. However, many of our ECR participants (across age, disciplines and doctoral models) demonstrated a wider range of objectives and ambitions for impact than the institutions, including but not limited to intellectual pursuit and knowledge contribution.

We acknowledge that many of our participants' perspectives on impact followed from the question which specifically prompted them to ponder impact, while the more generic questions on reasons for pursuing or the benefits of their doctorate yielded little impact-related content. Additionally, the universities (or their representatives) might have had more to say on the topic of research impact if they had been specifically prompted.

In any case, we were encouraged by the breadth and depth of our respondents' awareness of non-academic impact, as well as some of the actions they had already taken. This is more significant considering the lack of direct articulation of impact from the universities themselves. This forced us to revisit our hypothesis, namely that ECRs are novices in the knowledge hierarchy and, therefore, their doctoral training is the primary source through which they derive an understanding of the concept of research impact. Our data suggest that this is not necessarily the case. Instead, ECRs in South Africa have demonstrated an extensive and rich understanding of non-academic research impact, *independent* of their formal doctoral training. Some even seem to have taken it upon themselves to seek out developmental opportunities and activities to better understand and / or realise research impact. This is especially significant in countries like South Africa, where a national research assessment framework does not yet exist and the demonstration of research impact (academic and, to a lesser extent, social impact) is only required for more established researchers (e.g. in its National Research Foundation's researcher rating scheme; the rating scheme is not mandated for every researcher, however, but only for those who seek recognition). This is also significant because the current focus of South Africa's higher education policy is still largely on the quantity of graduates where its National Development Plan calls for a fivefold increase in annual PhD graduates, assuming an automatic correlation between the number of doctoral graduates and macroeconomic development (social impact). Little has been specifically said about either the quality of the doctoral programmes or the need to consciously prepare and assist these doctoral graduates to realise any social impact expected of them. We also see a similar lack of articulation from the higher education institutions themselves about social impact, as well as supports provided to their doctoral candidates in this regard.

Our data also suggested the added value of training / workshops / conferences in addition to the traditional apprenticeship model, both in terms of academic growth and the potential impact achieved through collaboration and networking. We note that supervisors still play an important role: one participant described his supervisor as a role model for his engagement in social issues. However, we also note the narrow focus of the training programmes. In fact, this limited exposure to topics beyond the narrow academic focus of thesis completion was a central concern among our participants, leading many to express desire for broader and more deliberate support for communication and public engagement. There were a few incidents of uncritical evaluation of one's impact. For example one participant claimed that 'my study…informed the implementation of a new curriculum in my country. The Minister of Education and other non-academics in my country were, to a large extent, guided by the finding of my thesis'. We suspect this may have something to do with the lack of exposure to, and critical engagement with, impact, as well as training in tools and techniques for the assessment and evidencing of research impact.

Conclusion

We are encouraged by the ambitions for impact that our ECRs have demonstrated. We believe that this should be deliberately acknowledged, encouraged and supported by universities and also possibly agencies funding doctoral studies.

On the other hand, we are concerned by the paucity of research impact both in policy (the country's National Development Plan and research assessment policy) and institutional practice, as well as the institutions' narrow focus on the academic pursuit of thesis completion and knowledge advancement (with little direct reference to or support for impact). We understand that this could partly be a result of the methodology we applied, but believe that this points to a need for both the policy experts and universities to engage and articulate a wider range of research impacts.

We believe that government policy, higher education institutions, as well as supervisors, need to pay greater attention to the interests (*motivation*) already exhibited by the ECRs and nurture this interest more deliberately and effectively (with support for *opportunities* and *capability* development). At the national policy level, this could mean more deliberate conceptualisation, articulation and incorporation of research impact alongside the target of a fivefold increase in PhD graduates, as well as a more clearly articulated theory of change from greater numbers of doctoral graduates to the intended societal impact. At the institutional level, there seems to be a great need for the institutions, as well as the supervisors, to acknowledge and encourage the impact work which some of their students have already engaged in, as well as to incorporate social impact components within the trainings the institutions organise and provide. This does not necessarily call for a new type of doctorate or a new doctorate training model. But to propel the impact trajectory of the ECRs, a change of focus and potentially change of training method seem to be much needed.

Learning points

- Early-career researchers' ambitions for impact should be acknowledged, encouraged and supported by universities and also possibly agencies funding doctoral studies.
- Discussion between policy experts, university leaders, and ECRs on a wider range of research impacts is needed.
- Supervisors should take an active role in acknowledging and encouraging the impact work of their doctoral candidates.

References

Academy of Science of South Africa (ASSAf) (2010). *An evidence-based study on how to meet the demands for high-level skills in an emerging economy.* Pretoria: Academy of Science of South Africa.

Bornmann, L. (2012). Measuring the societal impact of research. *EMBO Reports.* 13(8), 673–676.

CHET (2012). *South African higher education open data.* CHET. [Viewed 12 September 2017]. Available from www.chet.org.za/data/sahe-open-data

Council for Higher Education (2014). *Vital stats.* [Viewed 12 September 2018]. Available from: www.che.ac.za/sites/default/files/publications/VitalStats2014%20-%20webversion.pdf

Enders, J. (2002). Serving many masters: the PhD on the labour market, the everlasting need of inequality, and the premature death of Humboldt. Higher Education. 44(3–4), 493–517.

Federation for the Humanities and Social Sciences (2014). *Impacts of humanities and social science research.* Ottawa: Federation for the Humanities and Social Sciences.

Hockey, J. (1995). Change and the social science PhD: supervisors' responses. *Review of Education.* 21(2), 195–206.

Louw, J. and Godsell, G. (2015). Multiple paths to success. In: N. Cloete, J. Mouton, and C. Sheppard, eds., *Doctoral education in South Africa.* Cape Town: African Minds. pp. 125–172.

Louw, J. and Muller, J. (2014). *A literature review of the PhD, Centre for Higher Education Transformation.*Stellenbosch: CHET. [Viewed 16 March 2019]. Available from: www. idea-phd.net/images/doc-pdf/Louw_and_Muller_2014_Literature_-Review_on_Models_of_the_PhD.pdf.

Michie, S., van Stralen, M.M. and West, R. (2011). The behaviour change wheel: a new method for characterising and designing behaviour change interventions. *Implementation Science.* 6(42), 1–11.

Neumann, R. (2009). Policy driving change in doctoral education. In: D. Boud and A. Lee, eds., *Changing practices of doctoral education.* London: Routledge. pp. 211–224.

Ng'ambi, D. (2018). *PhD student and supervisor guide.* University of Cape Town. [Viewed 12 September 2018]. Available from: www.education.uct.ac.za/sites/default/files/image_ tool/images/104/2018%20PhD%20Student%20_%20Supervisor%20Guide%20_School% 20of%20Education.pdf

Purcell, K., Durbin, S., Warren, S., Elias, P., Behle, H. and Davies, R. (2005). *The employment of social science PhDs in academic and non-academic jobs: research skills and postgraduate training.* A report prepared for the ESRC Training and Development Board. [Viewed 24 August 2018]. Available from: https://warwick.ac.uk/fac/soc/ier/publications/2005/fina l_draft_socsci_phds_06_june_2005.pdf

Salter, A.J. and Martin, B.R. (2001). The economic benefits of publicly funded basic research: a critical review. *Research Policy.* 30(3), 509–532.

Samuel, M. (2016). Values and purposes of a PhD: comparative responses from South Africa and Mauritius. *Higher Education Forum.* 13, 1–23.

Scott, D., Brown, A., Lunt, I. and Thorne, L. (2004). *Professional doctorates: integrating professional and academic knowledge.* London: Open University Press.

University of Cape Town (2018). *Getting a PhD in sociology at UCT.* University of Cape Town. [Viewed 12 September 2018]. Available from: www.sociology.uct.ac.za/over view-phd

University of Johannesburg (2017). *Doctorate in sociology, industrial sociology or in urban studies.* University of Johannesburg. [Viewed 12 September 2018]. Available from: www.uj.ac.za/faculties /humanities/sociology/Courses-and-Programmes/Pages/Doctorate-in-Sociology,-Industria l-Sociology-or-in-Urban-Studies.aspx

University of Kwa-Zulu Natal (UKZN) (n.d.). *Guide to the procedures relating to the admission, registration and examination of research Masters and Doctoral Candidates and the responsibilities of the various parties concerned.* University of Kwa-Zulu Natal. [Viewed 12 September 2018]. Available from: https://doeh.ukzn.ac.za/Libraries/Documents/Postgrad_guide.sflb.ashx

Vitae (2013). *What do researchers do? Early career progression of doctoral graduates 2013.* [Viewed 9 May 2018]. Available from: www.sheffield.ac.uk/polopoly_fs/1.379269!/file/what-do-re searchers-do-early-career-progression-2013.pdf

Weiss, C.H. (1980). Knowledge creep and decision accretion. *Knowledge.* 1(3), 381–404

Wildy, J., Pedan, S. and Chan, K. (2015). The rise of professional doctorates: case studies of the Doctorate in Education in China, Iceland and Australia. *Studies in Higher Education.* 40 (5), 761–774.

Wolhuter, C. (2011). Research on doctoral education in South Africa against the silhouette of its meteoric rise in international higher education research. *Perspectives in Education.* 29(3), 126–138.

REFLECTION

International impact: What is the problem? Can I solve it and will anyone benefit?

Emma Heywood

Early career researchers (ECRs), and all researchers, are now faced with the obligation to incorporate the blurred concept of impact into their research. We all know that we have to generate research, publish papers and bring in income, but the additional pressure of being measured and judged by yet another component within the Research Excellence Framework (REF) is surely not making the task any easier. Becoming, or remaining, a productive researcher when faced with these new impact requirements involves planning from the early stages of any project, and a whole new mind-set. Simply put, it's the 'so what?' question. What is the problem? How am I going to solve it? And who will be the beneficiaries? Or more frighteningly – what is the worth of my research?

ECRs, who are already facing heightened stress at the seemingly ubiquitous and endless judgement of their own worth, leading to the various concepts of imposter syndrome, and aspirant and existentialist identities (Knights and Clarke, 2014), as discussed in greater detail by Hall et al. (Chapter 1), now have to justify and provide evidence of the worth of their research, which may not be measurable. It is little surprise that the systematised demands of the REF have been mentioned as a possible factor in increased work-related stress amongst those in academia (Kinman and Wray, 2014).

In this chapter, I highlight and reflect on my experiences of conducting research in another country. My project investigated the role of radio in the activities of non-governmental organisations (NGOs) in conflict-affected areas, with the West Bank as my case study. My previous research in this area had already demonstrated that NGOs in the West Bank rated radio as one of their most effective tools in reaching marginalised communities as part of their awareness and advocacy campaigns. This served to confirm established research regarding radio (Gilberds and Myers, 2012; Frère, 2013, 2016; Manyozo, 2012; Tacchi, 2005). Using quantitative and qualitative methods, I analysed the NGO-related output of selected radio stations over the course of a whole year and interviewed dozens of radio and NGO employees. Too little data would not be a problem. Information was gathered during several fieldtrips to the region and then analysed in the UK with additional queries being discussed remotely via Skype or Facebook messaging.

However, the delights of being awarded external funding for this project faded fast and I soon faced the reality of no longer being able to rely on my established UK-based networks. I instead had to tackle the complexities of working in a new culture, communicating in a different language, and then connecting remotely with the new network I'd had to create. However much of my research would contribute to my human experience and my 'research journey', I would now encounter the difficulties of being viewed as 'the other', a Westerner, and more importantly – as this region approached the 100th anniversary of the Balfour Declaration – someone who was British. I was also a woman, to which I received varying reactions in this patriarchal and misogynistic society. How could I, as an outsider, understand let alone accurately report their situation? Changing it – or having any impact – was beyond their comprehension. I would now be submitted to scrutiny and judgement by others, no longer just through the systematised and impersonal REF, but by people, in a different country with a better knowledge of the subject than me. This was alongside the need to build a recognised research identity within a crowded and sensitive subject area which inevitably would lead to widespread criticism of bias, all of which would only reinforce the abovementioned imposter syndrome (Clance and Imes, 1978). I was aware that my analysis would be published – this is part of the academic deal – but I faced the intellectual quandary of the extent to which academic research should, or even could be impartial. My work, however carefully written, could be interpreted as favouring one party over the other. Any impact from my findings could then be viewed as worthless.

And yet, surely, there would be a way I could combine my own learning, development and concerns into having a non-academic impact in the country I was researching. Could my work also be assessed, or judged, in terms of engagement and collaboration?

My aim was to assess how radios interacted with NGOs and make recommendations and suggest improvements. The impact of this study wasn't necessarily just to make changes here – however good this would be – but to be able to transfer the findings to other conflict-affected zones. I needed motivation and this was provided by the joy and excitement of travelling to the region I had learnt so much about. If I could make the slightest change in this small area of land, it would be worth it. The personal impact of working in a new environment, however welcoming the West Bank is, combined with anxiety of writing cautiously so as to not attract accusations of bias, nonetheless led to quick progress in my researcher development. I suddenly had to learn to not react negatively to criticism, how to identify positive criticism from emotionally based criticism, and how to filter out information which was not necessarily useful or relevant to my project but vital to the interviewees and which they were desperate to tell.

The simplicity of the initial task of 'what is the problem?' was nothing but reductive. Yet I could see the problem: radio works well but could be used more efficiently; this would lead to the better use of funding and more accurate targeting of particular audiences who were mainly marginalised communities. Using local radio stations whose reach is limited to the immediate vicinity and whose costs (shown by my research) were considerably lower than the large, expensive stations which cover the whole region, was one of my recommendations (Heywood, 2018). The lack of systematic audience surveys and market awareness had prevented this solution being found. My research has left its mark and has been taken on board by the NGOs. Large-scale solutions were beyond the realms of possibility and would require an overhaul of donor funding; significant and far-reaching changes to the institutional practices of radio stations; eliminating corruption within society; removing societal constraints and taboos, internal political divisions, and censorship; to say nothing, of course, of the occupation. But how could a single researcher with limited, albeit external, funding have an impact here?

This is the beauty of research and it is this that has had an impact on my research ability and behaviour. Research questions can and frequently have to be modified. What if, rather than trying to take on the world, I learn from this conflict, make certain, realistic suggestions resulting in some minor changes to NGO policies, and go on to take the positive knowhow of the NGOs and radio to other areas? Making huge changes in people's lives is only an aspiration and small achievable steps may be more realistic. Impact builds on impact.

References

Clance, P.R. and Imes, S.A. (1978). The imposter phenomenon in high achieving women: dynamics and therapeutic interventions. *Psychotherapy: Theory, Research and Practice*. 15(3), 241–247.

Frère, M.-S. (2013). Media sustainability in a postconflict environment: radio broadcasting in the DRC, Burundi, and Rwanda. In: T. Redeker Heper, and K. Omeje, eds., *Conflicts and peacebuilding in the African Great Lakes region*. Bloomington, IN: Indiana University Press. pp. 161–178.

Frère, M.-S. (2016). Audience perceptions of radio stations and journalists in the Great Lakes Region. In W. Willems, and W. Mano, eds., *Everyday media culture in Africa*. Abingdon: Routledge. pp 113–139.

Heywood, E. (2018). The work of women's NGOs on commercial radio in the West Bank: frustrations and shortcomings. *Radio Journal*. 16(1), 59–75.

Gilberds, H. and Myers, M. (2012). Radio, ICT convergence and knowledge brokerage: lessons from sub-Saharan Africa. *IDS Bulletin*. 43(5), 76–83.

Kinman, G. and Wray, S. (2014). Taking its toll: rising stress levels in further education. UCU Stress Survey 2014. [Viewed 29 January 2018]. Available at www.ucu.org.uk/media/7264/UCU-stress-survey-2014/pdf/ucu_festressreport14.pdf

Knights, D. and Clarke, C.A. (2014). It's a bittersweet symphony, this life: fragile academic selves and insecure identities at work. *Organization Studies*. 35(3), 335–357.

Manyozo, L. (2012). *People's radio: communicating change across Africa*. Penang: Southbound.

Tacchi, J.A. (2005). Radio and new media technologies: making technological change socially effective and culturally empowering. In: S. Healy, B. Berryman, and D. Goodman, eds., *Radio in the world: Radio conference, July, 2005, Melbourne, Australia*. [Viewed 31 January 2018]. Available from https://eprints.qut.edu.au/4397/

8

DOCTORAL EDUCATION AND THE IMPACT GAP

What we can learn from 'Prof Docs' and why it matters for early career researchers

Rebekah Smith McGloin

This chapter gives an overview of contemporary policy discourse around the doctorate, specifically looking at the question of impact in terms of the impact of education at a doctoral level on the knowledge economy. I start by providing an insight into policy drivers which have and continue to influence doctoral training programmes, models of doctorate, funder priorities and funding opportunities. I move on to explore the tension between policy and practice in doctoral education in the area of impact which stems from an aspiration in research and education policy to call for and evidence impact on the economy and a noticeable absence of data to prove it. I then go on to summarise examples in the UK of initiatives that have been designed to enhance the impact of the 'traditional' PhD on business, industry and third sector and then focus on key developments in professional doctorates, exploring the lingering uncertainties and unresolved anxieties about definition, value and fit of the professional doctorate, and – by extension – the evolving PhD.

The chapter aims to support ECRs to gain an understanding of policy and practice in doctoral education. This will help you to think about how you (co)-develop and (co)-design impactful doctoral projects which lead to high-quality research with impact for publication. It will give you the necessary context to shape enhanced funding applications for doctoral studentships which more easily fit funders' evolving agenda. It will also – hopefully – inspire you to challenge the current academic discourse which often struggles to define, locate and value newer evolutions of the traditional form of doctorates – such as the professional doctorate – where knowledge is more explicitly generated in the context of its application and impact is central to the research for supervisor and doctoral candidate.

Doctoral education, the knowledge economy and the impact gap

As ECRs, you will, no doubt, be thinking about trying to secure early experience on supervisory teams, building up your numbers of timely submissions and completions, undertaking supervisor training on a range of issues, from administrative paper trails and research degree regulations to the pedagogy of supervision and how best to support doctoral researchers to undertake one of the single most demanding projects of their life.

Ensuring that you are research active, and developing an excellent research track record, go without saying as effective ways to be invited onto supervisory teams and to have the opportunity to hone your supervisory skills and to learn from others with more experience. Depending upon your institution, there may be ringfenced funding for your own studentship, on a topic that is central to your research interests and expertise. You may also work in an area where you are able to attract high-quality self-funded doctoral candidates. However, despite these opportunities being available to some, for the majority of ECRs, securing a doctoral research project (or more) is a necessary but challenging item on the to-do list. This is central to producing high-quality research outputs with impact for the Research Excellence Framework or the equivalent research audit exercise in your own national context.

An understanding of the changing policy landscape of doctoral education, doctoral funding, and the challenges and opportunities of working closely with business, industry or the third sector are, therefore, all important to developing your research career, generating income, designing high-quality doctoral projects, and delivering research with impact.

This first section considers the question of the value of doctoral education as presented in UK and European policy discourse (education and skills and in research) and in the academic literature, alongside the case for impact from investment in doctoral training that is articulated by UK funders. In policy, through funders and within institutions we subscribe in many countries to the notion that graduate education 'builds on human capital to drive economic success' (RCUK 2014). The burden of proving this connection weighs heavy on higher education institutions, research funders and governments alike and has generated a body of policy documents, academic literature and a range of developments to the doctorate.

In the UK, doctoral education has been consistently tied into innovation and economic development at a national (Leitch 2006, p.68; Warry 2006; Smith et al. 2010), and supra-national (EC 2003, 2005; OECD 2010) level in terms of education and skills. Although the connection between higher education and a country's economic output is not uncontested. Rizvi and Lingard (2006) relate this policy theme to functionalist assumptions made at an Organisation for Economic Cooperation and Development (OECD) level that manifest in the educational policies of OECD members. Servage (2009) questions the validity of this approach, particularly in relation to doctoral education. Nevertheless, doctoral researchers frequently feature as a mechanism for better knowledge exchange in the research and innovation policy canon (Lambert 2003; Sainsbury 2007; Wilson 2012; Witty 2013; BIS 2015).

The impact of education to a doctoral level on the economy, the environment and society remains – as suggested by DTZ (2010) in their report for the Engineering and Physical Sciences Research Council (EPSRC) – arguably difficult to identify. Publications which can demonstrate explicit economic impact of doctoral education are rare. EPSRC (2015) is a relatively recent exception which sets out to quantify a return on investment in doctoral training as a part of research. Publications addressing economic impacts of research investment up to this point (such as Department of Business, Innovation and Skills [BIS] 2010, pp. 19–20) tended to mention the impact of investment in doctoral training in passing, implying rather than evidencing impact within the broader portfolio of research activity.

RCUK (2014) takes a more detailed, case-study approach which looks at the impact of doctoral education through the lens of doctoral graduate employment – outside of the higher education sector – rather than in terms of industrial engagement either in higher-level training awards or technology transfer outputs from doctoral research. The flow of PhD-qualified individuals from universities to business, industry and the third sector does play a significant part in the narrative of the economic impact of doctoral education. It is well-documented that it is more likely for a doctoral graduate to leave academia than to take up an academic post. Vitae (2013) shows that 56% of doctoral graduate respondents to the HESA 'Longitudinal' Destinations of Leavers from Higher Education in the United Kingdom (L DLHE) survey in November 2008 and 2010 had left higher education, although the data show a differentiated picture according to discipline. The Royal Society (2010) report highlights a flow of scientifically trained people into other sectors at various transition points following a PhD. Although one acknowledged weakness in the data is that they do not map returners into higher education.

Curiously, PhDs that remain within academia or return to higher education are less a part of this narrative of economic impact. RCUK (2014) focuses on how doctoral graduates who leave higher education help to foster innovation through ongoing collaboration and engagement with universities, foregrounding the 75% of doctoral graduates responding to the RCUK survey that stated that they had been engaged in collaborative projects, promoting knowledge exchange between universities and industry in their careers outside of academia.

Whilst this approach is successful in illuminating the broader picture there is, however, no published, quantified evidence of the scale and extent of these interactions and the report does not make a strong link back to doctoral-level education. To what extent, for example, are the skills and attributes identified by employers (problem–solving, creative thinking [RCUK 2014]) trained or developed as a result of doctoral education rather than common to a group of individuals who pursue a higher degree? There is also little acknowledgement of the impact of PhD-qualified people who choose to leave academia but stay in the higher education sector in leadership or management.

The challenge of maximising the impact of doctoral education and actualising the aspirations of policy rhetoric and theoretical conception has been the focus of another group of mainly UK-based reports which over the past decades have focused on locating the major blocks impeding the impact of doctoral students (exclusively traditional PhD) on mainly the economy but latterly also society at large. These include: lack of transferable skills training (Roberts 2002), which was also raised by the OECD as a challenge to governments and policy makers based on survey respondents from a number of European States, Canada, Australia, Korea, New Zealand and Turkey (OECD 2012); lack of mobility between university and industry (BIS 2015); graduates being unable to articulate their skills (Souter 2005); potential employers being ignorant of the skills doctoral students develop outside of specific technical skills in the sciences and engineering (CIHE 2010); and over-concentration of funding (Nurse 2015). In terms of research management and knowledge exchange more broadly the discourse has focused on a possible lack of capacity for business / industry in the UK to absorb new knowledge (RCUK 2014, p.5). The report cites the United Kingdom's comparatively weak performance in the Global Innovation Index findings on knowledge absorption. The 2018 Global Innovation Index shows the UK placed 4th overall but 30th for knowledge diffusion and 24th for knowledge absorption.

The impact gap in doctoral education is a key challenge for universities, businesses and policy-makers. We have traced the policy discourse which ties innovation and economic development to doctoral education and highlighted the lack of evidence which supports that in the UK context. Similar patterns of discourse can be identified in other developed national research environments which are outside the main focus of this chapter. Of note is the McGagh et al. (2016) review of Australia's research training system which highlights low levels of industry-university collaboration and foregrounds the important role that higher degree research training can play in addressing this challenge (through placements, industry-defined research problems, industry-based PhDs and industrial supervisors). The review also draws attention to the inadequate available data on the performance of the research training system and its value to Australia's economic and social wellbeing.

For ECRs, an awareness of this impact gap can give you a lens, as new supervisors, with which to view the broader doctoral training and development agenda and an understanding of the importance of development needs analysis for doctoral researchers, their attendance at both generic and research skills workshops, and their active participation in academic and non-academic placement opportunities, for example. It also offers food for thought when you are developing projects for doctoral research, with regard to finding the time and opportunity to work together with industry, business or third sector partners to co-create a project with impact embedded within the research design where possible.

Addressing the gap

Alongside the potential for individual supervisors to address the impact gap with their own practice, there have also been a variety of measures introduced in the UK over recent years at programme and funder level which have aimed to enhance and provide evidence for impact. It is useful for ECRs to be aware of these as examples of good practice and also potential avenues to find funding for doctoral candidates.

These initiatives have been largely focused on the PhD to-date. They have included: industry co-funded centres for doctoral training; mandatory placements for PhD students (PIP); industry-university partnerships to deliver staff training from continuing professional development to doctorate (ATP); national programmes of collaborative doctorates (CASE awards); and research council PhD funding awarded directly to industry (CTP). We might also consider recent smaller evolutions amongst some traditional PhDs on an individual or small-cohort basis which have included business, industry or third sector contribution to fees or stipend, representation on university steering groups or contribution to specialist workshops. In Europe, the Marie Curie European Industrial Doctorate Programme offers pan-European funding for collaborative doctorates between industry and universities.

Alongside this portfolio of activity in the UK to evolve the traditional PhD, the EPSRC has been the only research council to fund professional doctorates through its Engineering Doctorates (EngD) scheme. EPSRC-funded EngDs in industrial doctorate centres accounted for 18% of the doctoral training budget which it allocated to centres in 2012 (EPSRC 2012), building on early evidence of the 'major and beneficial effect on a wide range of companies and sectors' of this model (EPSRC 2007, p.1). Some business-facing universities, independently of EPSRC funding, have also developed or are currently developing a variety of professional doctorate programmes. This will be discussed in more detail later in the chapter.

Numbers of UK doctoral researchers who are undertaking a doctorate with an element of involvement from industry, business or third sector are difficult to ascertain as this is not recorded by the UK Higher Education Statistics Agency. However, it is clear that these are a small-scale (albeit growing) development compared to the national population of doctoral researchers.

Professional doctorates (of which Engineering Doctorates are a subset) are unusual within this range of initiatives in that arguably they have amongst the greatest potential to address many of the challenges thrown up by the imperative to tie innovation and economic development to doctoral education, yet they barely appear in UK policy documentation. For the ECR they may not be an obvious first option, however, there is evidence to suggest that they are a growing phenomenon in some parts of the sector; their structure and focus may have elements that could be incorporated into the more traditional doctorate, and an awareness of how professional doctorates have been received and discussed in the academic literature offers some interesting insight into the broader question of impact within doctoral education.

The professional doctorate

Professional doctorates emerged onto the scene in the UK in the late 1980s (Donn, Routh and Lunt 2000), around the same time as in Australia and significantly later than in the United States. They saw a rapid increase in programmes between 1990 and 2010 in the UK and in Australia. Mellors-Bourne et al. (2016) infer that this pattern of growth has continued at a steady rate from 2010 to 2015 within the UK, although the data are not directly comparable as the data used by Mellors-Bourne et al. excludes EngD programmes and focuses solely on English institutions, whilst the historical UKCGE surveys he compares with are UK-wide but only sent to member institutions (97% of total number documented by Universities UK). Response rates also differed significantly.

In terms of scale, these programmes are an emerging and evolving phenomenon. Mellors-Bourne et al. (2016) suggest a likely growth trajectory from 109 pro-grammes in 1998 to 320 in 2016. The Higher Education Statistics Agency (HESA) data does not differentiate between professional doctorates and PhDs so it is not possible to gain a clearer picture through HESA data in the UK. In Australia, professional doctorate programmes have undergone a similar pattern of growth in the first decade: from one in 1990 to 131 in 2001 (Neumann 2005). Maxwell (2011) uses a systematic analysis of the websites of all 39 Australian universities to demonstrate a continuation in the growth trajectory up to 2011 (202 programmes) and, although recent work suggests a retraction in Australia in overall population numbers (particularly in education) (Malloch 2016) Wallace et al. (2015) highlight an increase in enquiries in DBA which they pose as a rise in unmet demand. Wallace et al. (2015), like Servage (2009), specifically note signs of growth in professional doctorate programmes in less research-intensive institutions. This trend towards proliferation clustering in business-facing universities in the UK is also highlighted in Mellors-Bourne et al. (2016). Data recently collected as part of a project with a large UK university mission group of 19 business-facing universities indicated that the majority of universities intended to grow their professional doc-torate provision; both programme numbers and candidate numbers. In terms of programme development, 13 out of 17 responding institutions (70.6%) reported that they intended to increase the number of professional doctorate programmes. Regarding growth in candidate numbers, 15 out of 17 responding institutions (88.2%) suggested their intentions to grow the number of total enrolments on professional doctorate awards.

Definition and location

Professional doctorates have been the locus of contemporary academic debate over the past twenty-five years in terms of their university-industry connections, transdisciplinarity and knowledge generation for the knowledge economy. The following section is a brief review of the academic literature based on a literature search which was carried out using Google Scholar and Scopus with the search terms 'professional doctorate' and publication dates between 2005 and 2017. After duplicates and irrelevant materials were excluded a corpus was developed of 68 English Language journal articles, policy documents and book chapters. This predominantly focused on the United Kingdom, North America (mainly the United States) and Australia. Despite some differences in evolution, profile of programmes and key drivers between the national contexts (see Kot & Hendel 2012) two major themes emerged from the literature. These are: definition of the professional doctorate (often in terms of equivalency to and comparison with the 'traditional' PhD); and the conceptual location of the professional doctorate within the discourse of knowledge generation. These will be addressed in turn here.

Definition

The question of what a professional doctorate is and how it compares to a more 'traditional' PhD has been addressed in the academic literature for almost as long as the professional doctorate has existed. Two often-cited definitions in the UK are from the Quality Assurance Agency (QAA) and the UK Council for Graduate Education (Fell, Flint & Haines 2011), although neither definition captures the evolution of the professional doctorate over time that is set out by Maxwell (2003).

QAA doctoral degree characteristics (QAA 2015) describes a professional doctorate as suited for career purposes to mid-career professionals and in a few cases for entry to a specific profession. It also acknowledges that some candidates may undertake a professional doctorate for reasons beyond their career. It sets out in some detail the key characteristics of professional and practice-based doctorates which normally include a supervised research project and 'structured elements' that are taught and are relevant to professional practice. Research projects are normally situated within the candidate's profession but rooted in an academic discipline. The thesis may be of a shorter length than for the PhD and is assessed by viva.

The UKCGE definition focuses only on the professional doctorate for professional groups: 'A programme of advanced study and research which, whilst satisfying the university criteria for the award of doctorate, is designed to meet the specific needs of a professional group external to the university' (Hoddell 2002 cited in Fell et al. 2011, p.11). This works well for larger 'established brands' in England such as DBA, EngD and EdD but arguably the footprint of these programmes in reality is far smaller than one might expect if the professional doctorate is catering to a profession. This trend towards small-scale, responsive programmes will be discussed later. This definition also excludes two groups of candidates that have been identified as those seeking generic professional awards and those seeking niche awards (identified by Maxwell in an Australian context) – often associated with a specific interdisciplinary area such as biotech or sustainable agriculture.

Despite distinct definitions of the professional doctorate in its own right within the UK, Australian and North American contexts (Evans et al. 1998; Walker 2009; Fell et al. 2011) there is a sustained theme of benchmarking against the PhD, albeit predominantly from a 'separate but equal' (Salter 2013, p.1176) standpoint. Fink

(2006) exemplifies the approach and provides a snapshot of the major distinctions drawn between professional doctorate and PhD. These are focused around entry / exit pathways and degrees and types of connectedness to 'university' and to 'industry'; intended outcomes of the doctorate and how these outcomes are disseminated; and how, where and for whom knowledge is produced. This common comparative approach provides some clarity but risks creating a series of false dichotomies between ideas of inside and outside of the university which are not well-defined in the literature. This echoes weaknesses inherent in a number of the reports we discussed in the opening section where economic impact of PhD graduates is presumed to be realised only when the individual goes outside of the university.

Fink admits that the distinctions he makes may blur as the PhD develops to address the challenges and demands of the knowledge economy. We might go one step further to question whether these hard distinctions have ever existed in reality, given natural differences between disciplines and the heterogeneous nature of most higher education sectors (incorporating specialist institutions, business-facing universities with a focus on applied research, research-intensive organisations, and many with a blend of some elements of all of these).

The inside-outside spaces that are created in defining professional doctorates within the literature are also explored in work that focuses on the kind of knowledge that professional doctorates set out to generate. This is the second theme that we will explore.

Location

The academic literature on professional doctorates frequently frames them as an effective conduit within the triple helix model of the knowledge economy. That is to say that this kind of doctorate is put forward as a mechanism by which the university can realise its potential, through close interaction with industry and government, to deliver innovation and economic development in a Knowledge Society. Lee, Green and Brennan (2000) and Gallagher (2000) both look positively at the professional doctorate's connection with practice; closer integration between university and professions; encouragement of university-industry partnerships; and opening up of the process of knowledge production within the knowledge economy. The knowledge created within a professional doctorate is generally set out in the literature as distinctly different, following Gibbons et al. (1994) conception of Mode 2 knowledge. It is characterised as knowledge 'produced in (the) context of application; transdisciplinary; heterogeneous; [...] socially accountable and reflexive, including a wider and more temporary and heterogeneous set of practitioners, collaborating on problems defined in specific and localised context' (Lee, Green and Brennan 2000, p.124).

The extent to which types of knowledge can be neatly circumscribed is problematised in Neumann (2005, p.185): who points out that professional doctorate programmes are often developed and led by academics from a researcher perspective and they are undertaken inside a prescribed academic framework by candidates who must do the translation into their own professional context. The knowledge generated within practice as part of the doctorate is potentially somehow pre-shaped or constrained by existing academic thinking and cannot arguably be classified distinctly. We could add to this that the lead (and usually exclusive) role played by the academic in the final examination process is an indication of how even if a distinct kind of knowledge was produced within the professional context it becomes measured and assessed within academic boundaries. Although professional doctorates can emerge in areas where the community of academics themselves have developed from a practitioner and / or professional base rather than a more traditional academic career route and so may be developing their own hybrid identities whilst supervising professional doctorate candidates.

The complex and liminal nature of the territory inhabited by the professional doctorate is a point which is not explicitly addressed within much of the literature, which consistently restates the inside–outside binary framework. We can see this in the way the question of identity in professional doctorate candidates is handled. This theme is interwoven across discussions of definition and knowledge generation in the literature. A number of publications characterise professional doctorate candidates as hyphenated or paired individuals. Gregory (1997) in Wellington and Sikes (2006) sets out 'scholarly professionals' and 'professional scholars'. Bourner, Bowden and Laing (2001), Dreher and Montgomery (2009), Stew (2009) and Salter (2013) contrast the 'researching professional' (professional doctorate) with the 'professional researcher' (PhD). Dreher and Montgomery (2009) assert that most universities globally are still struggling to differentiate between the two. In the CPed Initiative in the United States (cpedinitiative.org), the Carnegie Foundation distinguishes the practitioner-scholar (professional doctorate), where scholarship and research are used to solve local problems in a way that is of value to fellow practitioners, from the practitioner-scholar (PhD) where 'generalizable knowledge is produced through research to inform the practice area'. What is interesting about these examples is that whilst each poses a fusion of some kind between research and its application they all restate a binary divide with an implied tipping point between one identity and the other; an inside space of the scholar or researcher and the outside space of the professional and the practitioner. The hyphen is, in these publications, a broadly unquestioned and unresolved space in between.

However, other publications explore and expand the practical challenges that link to this unresolved space. These are central to the critical discussion in the literature of whether professional doctorate programmes can in reality fulfil their ascribed impact potential in terms of delivering knowledge exchange, facilitating co-creation and producing applied research. They are also central to the question we posed regarding the professional doctorate's ability to address an impact gap in doctoral education more broadly or at least to provide better evidence than that currently available for it. The challenges cluster around three key themes: employer engagement, perceptions of relevance and esteem.

Burgess, Weller and Wellington (2011) suggest that the employer or sponsoring organisation to the professional doctorate are rarely acknowledged and remain under-utilised within the professional doctorate. Burgess et al. go on to explore how employers are sometimes ill-equipped to be 'learning organisations', and that employers can be resistant to implementing new knowledge and innovative products or practice that can arise from the work undertaken by candidates in a professional doctorate. In Neumann's empirical study on doctoral education in Australian universities, with specific reference to education, law, management and the creative arts, employers are characterised as being passively aware of the research undertaken by the professional doctorate candidates they employ. Mellors-Bourne et al., in their 2016 report, make a speculative link between small cohort sizes and the short-lived nature of some programmes that they find evident in the 63 institutional survey responses from English universities and possible weak employer engagement with professional doctorate programmes in England. Lester and Costley (2010) and Burgess, Weller and Wellington (2011) point to employers failing to grasp the relevance of the research to their organisation and professional doctorate candidates struggling to implement findings because of a perception that the research is rooted in or somehow belongs to the university. Research findings therefore have no direct connection to the workplace (even if the research question is rooted in it).

Whilst relevance can be questioned by employers there is also evidence of an ongoing lack of esteem accorded to professional doctorate programmes within the academic community. There are underlying suspicions which appear in the education press that the professional doctorate route is less rigorous than its conventional counterpart (Taylor 2008; Times Higher Education 2010; Grove 2017). We can add to this the theme of measuring the professional doctorate against the PhD in the literature already discussed.

In summary the academic literature on the professional doctorate reveals a hyphenated, qualified, interstitial space which tells us something of the challenges – practical and conceptual – of addressing the impact gap within doctoral education, either through a different award (professional doctorate) or through evolution within the traditional PhD.

Whether you are supervising, bid-writing or contributing to the training and development of doctoral researchers, be it related to the evolving PhD or the emerging professional doctorate, building close working between university and business, industry and third sector is a challenge that you are likely to have to face. For ECRs in the UK, there are many reasons why you should consider taking risks, making opportunities, engaging with existing innovations and creating new ones in the doctoral space.

The doctorate has evolved much from its Humboldtian origins and it will arguably need to continue to alter as the shape of the research landscape, the profile of the doctoral population and the needs of the knowledge economy change. As ECRs and the next generation of research leaders, you would do well to take a moment to consider what role you might play in driving further evolutions, in particular through being part of developing new models of doctorate that do not seek equivalency with the 'traditional PhD', that generate a new mode of knowledge and create a new space and identity for doctoral candidates. To do this would be to address the ongoing and fundamental issues of the impact gap in doctoral education that are so clearly articulated in policy and so challenging to address in practice.

Learning points

- **Securing funding**: The changes in UK research and innovation funding brought about by the establishment of UKRI may see new funding streams and funded opportunities to develop new models of work-based learning at doctoral level which extend and enhance the current national apprenticeship schemes.
- **Attracting high-quality candidates**: The implementation of postgraduate doctoral loans may generate new and different self-funded doctoral candidates with different skill sets and experiences, looking to answer perhaps different kinds of (co-created?) research questions with clearer impact and closer links to research end-users.
- **Supervising highly motivated doctoral researchers**: Anecdotally, most candidates for a doctorate will tell you that they are there to change the world in some way. Bridging the impact gap could bring you focused, highly motivated researchers who stay on track and on time.
- **Scoring career points**: With the increase in impact weighting in the UK's Research Excellence Framework 2021 and the possibility of a future 'KEF' (Knowledge Excellence Framework) for English universities, there is a sense – at least for now – that your ability to lead impactful research is going to continue to be central to your work as a researcher.
- **Supporting diversity in the research community**: Diversifying the current and future community of researchers is a sector priority and new models of doctorate could open up new pathways into research for candidates from non-traditional backgrounds, tapping into new markets of more mature mid-career professionals and / or those who have not taken a direct route through education.

Bibliography

Banks, G.C., Pollack, J.M., Bochantin, J.E., Kirkman, B.L., Whelpley, C.E. and O'Boyle, E. H. (2016). Management's science–practice gap: a grand challenge for all stakeholders. *Academy of Management Journal.* 59(6), 2205–2231.

Bartholomew, R., Disney, R., Eyerman, J., Mason, J., Newstead, S., Torrance, H. and Widdowfield, R. (2015). *Review of the ESRC doctoral training centres network (the Bartholomew report).* Swindon: Economic and Social Research Council Swindon. [Viewed 8 October 2018]. Available from https://esrc.ukri.org/files/skills-and-careers/doctoral-training/full-report-review-of-the-esrc-doctoral-training-centres-network/

BIS (Department of Business, Innovation and Skills) (2010). *Economic impacts of the UK Research Council system: an overview science and innovation analysis (SIA).* [Viewed 3 October 2018].

Available from: https://assets.publishing.service.gov.uk/government/uploads/system/uploa ds/attachment_data/file/32477/10-917-economic-impacts-uk-research-council-system.pdf

BIS (2015). *The Dowling review of business-university research collaborations.* [Viewed 3 October 2018]. Available from: https://assets.publishing.service.gov.uk/government/uploads/system/uploa ds/attachment_data/file/440927/bis_15_352_The_dowling_review_of_business-university_ rearch_collaborations_2.pdf

Bituskova, A. (2008). New challenges in doctoral education in Europe. In: D. Boud, and A. Lee, eds., *Changing practices of doctoral education.* Oxford: Routledge. pp. 200–210.

Borrell-Damian, L. (2009). *Collaborative doctoral education: university-industry partnerships for enhancing knowledge exchange; doc-careers project.* Brussels: European University Association.

Bourner, T., Bowden, R. and Laing, S. (2001). Professional doctorates in England. *Studies in Higher Education.* 26(1), 65–83.

Brown, K. and Cooke, C. (2010). *Professional doctorate awards in the UK.* Lichfield: UK Council for Graduate Education.

Burgess, H., Weller, G. and Wellington, J. (2011). Tensions in the purpose and impact of professional doctorates. *Work Based Learning e-Journal.* 2(1), 1–20.

CIHE (Council for Industry and Higher Education) (2010). What businesses want from postgraduates. [Viewed 12 December 2016]. Available from: www.ncub.co.uk/reports/ta lent-fishing-what-businesses-want-from-postgraduates.html

Costley, C. and Lester, S. (2012). Work-based doctorates: professional extension at the highest levels. *Studies in Higher Education.* 37(3), 257–269.

Costley, C. and Stephenson, J. (2008). Building doctorates around individual candidates' 'professional experience'. In: D. Boud, and A. Lee, eds., *Changing practices of doctoral education.* Oxford: Routledge. pp. 171–186.

Council of Deans and Directors of Graduate Studies (1998). Guidelines: professional doctorates. Unpublished paper prepared by T. Evans, A. Fisher and W. Gritchting.

Council of Graduate Schools and Educational Testing Service (2010). *The path forward: the future of graduate education in the United States. Report from the Commission on the Future of Graduate Education in the United States.* Princeton, NJ: Educational Testing Service.

DBA Compass (2015). *2015 report: professional doctorates in management.* [Viewed 3 October 2018]. Available from: www.dba-compass.com/News/Professional-doctorates-in-Mana gement-Report-2015

Donn, J.E., Routh, D.K. and Lunt, I. (2000). From Leipzig to Luxembourg (via Boulder and Vail): a history of clinical psychology training in Europe and the United States. *Professional Psychology: Research and Practice.* 31(4), 423–428.

Dreher, H.M. and Montgomery, K.A. (2009). Let's call it 'doctoral' advanced practice nursing. *The Journal of Continuing Education in Nursing.* 40(12), 530–531.

DTZ (2010). *'The economic impact of PhDs': report for the Engineering & Physical Science Research Council (EPSRC).* Swindon: EPSRC. Available from: https://epsrc.ukri.org/news events/pubs/the-economic-impact-of-phds/

EC (European Commission) (2003). *Realising the European Higher Education Area: communiqué of the Conference of Ministers responsible for higher education in Berlin, 19 Sept 2003.* [Viewed 3 October 2018]. Available from: www.eua.be/eua/jsp/en/upload/OFFDOC_BP_Berlin_ communique_final.1066741468366.pdf

EC (2005). Bologna seminar on 'Doctoral programmes for the European Knowledge Society': conclusions and recommendations. Salzburg, 3–5 Feb. [Viewed 3 October 2018]. Available from: www.eua.be/eua/jsp/en/upload/Salzburg_Conclusions.1108990538850.pdf

EC (2007). *Towards the European Higher Education Area: responding to challenges in a globalised world. London communiqué, 18 May 2007.* [Viewed 3 October 2018]. Available from: www.eua.be/fileadmin/user_upload/files/Publications/Londoncommunique.pdf

Enders, J. (2005). Border crossings: research training, knowledge dissemination and the transformation of academic work. *Higher Education*. 49(1–2), 119–133.

Enders, J. and De Weert, E. (2004). The international attractiveness of the academic workplace in Europe. In: J. Enders, and E. Weert, eds., *The international attractiveness of the academic workplace in Europe*. Frankfurt: Gewerkschaft Erziehung und Wissenschaft. pp. 11–31.

EPSRC (Engineering and Physical Science Research Council) (2007). *Report of a review of the EPSRC engineering doctorate centres*. [Viewed 3 October 2018]. Available from: https://www.epsrc.ac.uk/newsevents/pubs/report-of-a-review-of-the-epsrc-engineering-doctorate-centres/

EPSRC (2012). *The EPSRC industrial doctorate centre scheme good practice guidance*. [Viewed 3 October 2018]. Available from: https://web.archive.org/web/20121205140007/http://www.epsrc.ac.uk/SiteCollectionDocuments/other/IDCGoodPracticeGuidelines.pdf

EPSRC (2015). *Assessing the economic returns of engineering research and postgraduate training in the UK*. [Viewed 3 October 2018]. Available from: www.epsrc.ac.uk/newsevents/pubs/econreturnsengresreport/

Etzkowitz, H. and Leydesdorff, L. (1997). Introduction to special issue on science policy dimensions of the triple helix of university-industry-government relations. *Science and Public Policy*. 24(1), 2–5.

Fell, T., Flint, K. and Haines, I. (2011). *Professional doctorates in the UK, 2011*. Lichfield: UK Council for Graduate Education.

Fink, D. (2006). The professional doctorate: its relativity to the PhD and relevance for the knowledge economy. *International Journal of Doctoral Studies*. 1(1), 35–44.

Gallagher, M. (2000). New directions in Australian research and research training policy: some questions for researchers. Annual Conference for the Australian Network for Higher Education Policy Research, Australian National University, Canberra, 7–8 December.

Gibbons, M., Limoges, C., Nowotny, H., Schwartzman, S., Seot, P. and Trow, M., eds. (1994). *The new production of knowledge: the dynamics of science and research in contemporary societies*. London: Sage.

Gregory, M. (1997). Professional scholars and scholarly professionals: practical advice to prospective candidates for the Doctorate of Education. *New-Academic Birmingham*. 6, 19–21.

Grove, J. (2017). PhD or professional doctorate – which is better? *Times Higher Education*. 6 April.

Guthrie, J.W. (2009). The case for a modern doctor of education degree (EdD): multipurpose education doctorates no longer appropriate. *Peabody Journal of Education*. 84(1), 3–8.

Halse, C. and Malfroy, J. (2010). Retheorizing doctoral supervision as professional work. *Studies in Higher Education*. 35(1), 79–92.

Hoddell, S. (2002) *Professional doctorates*. Lichfield: UK Council for Graduate Education.

Hodsdon, L. and Buckley, A. (2011). *Postgraduate research experience survey 2011 results*. Higher Education Academy. [Viewed 3 October 2018]. Available from: www.heacademy.ac.uk/sites/default/files/pres_report_2011_0.pdf

Huisman, J. and Naidoo, R. (2006). The professional doctorate. *Higher Education Management and Policy*. 18(2), 1–13.

Kehm, B.M. (2006). Doctoral education in Europe and North America: a comparative analysis. In: U. Teichler, ed., *The formative years of scholars*. London: Portland Press. pp. 67–78.

Kot, F.C. and Hendel, D.D. (2012). Emergence and growth of professional doctorates in the United States, United Kingdom, Canada and Australia: a comparative analysis. *Studies in Higher Education*. 37(3), 345–364.

Lambert, R. (2003). *Lambert review of business-university collaboration: final report*. [Viewed 3 October 2018]. Available from: www.eua.be/eua/jsp/en/upload/lambert_review_final_450.1151581102387.pdf

LaRocco, D.J. and Bruns, D.A. (2006). Practitioner to professor: an examination of second career academics' entry into academia. *Education*. 126(4), 626–639.

Lee, A., Brennan, M. and Green, B. (2009). Re-imagining doctoral education: professional doctorates and beyond. *Higher Education Research & Development*. 28(3), 275–287.

Lee, A., Green, B., and Brennan, M. (2000). Organisational knowledge, professional practice and the professional doctorate at work. In: J. Carrick, and C. Rhodes, eds., *Research and knowledge at work: perspectives, case studies and innovative strategies*. London and New York: Routledge. pp. 117–136.

Leitch, S. (2006). *Leitch review of skills: prosperity for all in the global economy—world class skills.* London: HM Treasury.

Lester, S. and Costley, C. (2010). Work-based learning at higher education level: value, practice and critique. *Studies in Higher Education*. 35(5), 561–575.

Loxley, A. and Seery, A. (2012). The role of the professional doctorate in Ireland from the student perspective. *Studies in Higher Education*. 37(1), 3–17.

Malloch, M. (2016). Trends in doctoral education in Australia. In: V. Storey, ed., *International perspectives on designing professional practice doctorates*. New York: Palgrave Macmillan. pp. 63–78.

Maxwell, T. (2003). From first to second generation professional doctorate. *Studies in Higher Education*. 28(3), 279–291.

Maxwell, T.W. (2011). Australian professional doctorates: mapping, distinctiveness, stress and prospects. *Work based learning e-Journal*. 2(1), 24–43.

Maxwell, T.W. and Shanahan, P.J. (2000) Current issues in professional doctoral education in Australia and New Zealand. Third international conference on professional doctorates, 'Doctoral education and professional practice: the next generation?'Armidale, 10–12 September.

McGagh, J., Marsh, H., Western, M., Thomas, P., Hastings, A., Mihailova, M. and Wenham, M. (2016). *Review of Australia's research training system*. Melbourne: Australian Council of Learned Academies.

McWilliam, E., Taylor, P.G., Thomson, P., Green, B., Maxwell, T., Windy, H. and Simons, D. (2002). *Research training in doctoral programs: what can be learned from professional doctorates?*Canberra: Commonwealth Department of Education.

Mellors-Bourne, R., Robinson, C. and Metcalfe, J. (2016). *Provision of professional doctorates in English HE institutions: report for HEFCE by the Careers Research and Advisory Centre (CRAC), supported by the University of Brighton*. [Viewed 3 October 2018]. Available from: http://dera.ioe.ac.uk/25165/1/Professional_doctorates_CRAC.pdf

Neumann, R. (2005). Doctoral differences: Professional doctorates and PhDs compared. *Journal of Higher Education Policy and Management*. 27(2), 173–188.

Nurse, P. (2015). *Ensuring a successful UK research endeavour: a review of the UK Research Councils*. [Viewed 3 October 2018]. Available from: www.gov.uk/government/uploads/system/uploads/attachment_data/file/478125/BIS-15-625-ensuring-a-successful-UK-research-endeavour.pdf

OECD (Organisation for Economic Cooperation and Development) (2010). *Measuring innovation: a new perspective*. Paris: OECD.

OECD (2012). *Transferable skills training for researchers: supporting career development and research*. Paris: OECD.

Powell, S. and Long, E. (2005). *Professional doctorate awards in the UK*. Lichfield: UK Council for Graduate Education.

Quality Assurance Agency (2015). *QAA doctoral degree characteristics*. [Viewed 3 October 2018]. Available from: www.qaa.ac.uk/docs/qaa/quality-code/doctoral-degree-characteristics-15.pdf?sfvrsn=50aef981_10

RCUK (2014). *The impact of doctoral careers.* [Viewed 3 October 2018]. Available from: www.ukri.org/files/skills/Summaryidc-pdf

Rizvi, F. and Lingard, B. (2006). Edward Said and the cultural politics of education. *Discourse: Studies in the Cultural Politics of Education.* 27(3), 293–308.

Roberts, G. (2002). *Set for success: the supply of people with science, technology, engineering and mathematical skills.* London: HM Treasury. [Viewed 3 October 2018]. Available from: http://webarchive.nationalarchives.gov.uk/+/http:/www.hm-treasury.gov.uk/d/roberts review_introch1.pdf

Sainsbury, D. (2007). *The race to the top: a review of government's science and innovation policies.* [Viewed 3 October 2018]. Available from: www.rsc.org/images/sainsbury_ review051007_tcm18-103118.pdf

Salter, D.W. (2013). One university's approach to defining and supporting professional doctorates. *Studies in Higher Education.* 38(8), 1175–1184.

Servage, L. (2009). Alternative and professional doctoral programs: what is driving the demand? *Studies in Higher Education.* 34(7), 765–779.

Slaughter, S., Campbell, T., Holleman, M. and Morgan, E. (2002). The 'traffic' in graduate students: graduate students as tokens of exchange between academe and industry. *Science, Technology & Human Values.* 27(2), 282–312.

Smith, A., Bradshaw, T., Burnett, K., Docherty, D., Purcell, W. and Worthington, S. (2010). *One step beyond: making the most of postgraduate education. Report for UK Department for Business, Innovation and Skills.* London: HM Treasury.

Souter, C. (2005). *Empress: employers' perception of recruiting research staff and students. Survey report.* [Viewed 3 October 2018]. Available from: www3.imperial.ac.uk/pls/portallive/ docs/1/45265697.pdf

Stephenson, J., Malloch, M. and Cairns, L. (2006). Managing their own programme: a case study of the first graduates of a new kind of doctorate in professional practice. *Studies in Continuing Education.* 28(1), 17–32.

Stew, G. (2009). What is a doctorate for? In *Proceedings of the International Conference on Professional Doctorates.* Lichfield: UK Council for Graduate Education.

Taylor, J. (2008). *Quality and standards: the challenge of the professional doctorate.* Southampton: Centre for Higher Education Management and Policy, University of Southampton.

Tennant, M. (2004). Doctoring the knowledge worker. *Studies in Continuing Education.* 26(3), 431–441.

The Royal Society (2010). *The scientific century securing our future prosperity.* [Viewed 3 October 2018]. Available from: https://royalsociety.org/~/media/Royal_Society_Content/p olicy/publications/2010/4294970126.pdf

Thune, T. (2006). *Formation of research collaborations between universities and firms.* PhD Thesis. Norwegian School of Management.

Thune, T. (2010). The training of 'triple helix workers'? Doctoral students in university–industry–government collaborations. *Minerva.* 48(4), 463–483.

Times Higher Education (2010). Beware loss of respect for doctorates. *Times Higher Education.* 16 September.

Turner, G. (2015). *PRES 2015: The research student journey.* Higher Education Academy. [Viewed 3 October 2018]. Available from: www.heacademy.ac.uk/sites/default/files/ downloads/pres_report_2015.pdf

Usher, R. (2002). A diversity of doctorates: fitness for the knowledge economy? *Higher Education Research and Development.* 21(2), 143–153.

Vitae (2013). *What do researchers do? Early career progression of doctoral graduates 2013.* Vitae. [Viewed 8 October 2018]. Available from: www.vitae.ac.uk/vitae-publications/reports/ what-do-researchers-do-early-career-progression-2013.pdf/view

Walker, G., Golde, C., Jones, L., Conklin Bueschel, A. and Hutchings, P. (2009). *The formation of scholars: rethinking doctoral education for the twenty-first century.* [Viewed 3 October 2018]. Available from: http://archive.carnegiefoundation.org/pdfs/elibrary/elibrary_pdf_678.pdf

Wallace, M., Byrne, C., Vocino, A., Sloan, T., Pervan, S. and Blackman, D. (2015). A decade of change in Australia's DBA landscape. *Education & Training.* 57(1), 31–47.

Warry, P. (2006). *Increasing the economic impact of research councils: advice to the Director General of Science and Innovation DTI, from the Research Council Economic Impact Group.* [Viewed 3 October 2018]. Available from: http://webarchive.nationalarchives.gov.uk/20070603164510/http://www.dti.gov.uk/files/file32802.pdf

Wellington, J. and Sikes, P. (2006). 'A doctorate in a tight compartment': why do students choose a professional doctorate and what impact does it have on their personal and professional lives? *Studies in Higher Education.* 31(6), 723–734.

Wildy, H., Peden, S. and Chan, K. (2015). The rise of professional doctorates: case studies of the Doctorate in Education in China, Iceland and Australia. *Studies in Higher Education.* 40(5), 761–774.

Wilson, T. (2012). *A review of business–university collaboration.* [Viewed 3 October 2018]. Available from: http://dera.ioe.ac.uk/13842/1/wilson.pdf

Witty, A. (2013). *Final report and recommendations: encouraging a British invention revolution. Sir Andrew Witty's review of universities and growth.* [Viewed 3 October 2018]. Available from: https://assets.publishing.service.gov.uk/government/uploads/system/uploads/attachment_data/file/249720/bis-13-1241-encouraging-a-british-invention-revolution-andrew-witty-review-R1.pdf

REFLECTION

Knowledge transfer and the humanities early career researcher

Jessica Medhurst

This reflective narrative is drawn from my experience as an AHRC-funded Knowledge Transfer Partnership Research Associate, working with Seven Stories (the National Centre for Children's Books) and Newcastle University. In addition to giving an overview of the Knowledge Transfer Partnership (KTP) scheme, I briefly outline some of the ways in which humanities ECRs, and the universities that employ them, can use the scheme as a postdoctoral post, and suggest how the development of this area could challenge the marketization of higher education.

KTPs, under the auspices of Innovate UK, began in 1975 and aim to stimulate economic growth through 'the better use of [the] knowledge, technology and skills that reside within the UK knowledge base' (Innovate UK n.d. a). To this end, a KTP embeds research associates (RAs) – who may be recent graduates, PhD students or ECRs – in small- to medium-sized enterprises (SMEs) across the UK with these RAs supported by a university (called the Knowledge Base) and tasked with a specific research and development project designed to increase SME revenue. In the case of my KTP, this centred on archival research to contribute two exhibitions at the Seven Stories museum in Newcastle in order to increase adult audiences, and the use of this research, alongside my existing knowledge, in staff training and publicity materials.

Innovate UK defines the outcomes of a KTP as

> often deliver[ing] significant increased profitability for business partners as a direct result of the partnership through improved quality and operations, increased sales and access to new markets. Social enterprises see improved results, too. (Innovate UK n.d. b)

This satisfies the notion of research impact as defined by the UK Government's Research Excellence Framework (REF) exercise, which determines universities' national ranking, on the proviso that a REF-submissable publication is also an outcome. However, the abundance of buzzwords, easily dismissed as management speak, and the appended status of 'social enterprises' may be enough to repel any thoughtful ECR or potential KTP academic supervisor. In this reflective chapter, I will argue for the rejection of the marketization and the commercialisation of academia inherent in both the above quotation and in the current government's interpretation of such impact. In spite of this, I do argue that there is a place for humanities-based ECR-led KTPs – one that is founded specifically on an engagement with the assumptions of profitability on which the current KTP model relies.

Collaboration: Restrictions and opportunities

My KTP was supervised from within the Collections and Exhibitions department at Seven Stories and the English Literature department at Newcastle University; it ran from September 2015 to December 2016 and was unusual for a number of reasons. Firstly, it was somewhat shorter than most KTPs, which generally last at least two years and up to three. Secondly, it is more common for the RA to be a recent graduate who is working towards a Master's degree or a PhD than an ECR. Thirdly, KTPs were designed for the science, technology and engineering industries and are still massively dominated by SMEs in these fields. The Seven Stories–Newcastle University KTP was the first to be based within an arts organisation and the first to be partnered with an English Literature department.

The novelty of this kind of KTP and the questions raised about value and outcomes presented the opportunity to not only develop the aims of the project but also to act as a guinea pig for this emerging ECR role and, given the reflective nature of humanities research, to examine the notions of 'knowledge transfer' and 'value' on which the programme is founded. The project was also determined a success in other terms: it was judged as 'very good' by the Innovate UK assessors and it won the *Times Higher Education* Leadership and Management Award for 'Knowledge Exchange / Transfer Initiative of the Year' (*Times Higher Education* 2017).

In order to meet the project's aims of exhibition content development and embedding research skills at Seven Stories, the notion of academic research impact was turned on its head: rather than looking for impacts following the completion of research, the required impacts shaped the research agenda, something that continues to strike me as both dangerous and exciting. One of the most academically interesting items I found in the Seven Stories archive whilst researching for their Michael Morpurgo exhibition, for example, was a series of drafts for an uncommissioned film script for *War Horse* from the early 1990s. My work on the differences between the versions and their implications was truncated with the decision that the item was too obscure to include in the exhibition. In some ways, this was a deeply frustrating experience, which limited my personal academic freedom. It was, however, also incredibly useful in terms of Seven Stories, whose perceived needs were prioritised by the KTP model. Working in this way seems to help mitigate against partnership organisations feeling like they have been exploited by universities, who may more cynically use them to gain a high REF score without a meaningful understanding of what the organisations need.

Such negotiations worked in other ways too: I was, for example, given permission to use the generous 'personal development' portion of the KTP funding to undertake research in America that was not directly related to the project but that supported the development of my PhD thesis into a monograph. This was despite the difficulty I had in articulating the 'significant increased profitability [...] as a direct result of the partnership' in the final report. Whilst my work had both demonstrable and indemonstrable impacts (within the terms of the KTP), it was difficult to articulate these as a consequential financial gain. Attempting to do so allowed me to work through the difficulties in monetising research. This inability to demonstrate a numerical value increase did not prevent Innovate UK from reaching its favourable assessment of the project. Whilst the KTP scheme is certainly founded on financial profitability in its aims, it is not so restrictive as to disregard other ideas of value in its looked-for outcomes, suggesting the possibility of further using it to challenge the neoliberal move of marketization ratified in the Higher Education and Research Act 2017 (HM Government 2017).

Knowledge transfer

The construction of the knowledge from which the looked-for value originates and that is supposedly transferred in a KTP was, we discovered, of utmost importance to the success of the project for all three parties. In the definition of a KTP by Innovate UK, the knowledge originates from the Knowledge Base (the university) and from the RA undertaking the research, with the SME a somewhat passive partner: they make a demand for knowledge (that is, they define what is needed) and they are the primary beneficiary of that knowledge, but they do not produce it. In this, then, the business partner knows what is needed but not what it is that will fulfil this need. This suggests that what constitutes research in this model is a service or a product, provided to fulfil a lack; that is, knowledge is understood in concrete terms. In practice, in my KTP, we used this definition as our starting point but Seven Stories was very aware of not knowing what they did not already know and of responding to my research as challenging and informing what they understood themselves as needing.

The project model also underestimated, initially, the skill-set at Seven Stories and my ideas of what it means to be positioned as an expert. The level of expertise in the organisation is phenomenal and whilst, for example, the proposal expected the RA would not have museum experience (and built this education into the research plan), it overestimated the potential usefulness of this newly acquired exhibition design knowledge in comparison to Seven Stories' existing capabilities. In fact, the training I received in this area from Seven Stories surpassed what I gained through self-study and this was also 'transferred' to the so-called Knowledge Base through guest lectures delivered to postgraduate students and staff as well as in the progress meetings, attended by all the projects' supervisors on both sides of the transfer.

The questions this raised about the generation, transfer and direction of knowledge – and by implication the power assumptions within the KTP framework – bear more consideration, both here and beyond the scope of this short reflective narrative. In one sense 'knowledge *exchange*' seems to be a less problematic term for such a collaboration, since it does not privilege either party and suggests a more egalitarian idea of education, research and development. This still, however, finds itself invested in an idea of knowledge that is a concrete, delimited and exchangeable 'thing'. knowledge that is a predefined product. My experience on the KTP was certainly that new thinking was generated but it would be inaccurate to suggest that this was through a linear process of research and dissemination, as I found when attempting to write workflow models for future KTPs at the end of the project. Rather, I learnt and discovered as much through discussion and feedback as through archival study and reading. I do not mean to argue that a KTP is somehow better called a 'Knowledge *Discussion* Partnership', or some other variation, but rather that my experience suggests that humanities KTPs present a unique opportunity to engage with ideas of transfer, exchange and knowledge that have so far been overlooked in the scheme's articulations of its aims, outcomes and value.

Wider implications

This, then, speaks to wider issues within academia, particularly of the construction of education as something that can be bought and consumed. As many in our field have already argued, this trend does not put power in the hands of the so-called exchangers (lecturers and students) but always ends up being a reinforcement of neoliberalism and new managerialism (see, for example, Readings 1997 and Cocks 2016).

It would be easy to dismiss humanities KTPs as reinforcing these destructive constructions of education. To do this, however, would assume that we could somehow exempt ourselves from these problems through nonparticipation. KTPs are seen by universities as prestigious and often financially profitable schemes but, as I learnt during this post, a humanities-based engagement with them does not necessitate an acceptance of this view, just as a non-engagement does not destroy it. Similarly, humanities departments and individuals are already operating within structures that make these same assumptions about knowledge production, exchange and value.

This reflective narrative is not a ringing endorsement of the KTP model but hopes to be a call for participants from across the humanities to use the scheme as a way to fund postdoctoral research and to build meaningful and restructured links with non-academic institutions. Doing so will also help us to find ways in which our research can inform and support people beyond the educational environment and to challenge the ideas of value and knowledge outlined here. Although the KTP model is not perfect, the project was still a success on many terms: in my own career and research development, in a development of the relationship between the two institutions, in the quality and scope of the galleries, in staff development, and in widening the understanding that Seven Stories has of its own archive. Not-for-profit academic research is certainly possible within this structure but, given the currently sidelined construction of the humanities and social enterprises within how the KTP model constructs itself, it also presents an important opportunity to contest the structure's assumptions, a challenge that resonates in the current reshaping of the university sector.

References

Cocks, N. (2016). *Higher Education discourse and deconstruction: challenging the case for transparency and objecthood*. London: Palgrave.

Innovate UK. (n.d. a). *Overview*. Connect, Innovate UK. [Viewed 20 May 2018]. Available from: https://connect.innovateuk.org/web/ktp/overview

Innovate UK. (n.d. b) *Knowledge transfer partnerships*. Connect, Innovate UK. [Viewed 20 May 2018]. Available from: http://ktp.innovateuk.org/

Readings, B. (1997). *The university in ruins*. Harvard: Harvard University Press.

Times Higher Education (2017). 2017 Winners. [Viewed 20 May 2018]. Available from: www.thelmawards.co.uk/2017/en/page/2017-winners

HM Government (2017) *Higher Education and Research Act 2017*. c.29. Norwich: The Stationery Office. [Viewed 20 May 2018]. Available from: www.legislation.gov.uk/ukpga/2017/29/pdfs/ukpga_20170029_en.pdf

9

SITUATING EARLY CAREER RESEARCHERS WITHIN A DYNAMIC RESEARCH AND INNOVATION ECOSYSTEM

Kieran Fenby-Hulse

As I write in 2018, it feels we are still very much at the start of our impact journey. The policy push by funders, especially in the UK (but also elsewhere), for researchers to connect their research to wider society and effect economic, social and / or cultural change has certainly ushered in a new way of thinking about the research we do and the way we conduct research. It is undeniable that the effects of the impact agenda have been profound. For many early career researchers (ECRs) in the UK, impact is now 'part of the job' and for doctoral researchers an important part of their professional development. However, there is still much to learn and much to do. Achieving impact as an early career researcher is not easy. It can feel, at times, overwhelming, like throwing a stone into the ocean, any ripples of influence quickly indistinguishable from the incoming tide.

This feeling provides the inspiration for this final chapter that examines whether we are doing impact 'right' and whether an individualised focus on undertaking impact actually distracts us from the broader reach and significance, to use terms derived from the UK's Research Excellence Framework (see HEFCE 2011 and Research England 2018), of the research endeavour. By delving into theories of research ecosystems and collaborative working, as well as through an assessment of the current working practices and conditions for ECRs, I argue that to fully understand the impact of academic work, we first need to understand the role research and impact activities play within a complex innovation ecosystem that involves multiple actors, agents, and stakeholders. By thinking of impact from this perspective, we can reach new understandings of the contribution ECRs make to the impact agenda, contributions that when taken together and understood in context form not ripples, but influential waves that shape the incoming tide.

Research impact's long history

The idea that research should be of economic and social benefit is not new and links to established ideas of the knowledge economy, knowledge management, and knowledge transfer. For Peters, the idea of the knowledge or creative economy 'emerges from a set of claims that suggest the industrial economy is giving way to the creative economy based on the growing power of ideas and virtual value – the turn from steel and hamburgers to software and intellectual development' (Peters, Marginson and Murphy 2009, p. 13). In contrast, Mokyr (2002) argues that the knowledge economy isn't a recent development. Stemming from the Enlightenment movement of the eighteenth century, Mokyr claims the knowledge economy formed during the industrial revolution. As he states, 'the key to the Industrial Revolution was technology, and technology is knowledge' (Mokyr 2002, p. 29). In short, he argues that, while the mode of production and sale may have changed in recent times from 'hamburgers to software', technological development is still a mode of knowledge production. Etzkowitz and Zhou (2018) similarly give weight to the industrial revolution as a catalyst for the knowledge economy as it was at this time knowledge-creating institutions began to form. As they note, both the Massachusetts Institute of Technology (MIT), founded in 1861, and New York University, founded in 1831, were products of the industrial revolution. As they state, 'MIT's founding purpose was to infuse regional industry with scientific expertise' and New York University's was to promote 'commercial training in that quintessential locate' (Etzkowitz and Zhou 2018, p. 4).

Rooted in the idea of creating useable knowledge that was to be of benefit to society and economy, the industrial revolution connected propositional knowledge to prescriptive knowledge and, by proxy, science to society. Propositional knowledge Mokyr defines as that which documents and explains natural phenomena and regularities (Mokyr 2002). In short, the *what* and *why* of the world. Prescriptive knowledge, by comparison, is technical knowledge, invention. In this case, *making* things work by understanding *how* things work. Mokyr's two modes of knowledge map neatly onto the modes of knowledge production described in the influential study on knowledge production by Gibbons et al. (1994), propositional knowledge arising from what Gibbons et al. refer to as 'mode 1' research and prescriptive knowledge arising from 'mode 2' research. The authors define mode 1 research as:

[A] form of knowledge production – a complex of ideas, methods, values, norms – that has grown up to control the diffusion of the Newtonian model to more and more fields of enquiry and ensure its compliance with what is considered sound scientific practice. (Gibbons et al. 1994, p. 2)

By contrast, mode 2 knowledge is said to result from:

[A] broader range of considerations. Such knowledge is intended to be useful to someone whether in industry or government, or society more generally and this imperative is present from the beginning. Knowledge is always produced under an aspect of continuous negotiation and it will not be produced unless and until the interests of the various actors are included. (Gibbons et al. 1994, p. 4)

For Gibbons and colleagues, the difference between mode 1 and mode 2 research, and perhaps also between Mokyr's propositional and prescriptive knowledge, is that mode 2 research involves a far greater array of disciplines, actors, and influencers.

What differentiates Mokyr's work from that of Gibbons, though, is the assertion by Mokyr that the two types of knowledge are interdependent. For Mokyr:

> Knowledge can be in dispute and speculative, or it can be widely accepted, in which case I will call it 'tight'. Tightness is a measure of consenusalness of a piece of knowledge. It depends on the effectiveness of justification, the text to which rhetorical conventions accepted in a society persuade people that something is 'true', 'demonstrated', or at least determines the confidence that people have in the knowledge and – what counts for my purposes – thus their willingness to act upon it. (Mokyr 2002, p. 6)

In short, the boundaries between mode 1 and mode 2 may not always be clear, with propositional knowledge (or pure research) gaining acceptance and 'tightness' as a result of its use. In short, mode 1 research becomes accepted and normalised as a result of its application, conversion and translation into prescriptive, technical know-how and products. However, as he also notes, 'the existence of a knowledge base creates opportunities but does not guarantee they will be taken advantage of' (Mokyr 2002, p. 17); in other words, basic, pure research does not necessarily lead to innovation and impact. On the flip side, it is also true that 'in the absence of understanding of why and how a technique operates, further improvements run quickly into diminishing returns' (Mokyr 2002, p. 19). To, again, put this more succinctly, applied research is dependent on continued advances in pure research.

Mokyr's analysis of the knowledge economy provides a useful economic and historical context in which to situate contemporary discussions of research impact. For our purposes, Mokyr's research makes the case that if we are to move forward with the impact agenda, we need as researchers to have a critical understanding of the research ecosystem in which we work and an understanding of the role of pure and applied research and the synergies, connections, and opportunities for cross-fertilisation between the two.

During the years of the First and Second World Wars, the link between the two modes of knowledge production further cemented, although not necessarily just within the walls of academia. In the UK in 1915, Richard Haldane produced a report that argued that policymakers should undertake more research, that government should oversee policy-focused research, and that a council independent to government should govern research. However, as Edgerton (2009) has argued, developments at this time are not solely attributable to government policy or academic work, nor were they specific to the UK. As he states:

> [N]either radar nor the bomb were British inventions – nor did Britain alone work on them. So did nearly every major power. The idea of radar was widely known before 1935. The great and sudden interest in the possibility of

the bomb came from experimental work in Continental Europe. In neither case were British academics critical: they had to be inducted into radar; in the case of the bomb it is notable how few of the major British atomic physicists were involved at the beginning. Yet academics were to become essential to development, and as we know both projects needed and used people from many different scientific backgrounds. Universities produced people and knowledge, not inventions. (Edgerton 2009)

What we see during these years, then, is the emergence, perhaps unintentionally, of a dynamic research and development sector. This was the result a shared vision and aim, achieved through a confluence and flow of people and ideas between academia, industry and government.

In the US, it was the events of the Second World War that transformed the relationship between government and universities, and between pure and applied research. As Etzkowitz and Zhou (2018) state:

[A]cademics that had put aside their basic research interests to work as engineers on practical projects soon found that they had ideas for basic research that they would pursue after the war. This rediscovery of the interconnection between the practical and the theoretical, and the experience of working with virtually unlimited resources at their disposal, transformed academic scientists' anti-government attitudes that had led them to refuse support in the depth of the depression. (Etzkowitz and Zhou 2018, p. 108)

Whereas the industrial revolution led to an interconnection between knowledge, industry, and economic development, the war years highlighted the potential for a dynamic relationship between knowledge, government, and society. Following War World II, as Etzkowitz and Zhou note, university-government relationships changed significantly within the US and led to the establishment of government funding for research.

Despite the development of these relationships, all goes relatively quiet following the war, in both the UK and the US. A notable exception is the establishment of Stanford Science Park in 1951, which was not a government-led initiative, but the idea of Frederick Terman, Stanford University's Provost and Dean of Engineering. The park sought to support the development of Stanford University, the City of Palo Alto community, and regional business, all of which were struggling post war. This park provided the intellectual and entrepreneurial foundations for the later development of Silicon Valley. It wasn't until the 1970s, though, that the strategic relationships between the US government, universities, and businesses that had been tested during the War Years were given weight once again. Indeed, in 1973, led by the US government, three innovation centres were established in the US: one at MIT, one at Carnegie Mellon University, and one at the University of Oregon. These innovation centres sought to close the divide between business and universities, between research and its application. The Bahr–Doyle Act (1980) that permitted universities, for the first time, to obtain patent rights from federally funded research, followed this investment and further supported university-business collaboration. As Bozeman (2000) has suggested, as a result of these initiatives, a notable shift in the percentage of research and development supported by industry occurs in the period, rising from 2.6% in 1970 to 6.9% by 1990.

The UK sought to emulate US success through the development of science parks similar to the Stanford example. These regional clusters sought to bring businesses and universities together, within the same geographical space, to drive dialogue, collaboration, and invention. The Cambridge Science Park is the oldest in the UK. As their website states, the Cambridge Science Park was developed in response to:

> [A]n initiative of the Labour government following its election in 1964. Whitehall was urging UK universities to expand their contact with industry with the objective of technology transfer and to increase the payback from investment in basic research and an expansion in higher education in the form of new technologies. (Cambridge Science Park, n.d.)

Even as early as 1964, we see the government pushing, quite explicitly, for return on investment for research through knowledge translation and innovation. The Cambridge Science Park opened in 1971 and its first company, Laser–Scan, moved there in 1973. The park is still in operation today and continues to expand. As Brust (1991) has written on the development of UK science parks, 'whereas there were only two science parks with about 30 companies and 400 personnel in 1982, there were 28 parks with over 400 resident firms employing more than 5300 people in 1986' (Brust 1991, p. 4). The accelerated development of parks, incubators, and innovation centres in the 1980s were emblematic of the increasing understanding of the benefits of technology transfer to universities and to regional economies. As Berman states:

> One of the important changes of the 1980s was that market-oriented practices that had emerged somewhat organically from the activities of specific scientists and administrators were increasingly embraced by university leaders and framed explicitly in terms of their economic role. So one way that the expansion of these three practices helped to strengthen market logic throughout academic science was by providing very visible examples of how a market orientation could be successful, examples that university leaders would want to emulate. (Berman 2012, pp. 147–148)

The attention paid to the benefits of technology by universities, businesses and government intensified during the 1980s and 90s. For instance, in 1986, the Council for Industry and Higher Education was established in the UK to 'develop a shared agenda, influence Government policies and undertake joint projects' (NCUB, n.d.). In 1988, the Organisation for Economic Co-operation and

Development published a 'socio-economic' strategy for the development of new technologies (OECD 1988) and in 1991 a second publication focusing on the intersection between technology, productivity, and economic policy (OECD 1991). Within business, knowledge management was becoming increasingly important to business growth. Knowledge management has been defined as 'a way of managing work, paying due attention to the value and effect of an intangible asset, namely, knowledge' (Milton and Lambe 2016, p. 7). For Milton and Lambe, knowledge management consists of six key areas of work: connecting people; learning from experience; improved access to documents; retention of knowledge; creation of best practices; and innovation (Milton and Lambe 2016, p. 7). As Wiig has shown, although knowledge management practices expanded most dramatically in the 1990s, seeds can be traced back to as early as 1975, to Chapparel Steel, 'one of the first organisations to explicitly adopt a knowledge-focused management practice' (Wiig 1997, p. 6). This business concern with accounting for and managing institutional knowledge and intellectual property through systems, customer relations and talent management is, to my mind, another marker of the increasing importance attributed to knowledge and knowledge production as the twentieth century drew to its close.

Since the industrial revolution notions of the knowledge economy, knowledge production, knowledge transfer, and knowledge management have, to a greater or lesser extent, occupied the minds of those working in universities, government, industry, and business (albeit without any temporal or geographical consistency). The history of research impact assessment connects to this history. And like the history of knowledge production, the history of research impact assessment is neither linear, nor rooted in one geographical region. As shown in a comparative review of UK and Australian policy by Williams and Grant (2018), the history of the policy developments that led to research impact forming part of government research assessment in the UK (and later Australia) is linked to changes in political temperament and political priorities. For Williams and Grant, international influence, though, has been particularly profound in moving this agenda forwards. As they state, 'the evolution of impact assessment has been a back-and-forth process [between the UK and Australia]. Each country's policy development has been picked up on and developed through an ongoing process of international learning' (2018, p. 103).

According to Williams and Grant, the first specific mention of research being of explicit benefit to the UK economy and society was in a 1993 government whitepaper (2018, p. 97). While the authors do not identify any tangible outcomes of this whitepaper in their article, it is interesting to note that, whether a direct result of the whitepaper or not, in 1994 the membership organisation Unico was established in the UK to represent the technology exploitation companies of UK universities. And in 1995, the Association of University and Industry Links (AURIL) launched to support those working in the field of knowledge creation, development and exchange in the UK and Ireland. The appearance of both these organisations is no doubt connected to an increase in knowledge transfer and commercialisation activities in the UK at the time and the related surge in professional roles connected to this area of work. (The work of these organisations continues today in the revised and merged form of Praxis Auril.)

Following the establishment of these organisations, the landscape in the UK remained relatively static, perhaps a result of an economy doing well and there being little need for government intervention to support R&D activities. The recession of the early 2000s, though, resurfaced old discussions, with the role of research to the economy brought back on the policy agenda. Indeed, in 2002 the government commissioned a review of the skills and talent base for research in the UK. As the chancellor, Gordon Brown, stated in the forward to the report:

> The Government, in partnership with the Wellcome Trust, has done much in recent years to increase investment in scientific research in UK universities. There are already signs that this and the measures taken to stimulate the commercialisation of research are yielding fruit. Much has also been done to stimulate UK industry to invest more in research and development through the introduction of tax breaks and special partnership schemes linking universities and industry. The purpose of this Review has been to establish whether we have sufficient people to exploit these new facilities and technologies. (Roberts 2002, p. iii)

The report, *SET for success: The supply of people with science, technology, engineering and mathematics skills*, was undertaken by Sir Gareth Roberts (2002). The report stated that institutions were 'not adapting quickly enough to the needs of industry or the expectations of potential students' and that 'the training elements of a PhD, particularly training in transferable skills, need to be improved considerably' (Roberts 2002, p. 11). This led to a wave of government funding for universities (through the UK Research Councils) to develop expertise in this area and fill the gap in skills provision between Higher Education and industry.

The *Lambert Review of University-Business Collaboration* (Lambert 2003) followed swiftly. As stated in the forward, the biggest challenge identified was that:

> [C]ompared with other countries, British business is not research intensive, and its record of Investment in R&D in recent years has been unimpressive. UK business research is concentrated in a narrow range of industrial sectors, and in a small number of large companies. All this helps to explain the productivity gap between the UK and other comparable economies. (Lambert 2003, p. 1)

The two reviews, not mentioned in the paper by Williams and Grant, represent a renewed interest by government in the relationship between research and economic growth. The reports are likely a UK response to the Australian government's 2001 commitment to strengthening links between universities and industry announced in their strategy document *Backing Australia's ability: An innovation action plan for the future* (Commonwealth of Australia 2001).

It was also at this time that the UK's first national training programme aimed at technology transfer professionals working in universities, research institutions and industry was established, a programme funded by the Department of Trade and Industry. The aforementioned UNICO and AURIL were successful in receiving funding, again representative of the increasing commitment of the UK government to driving links between universities and business to meet the needs of the economy.

It is interesting to note that these developments were accompanied by an increasing interest within academia in university and academic entrepreneurship, with a significant increase in the number of publications in this area from the late 1990s onwards (Rothaermel, Agung and Jiang 2007). It wasn't, as Williams and Grant (2018) note, until later in the 2000s, however, that targeted policy initiatives on research impact began to shape the missions and strategies of universities and, in turn, the working practices and lives of researchers. Ultimately, it was the 2006 consultation on the research assessment exercise (that led to the inclusion of research impact in the 2014 Research Excellence Framework) and the incorporation of pathways to impact statements by the Research Councils in 2009 that led to the transformation in working practices of UK researchers that has become 'business as usual' in academia today.

As a result of these government-led initiatives, researchers started to dedicate time and resources to thinking through the possible effects their research may have on the economy and society and, in turn, to designing activities, events and initiatives to generate impact from their work. Institutions and research managers and leaders have also had to reflect on how to mobilise research and support impact initiatives. While it is true that universities have provided support for these activities in terms of funding and professionalised services, there is still much more that can be done. For instance, I remain unconvinced that universities (or funders) in the UK have sufficiently thought through the time, resources, and skills required to undertake impact work effectively. Neither am I convinced that universities have embedded appropriate recognition and reward mechanisms for these activities.

The drive for a dynamic research ecosystem

As noted above, the 'impact agenda' has its origins in the idea of the knowledge economy. As such, definitions and understandings of impact are inextricably wedded to national and global political systems and economies. While research impact has, to date, predominantly been discussed in the UK context (a direct result of the significant policy push), governments across the globe are also exploring how to best harness the outcomes of research. Australia, Canada, South Africa, the US and the European Commission have all developed their own understandings and approach to maximising the benefit of research to their respective economies and societies, as well as their own terms and language. Indeed, research impact sits alongside, above, and across related concepts such as knowledge mobilisation (Phipps and Shapson 2009) and evidence-based practice

(Gambrill 2018), as well as notions of public engagement, knowledge transfer and knowledge exchange (discussed by Maythorne in this collection).

Within changing national and international contexts, the funding to support research impact is likely to shift, change, and adapt. For ECRs, learning to adapt and seize emergent opportunities (whether in terms of careers, job opportunities, or funding) is key to thriving in this tumultuous environment. As universities become more entrepreneurial in nature, in response to the shifting policy priorities and resultant marketization of higher education, researchers too need to react and adapt to decide where they (and their research) fit into this picture (Berman 2012, Temple 2012, Taylor 2014, Etzkowitz and Zhou 2018). As Etzkowitz and Zhou note, universities are increasingly transcending their traditional education and research missions to become a 'knowledge-producing institution' through entrepreneurial strategies and approaches (Etzkowitz and Zhou 2018, p. 39). As they state:

> The entrepreneurial university, combining a 'third mission' of economic and social development, with teaching and research, is a growing contemporary phenomenon, in which academia takes a leading role in an institutional base of an emerging mode of production based on continuing organization and technological innovation. (Etzkowitz and Zhou 2018, p. 57)

The policy push from governments for research to be of social and economic benefit has been a key driver in this respect, encouraging a triple helix interaction that fosters multidirectional and dynamic relationships between universities, government, and business. In their comprehensive account of triple helix interactions, Etzkowitz and Zhou (2018) offer a range of detailed examples of triple helixes and the varied role played by government, universities and businesses in developing, in particular, regional economies. Silicon Valley is the oft-cited early example, the regional development of Silicon Valley a result of government pump-prime funding, cutting-edge university research and business investment, upscaling and development. As they note, though, this is not a linear process of government investment, leading to university research, leading to business commercialisation. As already noted in the case of Silicon Valley, Stanford University led the way through the establishment of the Science Park following World War II. In case of Linköping in Sweden, a triple helix interaction arose out of a grouping of regional high-tech firms. Instigated by an industrial liaison officer at Linköping University, an entrepreneurship club was established. This led to the establishment of a Centre for Innovation and Entrepreneurship at the University that taught students entrepreneurship skills, linking outcomes to the local economy. Regional authorities took this up as a model of good practice for regional economic development. In all the case studies discussed by Etzkowitz and Zhou, innovation occurs as a result of an ongoing relationship between government, universities, and businesses, although the catalyst for change is unique in each case and dependent on the local and regional context. In short, innovation occurs because of a multidirectional flow and exchange of people and ideas that are rooted in a shared sense of purpose.

Within the UK, the formation of UK Research and Innovation (UKRI) in 2018 signals yet another significant shift in the UK research landscape, particularly in terms of the relationship between government, universities and businesses. UKRI brings together the research and innovation strands of the previous funding system, as well as the work of Research England. The aim is to create a whole-system approach to research and development. Their most recent *Strategic prospectus* (UKRI 2018) provides a clear overview of the intended trajectory. In the prospectus, the economic and social benefit of research constitutes a core pillar of their strategy, sitting alongside pushing the frontiers of knowledge. The prospectus also outlines a raft of new funding schemes that, while broad in nature, align to the current government's industrial strategy and regional, national, and international development agendas. Perhaps most interesting, though, is the shift in language throughout the document from *research* to *research and development*, emphasising the focus on innovation and impact. The establishment of UKRI signals another step change in the UK government's ambition for research to support economic development and adapt to the changing needs of society.

Locating early career researchers within the impact agenda

For ECRs who are often in precarious employment and attempting to navigate a radically shifting research landscape, nationally and globally (Jaeger and Dinnin 2018), the pressure to produce research with impact can feel unsettling and daunting (as discussed by Hall, Morley and Bromley in this collection). As the narratives in this collection have shown, expectations of research impact are complex and context-specific, with appropriate methodologies and support either lacking or in development. In addition, the very notion of strategic, high-level triple helix interactions between government, business, and universities might seem an impossible future – an intangible, neoliberal sublime – for those at the start of their research career. As such, it is entirely appropriate for ECRs to ask pointed questions such as: how do I, an ECR with seemingly little institutional power and influence, play a part in the development of those kind of relationships; and will any work in this area be recognised and rewarded by peers, employers and promotion panels?

Research impact asks difficult questions of the ECR population and those who manage and support them. Indeed, it asks ECRs to consider the very purpose of their research and to shift their thinking from a preoccupation with advancing knowledge to thinking about how the knowledge they produce intersects with economic or social development and change. While this is challenging, it can also be empowering and stimulate new ways of thinking about research and research careers (as Hayes describes in this collection). It is important to remember, though, that impact remains contested, with definitions of impact subject to change. For example, there has already been a notable change in the assessment guidance for REF2021. For REF2021, 'impacts on students, teaching or other activities both within and beyond the submitting HEI are included' (Research England 2018, p. 84). Previously, it had been stated that: while 'impacts within the higher education sector, including on teaching or students, are included where they extend significantly beyond the submitting HEI', 'impacts on students, teaching or other activities within the submitting HEI are excluded' (HEFCE 2011, p. 27). For 2021, institutions are able to examine, evaluate and submit impact of research through teaching. This is a significant development, especially for those working in the arts and humanities where research-led teaching could offer a particularly fruitful pathway to impact. How to evidence a chain of influence and change that is rooted in original research, though, may still be problematic.

The broad definitions of impact are also revised. For the 2014 assessment exercise, impact was described as 'the "reach and significance" of impacts on the economy, society and / or culture' (HEFCE 2011, p. 26). For the 2021 assessment, a broader and more inclusive definition is given, impact now described as 'the "reach and significance" of impacts on the economy, society, culture, public policy or services, health, the environment or quality of life' (Research England 2018, p. 12). While the REF2014 team throughout the pilot and assessment period stressed that they were open to all types of impact, the 2021 amendments emphasise the point we should remain alive to new possibilities for impact, resist rigid definitions and finite notions of best practice, and continue to explore what impact means to our respective disciplinary areas. In addition, we must scrutinise how impact intersects with research careers, career pathways and equality, diversity and inclusion to understand how impact affects the working lives and practices of researchers. We must also continue to assess and analyse the role impact plays within research policy and the higher education landscape. Finally, we need to advance our understanding of research impact and the mechanisms that underpin it so that we ensure research has the desired social and economic benefit. Research on research impact is crucial to achieving this.

The role ECRs play in the impact ecosystem is one area where we need in-depth research studies, given the often fragmented and precarious nature of employment at the start of many research careers. Precarious employment because of fixed-term contracts, often tied to time-limited funded research projects or hourly paid teaching positions, has become a tortuous rite of passage for ECRs, with this having the effect that many talented researchers are lost or pushed out along the way (White 2004, Ackers and Gill 2005, Jaeger and Dinnin 2018). The almost necessary mobility that is expected of early career researchers (which has implications for the diversity of the research base in terms of penalising those who are not able to move around the country or globe for their next position) can make contributing to the research impact agenda seem like an impossible feat. Indeed, as soon as one establishes a set of research relationships at one university, these relationships are replaced (or put to one side) when taking up a new role at another institution. The short nature of many contracts further problematises the ability of ECRs to contribute to the impact agenda, as it is difficult to achieve deep and meaningful relationships in such a short space of time. Rules around institutional ownership for impact work also can inhibit impact planning for those in more transient employment (Research England 2018). Due to this combination of instability and precarity, ECRs can struggle to embed themselves within departmental and institutional cultures, thus turning to disciplinary societies instead to support their development (where support for impact is sometimes lacking and out of remit). Given the focus in national audits on excellence, high performance and long-term impact, the impact ambitions of ECRs are low on institutional priority lists. If the valuable impact work of ECRs continues to be under supported and unacknowledged, this will damage the sustainability of the research base and the ability of our future research leaders to deliver research impact with both reach and significance. It is, ultimately, the responsibility of research and higher education institutions to support researchers to develop their understanding of impact and their impact practice (regardless of career stage and contractual status).

The danger is that, within the current context, impact for ECRs can quickly become a burden. It is something that requires considerable time and effort, but something that remains of little obvious benefit in terms of career progression and professional recognition (as Graham et al. have described elsewhere in this collection). This lack of reward and recognition also comes across clearly in the recent book *What every postdoc needs to know* (Elvidge, Spencely and Williams 2017). The key argument the authors make is that a postdoc is a developmental position, an opportunity to acquire and practice new skills, a stepping-stone in a research career. Although impact is mentioned, it gets relatively little attention, perhaps confirming the above idea that delivering research impact, while important, isn't something expected (or useful) at this career stage. Where impact is discussed, it is in relation to grant applications, suggesting, albeit implicitly, that impact is something that is bound to projects, rather than part of a wider disciplinary, departmental or institutional mission.

As well as career-specific texts, there are also a number of 'how-to' guides on research impact (Denicolo 2014; Reed 2018). Reed's handbook and Deniclo's edited collection both offer the reader a textbook approach to research impact, acting as self-help guides for researchers, through advice, guidance, best practice and case studies. Denicolo's collection provides a kaleidoscopic array of perspectives on impact, providing definitions, understanding and challenges. Reed's book focuses more on offering concrete advice. While both books are useful and have their place, neither book considers the intersection between research impact and career stage. Moreover, neither discusses how impact work may differ depending on whether you are an established professor or ECR. With little time, short-term contracts, competing pressures from teaching, administration and writing, as well as an already taut and potentially damaging and detrimental work-life balance (with increasing sector discussions on poor staff mental health and wellbeing within the research staff base, see Levecque et al. 2017 and Guthrie et al. 2017), research impact for ECRs remains an elusive concept and, for some, an unwelcome distraction from the day job.

Recent UK-based surveys on the career prospects of ECRs and doctoral researchers have suggested, though, a significant increase in the percentage of ECRs having undertaken training and development in the areas of public engagement and knowledge exchange over the last eight years (Vitae 2017). Perhaps more interestingly, the 2017 survey also revealed that there is a significant appetite for undertaking development in this area (Vitae 2017). And this isn't peculiar to the UK, as Yu, Edelstein and Shandu have shown in this collection. With ECRs perhaps more open to engaging critically and reflectively with notions of research impact (partly as a result of the competitive career climate and the need to develop new and alternative ways of working), it seems that institutions (and government) are not effectively harnessing the enthusiasm, knowledge, and expertise of this group.

Reed's handbook focuses predominantly on impact arising from research projects and, to a lesser extent, bodies of work. In the context of the UK Research Excellence Framework, this is appropriate advice. This focus, though, can lead to impact being understood as an individualised activity or the work of a research group (and I deliberately use the term group here, rather than team, for reasons I'll discuss below).

From my own experience of writing impact case studies for REF2014 and supporting researchers with planning pathways to impact, I have found that a focus on research projects and the work of individuals, while helping give focus to impact activities, can also severely limit our understanding of how research effects change. To my mind, the individualised and project-based approach reduces the role and importance of collaborative thinking, of research teams, networks and communities, and the role of departments and faculties in nurturing and developing research and research relationships. To focus impact on single projects or the legacy of the professoriate, while important, undermines the crucial role ECRs play in impact through their contributions to research impact cultures and communities. Worse, it renders invisible the invaluable contribution of ECRs who regularly work outside the confines of academia's ivory tower and who are developing new relationships with a wide range of communities and businesses. By ignoring these contributions, we fail to cultivate the impact of the future, focusing instead on 'quick wins' and tangible outcomes.

Realising impact through collaborative working and collaborative advantage

To understand the important contribution ECRs make to the impact agenda, we need to learn more about how knowledge economies, knowledge networks and knowledge flows work. And this means thinking of research as a collaborative and engaged mode of knowledge production, rather than the work of isolated individuals and investigators. Indeed, impact is not a result of letting down one's golden academic hair for the world to admire, nor does it result from stories told of research of old. Impact is the result of agency and a desire for change. The idea of impact requires us to escape the ivory tower and to go on to dismantle it brick by brick. The ECRs already undertaking this work need to be encouraged and supported, not undermined and undervalued. Institutions and funders need to actively support this agency and recognise this work through an approach that is inclusive and that recognises that impact forms part of a complex and dynamic research ecosystem.

Research has already shown that PhD students and postdocs embed within academic knowledge networks at a very early stage, primarily through their supervisors and their collaborators and contacts (Abbasi, Hossain and Leydesdorff 2012). Further research, though, is needed on research and innovation networks that exist within and across academia, industry and government. A recent issue special issue of the journal *Evidence & Policy* offers a useful starting point, providing an insight into the networks, structures and mechanisms that can support the take-up of research within the policy arena (Oliver and Faul 2018). Understanding impact networks and the way in which knowledge moves within and beyond the academy can also help us to understand the important role knowledge brokers and intermediaries play in delivering and enhancing research impact. As Martinuzzi and Sedlačko (2016) have argued, boundary work is an essential element of impact work and requires experienced facilitators and translators who create spaces for dialogue so that knowledge is more accessible and relevant. Indeed, as Streffen and Meckin and Soubes have shown in this collection, intersections between disciplines, practices and sectors are all important in designing and delivering research impact.

Research impact is a necessarily collaborative and networked endeavour. However, as Mokyr (2002) has argued, knowledge is political, and the politics surrounding knowledge production and acceptance can dramatically affect how knowledge is used, deployed, and taken up. This is worth bearing in mind in the current context of research impact, as some research may not be socially, politically, or economically desirable and, as such, the pathway to impact more tortuous and more dependent on negotiation, influence and collaborative working (as Warira articulates in this collection). In short, impact work involves engagement with interested parties, facilitators and brokers, and gatekeepers and dissenters. At the heart of impact, though, is collaboration.

The marketised context for higher education (Berman 2012), combined with the proliferation of league tables, finite funding for grants, and pressure to publish high-quality papers or perish, has led to work environments where individualised competition thrives. As Lines and Rhodes have said, if the environment 'values individual over collective excellence, and the level of trust between individuals and teams is poor, this can lead to the individual protecting and isolating him or herself' (Lines and Scholes-Rhodes 2013, p. 15). While competition can encourage creative thinking and increase performance, it can also lead to isolation and siloed working, with employees disconnected from the teams and institutions in which they work. The danger here is that research impact also becomes understood as a product, as something that is to be protected and owned by an individual, rather than as something shared through collaborative endeavour. As Martinuzzi and Sedlačko argue, while knowledge exchange can furnish researchers with a stronger sense of social responsibility and support in making knowledge more accessible, it can also lead to commodification of knowledge, knowledge becoming subordinated 'to interests of capital accumulation with scientists disciplined through neoliberal reforms into the role of individualised "knowledge workers" in precarious working conditions' (Martinuzzi and Sedlačko 2016, p. 8). A fine balance must be struck between competition and collaboration for an effective research and innovation system. As Gardner has stated of collaborative working within business firms: 'If your high-performing professionals are not collaborating effectively today, it's surely not because they're stupid or obstinate; it's often because you are holding them to the kinds of short-term metrics that work against collaboration' (Gardner 2017, p. 18). For ECRs, it is essential that research managers and leaders interpret and contextualise metrics and key performance indicators so as not to reinforce siloed working. With respect to research impact, it is all the more important that motivations and measures are clear. For Reed, 'the concept at the heart of the impact agenda [is] empathy' (Reed 2018, p. ii). Indeed, impact is not owned by the higher education sector (although it can, at times, feel as such), but is something that connects us to, and that is shared with, the communities and stakeholders with which we work. Collaborative working requires ethical working.

In some respects, the business sector is much further ahead in terms of how to support collaborative work. For Skinner, a business consultant and entrepreneur, the 'core assumption that value should be created exclusively inside the business no longer stands' (Skinner 2018, p. 9). As he argues, insular models of competitive advantage based on trade secrets, assets and human resources are falling out of favour, with collaborative practices based on fluid knowledge flows and cross-company teamwork more suited to the increasingly interconnected world in which we live. Skinner's viewpoint echoes that of Hansen (2009) and Gardner (2017), both of whom have written on how collaboration isn't just important, but essential to business success. However, as they both also note, collaboration needs to be done for the right reasons; bad collaboration can be worse than no collaboration at all. As Hansen states: 'The solution is not to get people to collaborate more, but to get the right people to collaborate on the right projects' (Hansen 2009, p. 17).

The tension between collaboration and competition is something that requires further thought by research leaders, institutions and funders. The increase in professional doctorates is, in a number of ways, an example of university-business collaboration, the doctorate repurposed to align to business problems and needs (as Smith McGloin has shown in this collection). Another example is the shift, in the UK, from funding individual doctorates to funding cross-institutional doctoral training centres and partnerships. According to the EPSRC, doctoral training centres:

> bring together diverse areas of expertise to train engineers and scientists with the skills, knowledge and confidence to tackle today's evolving issues, and future challenges. They also provide a supportive and exciting environment for students, create new working cultures, build relationships between teams in universities and forge lasting links with industry [EPSRC, n.d.].

The aim of doctoral training centres is to provide doctoral researchers with a more dynamic environment in which to work, bringing the best elements of individual institutions together. A recent report, however, has suggested that doctoral training centres and partnerships may not be achieving their aims and that further research is needed to understand: 1) the nature of these collaborations; 2) the value attributed to the collaboration by doctoral researchers; and 3) how future iterations could enhance the nature of the collaboration for all those involved (Budd et al. 2018). Effective collaboration is not easy and requires an iterative and reflective process.

Nevertheless, encouraging collaboration within, across, and outside of academia remains a priority for government and, in turn, universities. This is evident in the increased focus on longer and larger research grants, shifting the focus from small-scale individual projects to larger, collaborative and interdisciplinary projects. It is also evident in UKRI's *Strategic prospectus*, which focuses the reader's attention on interdisciplinary global challenges, research with and for industry, as well as regional development initiatives (UKRI 2018). Problems, though, persist, through the continued focus on principal investigators, individual research leaders, and the idea of independent research. In all these cases, the language is not one of collaboration, shared leadership, networks and teamwork, but of individual success and achievement.

To ensure research, both in the UK and internationally, is of the greatest benefit to society and international economies, we need to encourage a more collaborative approach to research and to delivering research impact. This is not a simple task, as it requires us to engage at the 'touchpoint' between the needs, aims and values of government, the needs, aims and values of researchers and research institutions, and the needs, aims and values of business, society, and the economy. Lines and Rhodes' theory of touchpoint leadership is based on mutual learning and growth, attending to points of difference between people and groups, igniting collective energy, and trusting individuals to act freely and responsibly. It's about being permanently at the 'learning edge', being comfortable with not knowing, thinking together, and learning to ask the right questions (Lines and Scholes-Rhodes 2013). Rather than smoothing over conflict or reducing complexity, a touchpoint approach to leadership is rooted in the idea of seeking out new and creative solutions to address the challenges in front you. By acknowledging the tension between collaboration and competition, between pure and applied research, and between public sector, business and government values and priorities, we can start to seek out new ways of working, develop new career pathways, and recognise the contributions of everyone involved in the research process.

This requires that we move from working as research groups to multidisciplinary and cross-sectoral teams. Leary-Joyce and Lines argue that a team has 'a collective purpose and objective which its members are jointly responsible for fulfilling', whereas a group, although having a reason for coming together, consists of individuals with their own objectives and responsibilities (Leary-Joyce and Lines 2018, p. 3). Impact requires a team-based ethos and approach and, therefore, institutions and funders need to work towards team-based recognition and rewards and sustainable collaborative and cross-sector relationships. To achieve this, we first need to consider whether current business and funding models enable or inhibit our ability to deliver on research impact. Second, we need to recognise and understand the types of contributions that lead to research impact (which will involve people working within, between, and outside of academia). Casrai, the Consortia Advancing Standards in Research Administration Information, has already done some work in giving name to the various roles and contributions researchers make towards a publication (see Casrai 2015). A similar project for research impact might also be worthwhile.

For Skinner, a collaborative approach can increase value by 'building clarity of purpose, accessing external resource to drive growth, enabling a better response to a changing environment, identifying disruptive business models, lowering costs, increasing customer value and building more ambitious partnerships' (Skinner 2018, p. 47). To rewrite this in terms relevant to research impact: collaborative approaches increase the reach and significance of our work by aligning more closely the aims of our research with the needs of our stakeholders and publics. Collaboration provides us with new and renewed perspectives, ensuring that we ask the right questions, so that we can provide the most appropriate answers and solutions. Collaboration, in short, helps us to rethink the way we work, so that we are more able to build sustainable relationships with publics, businesses, and governments, all based on trust, shared values and mutual respect.

Conclusion

Impact is here to stay (at least for the near future). It has already shaped the way we think about research, the way we conduct research, and perhaps the value we attribute to the research endeavour. For some, it makes the motivation for undertaking research clear; for others, it challenges them to think about where their research sits within the broader academic landscape. However, there is still much to learn and still some way to go. To truly understand and evidence the impact of research within higher education, we need to understand research as part of a complex and changing ecosystem. We need to consider our place within this ecosystem through a critical evaluation of who we work with and why. We need to understand the opportunities we create (as well as the barriers we put in place) for ensuring knowledge flows across disciplinary, institutional, and sectoral boundaries. And we need to wrestle with the tensions that arise from conflicting values and understandings of knowledge, from conflicting political standpoints and worldviews, and from seemingly contradictory ways of working and thinking.

To usher in this change, we must move to an understanding of research as a collaborative endeavour, knowledge not beholden to disciplinary limitations or locked within institutional walls. Opening up research will help us to understand: 1) our place, as researchers, within a dynamic innovation ecosystem; 2) the nature of relationships we create and foster; and 3) where knowledge flows and where knowledge is blocked. This requires research and institutional leaders to think about researcher roles and responsibilities and the activities that are recognised and rewarded. At the very least, we need to acknowledge the time it takes to forge, negotiate and sustain relationships. At our most ambitious, we need to ask whether there is a place in the academy for a new type of researcher and new types of research-related roles. Indeed, is there the opportunity to create new hybrid roles, which combine research skills with brokerage, communication, and negotiation skills? Is there the opportunity to develop roles that exist in-between and across organisations to drive deep and strategic relationships? Is there the opportunity to re-evaluate the relationship between teaching, research, engagement, enterprise and impact?

To move forward with this it is important that we move beyond linear models of knowledge transfer and think of research as part of an innovation ecosystem where timelines of influence are complex and boundaries between social, economic and cultural benefit are often blurred. This requires us to rethink how we develop partnerships with other universities, with businesses, and with government, at regional, national, and international levels. Crucially, we will need to shift from the idea of competitive advantage to collaborative advantage. This doesn't require a nudge in our thinking, but a paradigm shift. It asks us to rethink notions of authorship and ownership and of sharing and commercialising intellectual property. It may even require a rethink of existing legal frameworks for research exploitation and an overhaul of government incentivisation for regional, national and international enterprise activities.

For ECRs, impact presents both a challenge and an opportunity. The challenge is in determining what impact means for you, your field, and the teams and communities in which you work. These are not easy questions and require critical and considered reflection. The opportunities lie in defining the impact agenda, in redefining academic roles, and renewing the role of academia within society today. It is now time to start shaping and creating the research and roles that will underpin the future of the academy.

Learning points

- Critically reflect on your current networks to understand the reach of research.
- Engage and collaborate to align your research to the needs of your stakeholders and beneficiaries.
- Think together and actively foster a team-based culture rooted in trust, shared leadership and respect.
- Come together as ECRs to make your contributions as a community visible.
- Be bold and take risks; create your own impact future.

References

Abbasi, A., Hossain, L. and Leydesdorff, L. (2012). 'Betweenness centrality as a driver of preferential attachment in the evolution of research collaboration networks', *Journal of Informetrics*, 6(3), pp. 403–412.

Ackers, L. and Gill, B. (2005). 'Attracting and retaining "early career" researchers in English higher education institutions', *Innovation: The European Journal of Social Science Research*, 18 (3), pp. 277–299.

Berman, E.P. (2012). *Creating the Market University*. Princeton: Princeton University Press.

Bozeman, B. (2000). 'Technology transfer and public policy: a review of research and theory', *Research Policy*, 29(4), pp. 627–655.

Brust, M.F. (1991). 'Technolgy transfer and the university', *The Journal of Applied Business Research*, 7(1), pp. 1–5.

Budd, R., O'Connell, C., Yuan, T. and Ververi, O. (2018). *The DTC Effect: ESRC Doctoral Training Centres and the UK Social Science Doctoral Training Landscape*. Liverpool: Liverpool Hope University Press.

Cambridge Science Park (n.d.) *Cambridge Science Park: About the Park*. Available at: www.cambridgesciencepark.co.uk/about-park/past/ (Accessed: 20. 11. 2018).

Commonwealth of Australia (2001). *Backing Australia's Ability: An Innovation Action Plan for the Future*. Canberra: Paragon Printers Australasia.

Consortia Advancing Standards in Research Administration Information (Casrai) (2015). *Casrai: Contributor Roles*. Available at: https://dictionary.casrai.org/Contributor_Roles (Accessed: 28. 11. 18).

Denicolo, P. (ed.) (2014). *Achieving Impact in Research*. London: Sage Publications.

Edgerton, D. (2009). *The 'Haldane Principle' and Other Invented Traditions in Science Policy*. Available at: www.historyandpolicy.org/policy-papers/papers/the-haldane-principle-and-other-invented-traditions-in-science-policy (Accessed: 20. 11. 2018).

Elvidge, L., Spencely, C. and Williams, E. (2017). *What Every Postdoc Needs To Know*. Singapore: World Scientific Publishing Company.

Engineering and Physical Sciences Research Council (EPSRC) (n.d.) *EPSRC: Doctoral Training Centres*. Available at: https://epsrc.ukri.org/skills/students/centres/ (Accessed: 28. 11. 2018).

Etzkowitz, H. and Zhou, C. (2018). *The Triple Helix: University-Industry-Government Innovation and Entrepreneurship* (2nd edition). London: Routledge.

Gambrill, E. (2018). *Critical Thinking and the Process of Evidence-Based Practice*. Oxford: Oxford University Press.

Gardner, H.K. (2017). *Smart Collaboration: How Professionals and Their Firms Succeed by Breaking Down Silos*. Boston: Harvard Business Review Press.

Gibbons, M., Limoges, C., Nowotny, H., Schwartzman, S., Scott, P. and Trow, M. (1994). *The New Production of Knowledge: The Dynamics of Science and Research in Contemporary Societies*. London: SAGE Publications.

Guthrie, S., Lichten, C.A., van Belle, J., Ball, S., Knack, A. and Hofman, J. (2017). *Understanding Mental Health in the Research Environment: A Rapid Evidence Assessment*. Santa Monica: RAND Corporation. Available at: www.rand.org/pubs/research_reports/RR2022.html (Accessed: 28. 11. 18).

Hansen, M.T. (2009). *Collaboration: How Leaders Avoid the Traps, Create Unity, and Reap Big Results*. Boston: Harvard Business School Publishing.

Higher Education Funding Council England (HEFCE) (2011). *Research Excellence Framework 2014: Assessment Framework and Guidance on Submissions*. Bristol: HEFCE. Available at: www.ref.ac.uk/2014/pubs/2011-02/ (Accessed: 28. 11. 18).

Jaeger, A.J. and Dinnin, A.J. (eds.) (2018). *The Postdoc Landscape*. London: Academic Press.

Lambert, S.R. (2003). *Lambert Review of Business–University Collaboration*. Norwich: Her Majesty's Stationery Office. Available at: http://webarchive.nationalarchives.gov.uk/+/http://www.hm-treasury.gov.uk/consultations_and_legislation/lambert/consult_lambert_index.cfm (Accessed: 20. 11. 18).

Leary-Joyce, J. and Lines, H. (2018). *Systemic Team Coaching*. St Albans: AoEC Press.

Levecque, K., Anseel, F., De Beuckelaer, A., Van der Heyden, J. and Gisle, L. (2017). 'Work organization and mental health problems in PhD students', *Research Policy*, 46(4), pp. 868–879.

Lines, H. and Scholes-Rhodes, J. (eds.) (2013). *Touchpoint Leadership: Creating Collaborative Energy across Team and Organizations*. London: Kogan Page.

Martinuzzi, A. and Sedlačko, M. (eds.) (2016). *Knowledge Brokeredge for Sustinable Development: Innovative Tools for Increasing Research Impact and Evidence-Based Policy-Making*. Saltaire: Greenlead Publishing.

Milton, N. and Lambe, P. (2016). *The Knowledge Manager's Handbook*. London: Kogan Page.

Mokyr, J. (2002). *The Gifts of Athena: Historical Origins of the Knowledge Economy*. Princeton: Princeton University Press.

National Centre for Universities and Business (NCUB) (n.d.) *NCUB: Our History*. Available at: www.ncub.co.uk/who-we-are/history.html (Accessed: 28. 11. 18).

Oliver, K. and Faul, M. (eds.) (2018). 'Networks and network analysis in evidence'. *Evidence & Policy: A Journal of Research, Debate and Practice*, 14(3), pp. 369–379.

Organisation for Economic Cooperation and Development (OECD) (1988). *New Technologies in the 1990s: A Socio-Economic Strategy*. Paris: OECD.

Organisation for Economic Co-operation and Development (OECD) (1991). *Technology and Productivity: The Challenge for Economic Policy*. Paris: OECD.

Peters, M.A., Marginson, S. and Murphy, P. (2009). *Creativity and the Global Knowledge Economy*. Bern: Peter Lang.

Phipps, D.J. and Shapson, S. (2009). 'Knowledge mobilisation builds local research collaborations for social innovation', *Evidence & Policy: A Journal of Research, Debate and Practice*, 5(3), pp. 211–227.

Reed, M.S. (2018). *The Research Impact Handbook* (2nd edition). Huntley: Fast Track Impact.

Research England (2018). *Research Excellence Framework 2021: Draft Guidance on Submissions*. Bristol: HEFCE. Available at: www.ref.ac.uk/publications/draft-guidance-on-submissions-201801/ (Accessed: 28. 11. 18).

Roberts, S.G. (2002). *SET for Success: The Supply of People with Science, Technology, Engineering and Mathematics Skills*. London: Department for Trade and Industry. Available at: https://webarchive.nationalarchives.gov.uk/+tf_/http://www.hm-treasury.gov.uk/documents/enterprise_and_productivity/research_and_enterprise/ent_res_roberts.cfm (Accessed: 28. 11. 18).

Rothaermel, F.T., Agung, S.D. and Jiang, L. (2007). 'University entrepreneurship', *Industrial and Corporate Change*, 16(4), pp. 691–791.

Skinner, P. (2018). *Collaborative Advantage: How Collaboration Beats Competition as a Strategy for Success*. London: Robinson.

Taylor, Y. (ed.) (2014). *The Entrepreneurial University: Engaging Publics, Intersecting Impacts*. Basingstoke: Palgrave Macmillan.

Temple, P. (ed.) (2012). *Universities in the Knowledge Economy: Higher Education Organisation and Global Change*. Abingdon: Routledge.

UK Research and Innovation (UKRI) (2018). *Strategic Prospectus: Building the UKRI Strategy*. Bristol: UKRI. Available at: www.ukri.org/about-us/strategic-prospectus/ (Accessed: 28. 11. 18).

Vitae (2017). *Five Steps Forward: Progress in Implementing the Concordat to Support the Career Development of Researchers*. Cambridge: Careers Research & Advisory Centre (CRAC) Ltd.

White, K. (2004). 'The leaking pipeline: Women postgraduate and early career researchers in Australia', *Tertiary Education and Management*, 10(3), pp. 227–241.

Wiig, K.M. (1997). 'Knowledge management: where did it come from and where will it go?', *Expert Systems with Applications*, 13(1), pp. 1–14.

Williams, K. and Grant, J. (2018). 'A comparative review of how the policy and procedures to assess research impact evolved in Australia and the UK', *Research Evaluation*, 27(2), pp. 93–105.

REFLECTION

Putting social responsibility at the heart of the institution: The research experience and career development of early career researchers

Rachel Cowen, Judith Gracey and Dee-Ann Johnson

> Our first two goals of world class research and outstanding learning and student experience might be characterised by the question 'what are we good at?' In contrast, social responsibility can be characterised by a different question; 'what are we good for?' (Prof Dame Nancy Rothwell, University of Manchester President and Vice Chancellor)

The University of Manchester championed 'research with impact' well before its inclusion in the UK REF. We were one of the first HEIs in the UK to make social responsibility (SR) a core strategic goal (The University of Manchester 2012). Our institutional aim is to embed social responsibility as a highly valued academic activity supported by strategic priorities and monitoring processes, governance structures, researcher development programmes, career progression and reward systems.

This provides reflections on the institutional journey we have taken to provide the infrastructure and support to enable social responsibility to flourish. The chapter highlights good practice and challenges and the impact on research experiences and career development opportunities from an early career researcher (ECR) and researcher developer perspective.

Vision, strategy and governance to drive the SR agenda

The university embraces a broad view of social responsibility encompassing all disciplines (Humanities, Science and Engineering and Biology, Medicine and Health), our professional support services and cultural institutions, and includes widening participation (WP), community engagement, public engagement (PE) and sustainability. Consequently, it covers a myriad of approaches ranging from individual activities to university-wide programmes. The challenge of capturing and communicating the full extent of our SR activities is compounded by our institutional scale, with 12,315 staff and 39,700 students, of which 5,615 identify as ECRs (PGR and research staff) (The University of Manchester 2017a). To ensure SR opportunities and impact are visible both internally and externally, we have worked hard to develop a clear governance and support infrastructure (Figure 9.1).

The implementation of the SR goal has been overseen by the Social Responsibility Governance Group chaired by the University President, who is an inspiring SR role model. She was the first female head of a Russell Group university and is passionate about connecting the institution to the community, furthering public awareness of science and encouraging women to pursue careers in science and academia. The group commissioned a pivotal external review of the institutional SR approach in 2013, which resulted in our commitment to SR being significantly renewed. Recommendations led to the launch of an SR strategy, our 'making a difference' mission statement and five priority themes (Figure 9.1) (The University of Manchester 2013a), and the appointment of the Vice President for SR as a key member of the senior leadership team. We also commissioned an independent baseline report to assess the overall economic and social impact of the university to allow us to 'measure the difference' through a longitudinal evaluation (The University of Manchester 2013b). To reflect our size and faculty structure, we have a devolved model of SR leadership and management. The Vice President for SR, in partnership with the Operational Director for SR, leads a central SR team. In faculties and schools, SR is cascaded through local strategic and operational structures. This underlying governance and support are clearly effective, as we have strong evidence that the SR goal is highly visible across all staff groups including ECR research staff. Indeed, 90% of staff are aware of the SR goal and 98% of those who are aware agree with its principle to make a positive contribution to society (University of Manchester 2017c).

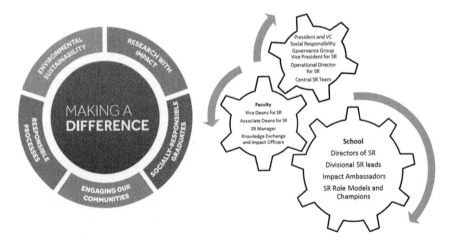

FIGURE 9.1 University of Manchester SR strategic priorities and SR governance structure

Social responsibility training and development provision for ECRs

We have been responsive to the impact agenda as it has emerged from our various funders. It has proved to be a useful vehicle to evolve our SR training and development provision so that we are able to promote SR at the earliest opportunity and at the grassroots level. This has resulted in an institutional expectation and the necessary support infrastructure to encourage all under-graduates and postgraduates to step up to 'make a difference' to our local and global communities. This has been achieved through various successful discrete programmes, including the Manchester Leadership Programme, student volunteering and ethical, global and enterprise grand challenges. To promote communication and visibility these activities have been packaged together into the 'Stellify' programme which asks all students to make a personal and public pledge to SR. The aim is to embed SR as a core value and a distinctive mark of all Manchester graduates in support of the SR strategic key priority 'Responsible Graduates' (The University of Manchester 2018a).

> I set a goal for myself. I must spread as much knowledge as I can regarding our planet Earth and its rocks. (Earth Science PhD student – Stellify pledge)

To support the 'Research with Impact' SR priority, we have invested in a continuum of development opportunities for ECRs ranging from online training and short learning lunches, through to intensive accredited training programmes. These are delivered centrally and within discipline at the faculty level where, dependent on research experience and career stage, staff and students are supported through doctoral training, research staff development and / or new academics and research fellows programmes. Programmes are delivered by dedicated researcher developers, faculty SR leads and local SR role models from the academic and professional support services (The University of Manchester 2018b, 2018c).

Annually, doctoral training provides access to over 45 SR training workshops including social impact, public engagement, patient and public involvement in research. PGR research is celebrated at the university-wide annual Postgraduate Summer Research Showcase, where research is presented as a poster with a research impact statement, a short video 'Research Digital Stories' or a 'Research in Action' image. The event highlights the collective output and impact of the PhD community, alongside development of communication, presentations skills and interdisciplinary networking (The University of Manchester 2018d).

> I highly recommend other researchers to take part. In today's fast-paced world, capturing research in one image is a creative way to communicate your research to an interdisciplinary audience and to the general public in a way that is highly accessible and easy-to-understand, and remember, a picture is worth a thousand words. (PGR student, School of Arts, Languages and Cultures)

Using the 'Gradschool' training model (Vitae 2018), we provide an immersive, three-day team learning experience to late-stage PhD and ECR staff, focusing on the themes of research impact and enterprise. Teams are facilitated by experienced tutors helping them connect their experiences to important transferable skills, e.g. communication, leadership and networking, and broaden their horizons on future career choices within and outside academia. It has been documented that 65% of participants felt more likely to start a business having participated in the enterprise school (University of Manchester 2017c).

> Gained a better understanding of factors to consider for business (solutions to problems, market research, finance, intellectual property etc.) and how to manage these as a team as well as meeting very helpful business contacts. (Feedback from GradSchool: Enterprise)
>
> Enriching and empowering. Inter-disciplinary ideas. Energy oriented and skill oriented tasks. Valuable networking with regional researchers.
>
> Inspired me to see beyond research and more into the impact researchers have. Has changed me for the better as a researcher. (Feedback from Grad-School: Making an Impact: Personal, Group & Research)

Perceptions gathered through the national Postgraduate Research Experience Survey (PRES) show that 84% of Manchester postgraduates state that 'their ability to communicate information effectively to diverse audiences has developed during their programme'; this is 3% higher than the national average (Advance HE 2017). Qualitative comments reinforce this, such as: 'The research environment is very conducive for public engagement with many opportunities'; and 'Good post-graduate research programme of workshops fulfilling all requirements'

Additionally, research staff have access to public engagement masterclasses, pathways to impact grant writing and Vitae national resources including 'Making your Mark' training. All staff and students have access to hubs of SR expertise including engagement@manchester, policy@manchester and the Centre for Engagement and Involvement providing shared learning and best practice, local advice, networking and mentoring.

> Inspiring – helped me consider the wider impact of my research and ways to create impact right from the start of my research project. (Research staff member, Faculty of Biology, Medicine and Health)

We encourage and coach ECRs to enter institutional SR competitions such as Venture Out, Venture Further and national competitions such as Biotechnology YES, Engineering YES and international competitions including, Three Minute Thesis and Famelab.

> The support and encouragement to participate in networking and business related activities such as the 'YES competition' by the university improved and expanded my development on the professional level.

I had an excellent opportunity for a secondment to a government department which was a fantastic experience and very useful for professional development. I have also attended an international conference which provided excellent opportunity for professional networking and presenting my work to a diverse audience. Involvement in outreach has also developed my communication skills. (Postgraduate Researcher, University of Manchester 2017b)

Funding, reward and recognition mechanisms promoting SR

The institution has recognised the need to link our SR goal with funding and reward mechanisms at faculty and university level. The university 'Widening Participation Fellows' internal awards support the SR strategic priority 'Engaging our Communities'. Focusing on young people (from primary through to sixth form), their parents, carers and teachers, WP fellows act as ambassadors, bridging the gap between local communities and higher education. Internally, fellows lead staff and student WP initiatives, and externally, they raise awareness of their discipline through taster workshops, study skills and careers events. In the last five years, the scheme has supported over 150 fellows, providing paid work experience, training and networking, motivating several fellows to go on to work in education and public engagement roles. A cascade effect is created in which experienced WP fellows feed into the training of new fellows to inspire and maintain momentum.

As a WP fellow I have been privileged to work with young people and I feel I have developed many skills needed to become a good doctor and teacher. (WP fellow and MRes student, Faculty of Biology, Medicine and Health)

It was excellent, perfectly pitched, engaged and informed. (Headteacher, Primary School Careers Event)

ECRs can also apply for funding for SR activities, including Wellcome Trust Institutional Strategic Support Funding and Faculty SR funding, to promote SR in the curriculum, Engaging our Communities, or Research with Societal or Environmental Impact. Anecdotally, the ability to secure competitive internal funding for SR activity can be confidence- and CV-boosting for ECRs, informing their approach to preparing applications and securing external research funding, and providing an opportunity to build a funding track record.

Excellence in SR is celebrated through the Manchester Doctoral College 'Best Contribution to Society' (The University of Manchester 2018b). The 2017 recipient Kelly Pickard-Smith, Faculty of Humanities, is an example of a new generation of ECRs who take advantage of multiple SR opportunities to maximise their PhD, and to raise their profile and employability. Throughout her PhD, Kelly has looked outward and is concerned that her research and the research of others has impact. She embraces diverse engagement activities including science communication in schools, museums and festivals, and is a school governor. Her goal of making her research findings accessible led her to submit an alternative format thesis including an educational film engaging over 300 people with research into mathematical identity. Kelly's career choices have been heavily influenced by her ECR experiences and she is now passing on her passion and commitment to SR as a researcher developer.

The Faculty of Science and Engineering host the 'Better World Showcase' recognising the SR efforts of 50+ staff and students annually inspiring others to do the same. Faculty-level schemes act as a pipeline to the prestigious institutional 'Making a Difference Awards'. In 2016 this attracted 150+ nominations resulting in 9 award winners (The University of Manchester 2018e).

Lidja McKnight, Research Staff, Faculty of Science and Engineering was in the team awarded outstanding public engagement activity for the development of a travelling exhibition providing an immersive and interactive experience to explain cutting-edge research into the role of animals in life and death in ancient Egypt.

> It was great for the team's efforts to engage the public with scientific research to be recognised with a Making a Difference Award, confirming the University's commitment to making social responsibility a vital element of our work here in Manchester. (Lidja McKnight, Research Staff, Faculty of Science and Engineering)

Lidja is an example of an ECR who has gone on to use their portfolio of SR activity as strong evidence of teaching and learning within and outside HE. Supported by our Leadership in Education Awards Programme (LEAP) launched in 2016, ECRs are mentored and supported to apply for formal national teaching accreditation (The University of Manchester 2018f). To date, 25 ECRs have successfully completed LEAP and been awarded Fellowship status of the Higher Education Academy; 180 ECRs are currently going through the application process.

Evidence of SR activity is also well-embedded in the annual Academic and Research Staff promotion process. Key criteria include research impact, enterprise, knowledge transfer and public engagement. Several ECRs have been promoted, and their significant contribution to SR recognised – most notably Sheena Cruickshank, an immunologist whose PE activities have involved over 300,000 participants at approximately 70 events nationally and who holds numerous university and national research and engagement awards and fellowships. Sheena was promoted to Professor of Public Engagement and Biomedical Sciences in 2017, recognising her research and engagement profile and the difference she has made as University Academic Lead for PE, developing leadership and PE strategy.

Through our reward and recognition mechanisms we are creating a network of SR role models and academic research impact ambassadors who act as advocates for how SR can enhance careers. A significant recent step forward has also been the appointment of research impact ambassadors in every school. These people and other inspiring SR news stories are promoted through engagement@manchester and policy@manchester networks, newsletters and blogs which are also effective communication channels for SR funding calls.

What have we learned so far?

- It's essential that there is a designated member of the senior leadership team with responsibility for SR strategy working alongside a network of local champions to embed SR as a core activity and connect and share good practice.
- A clearly communicated strategy which we have bolstered with a simple memorable mission statement and visual SR wheel covering the key themes and priorities have been critical in gaining SR traction across the organisation.
- You need a mechanism to independently evaluate the impact of your SR commitment and activity including a thorough baseline assessment, longitudinal evaluation, annual reporting on progress and benchmarking against the sector.
- To make SR sustainable, it is better to have overarching programmes that have continuity and significant investment, rather than pump-priming lots of smaller initiatives. This has also helped to make sure that SR is embedded in everyday academic practice.
- There need to be carrots for people to fully engage in SR activity such as personal funding, career advancement and professional recognition.

What do we need to do more of?

- We need to improve the quality assurance of our SR training and development provision to ensure it meets the needs of our diverse community of staff and students and provide better mechanisms for researcher developers to share good practice.
- We need to further develop SR practices, networking and support across faculties and disciplinary silos. This would connect communication strategies and SR functions so we can maximise available resources and avoid overlapping activities that could have increased impact through coordination.
- We need to increase the visibility of reward and recognition mechanisms for ECRs and increase the granularity of the data we are capturing so that we know which researchers are not as engaged and / or are under-represented.
- To keep the SR momentum we need ECRs to unconsciously plan SR activity into their research and teaching practices, while maintaining our clear SR goals and leadership.

Challenges and future development

Robust evaluation of SR activity represents a major challenge for higher education. We commissioned a three-year follow up independent review which showed the significant progress and social and economic impact we are making, particularly in the Greater Manchester region (University of Manchester 2018g). Our faculties are required to provide evidence of public engagement in our annual performance review process. Qualitative data is captured through appraisal, promotion and faculty email audits. Research impact is captured in impact case studies for future national research assessment exercises, e.g. REF, but this does not capture all SR activity. Therefore, we are also developing PE case studies that are broader than those for REF. To date ECR involvement in SR activities has been sporadically captured, is open to individual interpretation and will have overlap in reporting of activity. However, we will be able to take a more evidenced-based approach with the recent introduction of our integrated research database (PURE).

The investment in strong SR governance and training and development at all levels of the university has resulted in a step change in the SR culture. Emerging evidence for this includes the 2017 staff survey showing 51% of our research staff take part in public engagement activities compared to 50% nationally (Vitae 2017), and 55% say that the university recognises and values the contribution they make to public engagement (University of Manchester, 2017c).

However, some pockets remain in the university where a more traditional view of research, in the pre-impact era, still exists.

> There are plenty of opportunities to get involved in the wider research community, and particularly outreach events, which I really enjoy however…often supervisors are not too keen on it…Maybe some more awareness for supervisors to realise that outreach / wider research events are useful additions to PhDs would be good. (PGR student, PRES 2017)

In 2014, Sheena Cruickshank in her capacity as Academic Lead for Public Engagement with Research conducted a university-wide review presenting a similar picture showing the need to create uniformity of expectations of SR practice whilst still allowing for creativity in SR (Cruickshank 2017).

We will continue to respond to the changing research landscape and to evolve our SR strategy and researcher development approach. Our role as researcher developers is to embed good practice and connect the ECR experience with this changing landscape whilst engendering supervisory practices that support the SR agenda.

References

Advance HE. (2017). *Postgraduate Research Experience Report*. Advance HE. [Viewed 10 September 2018]. Available from: www.heacademy.ac.uk/knowledge-hub/postgraduate-research-experience-survey-report-2017

Cruickshank, S. (2017). *From Piecemeal to Purpose: An Initial Review of Public Engagement with Research*. The University of Manchester. [Viewed 10 September 2018]. Available from: www.engagement.manchester.ac.uk/about/PE%20with%20Research%20Initial%20Findings.pdf

The University of Manchester. (2012). *Manchester 2020: The University of Manchester Strategic Plan*. The University of Manchester. [Viewed 10 September 2018]. Available from: http://documents.manchester.ac.uk/display.aspx?DocID=25548

The University of Manchester. (2013a). *The University of Manchester's Social Responsibility Strategic Priorities*. The University of Manchester. [Viewed 10 September 2018]. Available from: www.socialresponsibility.manchester.ac.uk/strategic-priorities/

The University of Manchester. (2013b). *Measuring the Difference: The Economic and Social Impact of the University of Manchester, Summary Report*. The University of Manchester. [Viewed 10 September 2018]. Available from: http://documents.manchester.ac.uk/display.aspx?DocID=21569

The University of Manchester. (2017a). *The University of Manchester's Facts and Figures*. The University of Manchester. [Viewed 10 September 2018]. Available from: http://documents.manchester.ac.uk/display.aspx?DocID=31312

The University of Manchester (2017b). *Postgraduate Research Experience Survey 2017*. The University of Manchester. [Unpublished internal report].

The University of Manchester (2017c). *Staff Survey*. The University of Manchester. [Unpublished internal report].

The University of Manchester. (2018a). *Stellify Programme*. The University of Manchester. [Viewed 10 September 2018]. Available from: www.dse.manchester.ac.uk/our-projects/stellify/

The University of Manchester. (2018b). *University of Manchester Doctoral Training*. The University of Manchester. [Viewed 10 September 2018]. Available from: www.manchester.ac.uk/study/postgraduate-research/why-manchester/doctoral-college/

The University of Manchester. (2018c). *University of Manchester Support for Academic Staff and Researchers*. The University of Manchester. [Viewed 10 September 2018]. Available from: www.staffnet.manchester.ac.uk/staff-learning-and-development/academicandresearch/

The University of Manchester. (2018d). *Postgraduate Summer Research Showcase*. The University of Manchester. [Viewed 10 September 2018]. Available from: www.psrs.manchester.ac.uk/

The University of Manchester. (2018e). *Making a Difference Awards*. The University of Manchester. [Viewed 10 September 2018]. Available from: www.socialresponsibility.manchester.ac.uk/get-involved/awards/

The University of Manchester. (2018f). *Leadership in Education Awards Programme*. The University of Manchester. [Viewed 10 September 2018]. Available from: http://documents.manchester.ac.uk/display.aspx?DocID=29569

The University of Manchester. (2018g). *Measuring the Difference: Summary Report 2016/17*. The University of Manchester. [Viewed 10 September 2018]. Available from: http://documents.manchester.ac.uk/display.aspx?DocID=32801

Vitae (2017). *Five Steps Forward: Progress in Implementing Concordat to Support the Career Development of Researchers 2008–2017*. Vitae. [Viewed 10 September 2018]. Available from: www.vitae.ac.uk/vitae-publications/reports/vitae-5-steps-forward-web.pdf

Vitae (2018). *Vitae GradSchool Model*. Vitae. [Viewed 10 September 2018]. Available from: www.vitae.ac.uk/vitae-publications/vitae-library-of-resources/about-vitae-researcher-development-programmes/gradschools

INDEX

Note: page references in italics indicate figures; bold indicates tables.